Ninth Workshop on Noisy User-generated Text (W-NUT 2024)

St. Julian's, Malta
22 March 2024

ISBN: 978-1-7138-9465-0

Printed from e-media with permission by:

Curran Associates, Inc.
57 Morehouse Lane
Red Hook, NY 12571

Some format issues inherent in the e-media version may also appear in this print version.

Association for Computational Linguistics
209 N. Eighth Street
Stroudsburg, Pennsylvania 18360

Phone: 1-570-476-8006
Fax: 1-570-476-0860

acl@aclweb.org

Additional copies of this publication are available from:

Curran Associates, Inc.
57 Morehouse Lane
Red Hook, NY 12571 USA
Phone: 845-758-0400
Fax: 845-758-2633
Email: curran@proceedings.com
Web: www.proceedings.com

WNUT 2024

The Ninth Workshop on Noisy and User-generated Text (W-NUT 2024)

Proceedings of the Workshop

March 22, 2024

Order copies of this and other ACL proceedings from:

Association for Computational Linguistics (ACL)
209 N. Eighth Street
Stroudsburg, PA 18360
USA
Tel: +1-570-476-8006
Fax: +1-570-476-0860
acl@aclweb.org

Introduction

The W-NUT 2024 workshop focuses on a core set of natural language processing tasks on top of noisy and user-generated text, such as those found on social media, web forums and online reviews. The internet has democratized content creation leading to an explosion of informal user-generated text, publicly available in electronic format, motivating the need for NLP on noisy text to enable new data analytics applications. We have received a total of 15 main workshop submissions, of which 10 are included in the proceedings. The workshop will be held in hybrid in-person and virtual modes. We have two invited speakers: Jennifer Foster and Yvette Graham, who have generously agreed to share their ongoing research work. We're very thankful to have them in our workshop. We would like to thank the Program Committee members who reviewed the papers, as well as all of the workshop participants for submitting their work.

Rob van der Goot, JinYeong Bak, Max Müller-Eberstein, Wei Xu, Alan Ritter, and Tim Baldwin
W-NUT Co-Organizers

Organizing Committee

General Chair

Rob van der Goot, IT University of Copenhagen, Denmark

Program Chair

JinYeong Bak, Sung Kyun Kwan University, Republic of Korea

Publication Chair

Max Müller-Eberstein, IT University of Copenhagen, Denmark

Co-Organizers

Wei Xu, Georgia Institute of Technology, United States of America
Alan Ritter, Georgia Institute of Technology, United States of America
Tim Baldwin, Mohamed bin Zayed University of Artificial Intelligence, United Arab Emirates and The University of Melbourne, Australia

Program Committee

Invited Speakers

Jennifer Foster, Dublin City University
Yvette Graham, Trinity College Dublin

Reviewers

Diana Inkpen, University of Ottawa
Yuval Pinter, Ben-Gurion University of the Negev
Wei Gao, Singapore Management University
Ayah Zirikly, Johns Hopkins University
Maria Antoniak, Allen Institute for Artificial Intelligence
Richard Sproat, Google
Dianna Radpour, University of Colorado at Boulder
Yogarshi Vyas, Amazon
A. Seza Doğruöz, Ghent University
Naoki Otani, Megagon Labs
Aron Culotta, Tulane University
Shi Zong, University of Waterloo
Mika Hämäläinen, Rootroo Ltd
Eduard Dragut, Temple University
Mirco Schönfeld, Universität Bayreuth
Sweta Agrawal, University of Maryland, College Park
Maximilian Mozes, Cohere
Roman Yangarber, University of Helsinki
Kwan Hui Lim, Singapore University of Technology and Design
Lucy H. Lin, Spotify
Yansong Feng, Peking University
Yoshinari Fujinuma, AWS AI Labs
Nikola Ljubešić, Jožef Stefan Institute
Dan Simonson, BlackBoiler, Inc.
Dan Goldwasser, Purdue University
Marina Danilevsky, International Business Machines
Hamdy Mubarak, Qatar Computing Research Institute
Shubhashis Roy Dipta, University of Maryland, Baltimore County
Micha Elsner, Ohio State University
Yasuhide Miura, FUJIFILM
Xingyi Song, University of Sheffield
Monojit Choudhury, Mohamed bin Zayed University of Artificial Intelligence
Maria Nadejde, Amazon
Kevin Small, Amazon
Chao Jiang, Georgia Institute of Technology
Kokil Jaidka, National University of Singapore
Joel R. Tetreault, Dataminr
Jennifer Foster, Dublin City University
Manuel Montes, Centro de Investigación en Computación, IPN, Mexico
Soroush Vosoughi, Dartmouth College
Reno Kriz, Johns Hopkins University

Anna Wegmann, Utrecht University
Mike Zhang, IT University of Copenhagen
Sai P Vallurupalli, University of Maryland, Baltimore County
Eduardo Blanco, University of Arizona
Jeniya Tabassum, Amazon
Paolo Rosso, Universitat Politècnica de València
Xiaojun Wan, Peking University
Abhinav Singh, Bloomberg
Vinodkumar Prabhakaran, Google
Dhivya Chinnappa, Thomson Reuters
Hamid Beigy, Sharif University of Technology
Alice Oh, Korea Advanced Institute of Science and Technology
Zeerak Talat, Mohamed bin Zayed University of Artificial Intelligence
Daniel Varab, Novo Nordisk, IT University of Copenhagen
Gabriel Stanovsky, Hebrew University of Jerusalem
Fajri Koto, Mohamed bin Zayed University of Artificial Intelligence
Ori Shapira, Amazon
Biaoyan Fang, CSIRO
Marcos Zampieri, George Mason University
Paul Cook, University of New Brunswick
Christine de Kock, University of Melbourne
Vicky Zayats, Google
Guangzeng Han, University of Memphis
Tanmay Parekh, University of California, Los Angeles
Lisheng Fu, New York University
Danae Sanchez Villegas, University of Sheffield
Patrick Littell, National Research Council of Canada
Günter Neumann, German Research Center for AI
Jing Jiang, Singapore Management University
Kristen Johnson, Michigan State University
Cagri Coltekin, University of Tuebingen
Emily Allaway, Columbia University
Anthony Rios, University of Texas at San Antonio
Chiyu Zhang, University of British Columbia
Peter Makarov, Amazon
Ishan Jindal, IBM Research
Sihao Chen, University of Pennsylvania
Alla Rozovskaya, City University of New York
Rahmad Mahendra, Royal Melbourne Institute of Technology
Sara Tonelli, Fondazione Bruno Kessler
Vincent Ng, University of Texas at Dallas
Vasileios Lampos, University College London, University of London
Alexander Fabbri, SalesForce.com
Vivek Kulkarni, Grammarly
Andreas Spitz, Universität Konstanz
Zhiyang Teng, Nanyang Technological University
Yitong Li, Huawei Technologies Co., Ltd.
Sai P Vallurupalli, University of Maryland, Baltimore County

Table of Contents

Program

Friday, March 22, 2024

09:00 - 09:05 *Opening Remarks*

09:05 - 10:00 *Keynote: Yvette Graham*

10:00 - 10:30 *Oral Session 1*

Correcting Challenging Finnish Learner Texts With Claude, GPT-3.5 and GPT-4 Large Language Models
Mathias Creutz

Effects of different types of noise in user-generated reviews on human and machine translations including ChatGPT
Maja Popovic, Ekaterina Lapshinova-Koltunski and Maarit Koponen

10:30 - 11:00 *Coffee Break*

11:00 - 12:30 *Poster Session*

The Effects of Data Quality on Named Entity Recognition
Divya Bhadauria, Alejandro Sierra Múnera and Ralf Krestel

Context-aware Adversarial Attack on Named Entity Recognition
Shuguang Chen, Leonardo Neves and Thamar Solorio

CODET: A Benchmark for Contrastive Dialectal Evaluation of Machine Translation
Md Mahfuz Ibn Alam, Sina Ahmadi and Antonios Anastasopoulos

Label Supervised Contrastive Learning for Imbalanced Text Classification in Euclidean and Hyperbolic Embedding Spaces
Baber Khalid, Shuyang Dai, Tara Taghavi and Sungjin Lee

Stanceosaurus 2.0 - Classifying Stance Towards Russian and Spanish Misinformation
Anton Lavrouk, Ian Ligon, Jonathan Zheng, Tarek Naous, Wei Xu and Alan Ritter

Stars Are All You Need: A Distantly Supervised Pyramid Network for Unified Sentiment Analysis
Wenchang Li, Yixing Chen, Shuang Zheng, Lei Wang and John P. Lalor

Friday, March 22, 2024 (continued)

Effects of different types of noise in user-generated reviews on human and machine translations including ChatGPT
Maja Popovic, Ekaterina Lapshinova-Koltunski and Maarit Koponen

Barriers to Effective Evaluation of Simultaneous Interpretation
Shira Wein, Te I, Colin Cherry, Juraj Juraska, Dirk Padfield and Wolfgang Macherey

When do Generative Query and Document Expansions Fail? A Comprehensive Study Across Methods, Retrievers, and Datasets
Orion Weller, Kyle Lo, David Wadden, Dawn Lawrie, Benjamin Van Durme, Arman Cohan and Luca Soldaini

12:30 - 14:00 *Lunch*

14:00 - 15:00 *Keynote: Jennifer Foster*

15:00 - 15:30 *Oral Session 2*

The Effects of Data Quality on Named Entity Recognition
Divya Bhadauria, Alejandro Sierra Múnera and Ralf Krestel

Stars Are All You Need: A Distantly Supervised Pyramid Network for Unified Sentiment Analysis
Wenchang Li, Yixing Chen, Shuang Zheng, Lei Wang and John P. Lalor

15:30 - 16:00 *Coffee Break*

16:00 - 17:00 *Oral Session 3*

Topic Bias in Emotion Classification
Maximilian Wegge and Roman Klinger

A Comparative Analysis of Noise Reduction Methods in Sentiment Analysis on Noisy Bangla Texts
Kazi Toufique Elahi, Tasnuva Binte Rahman, Shakil Shahriar, Samir Sarker, Md. Tanvir Rouf Shawon and G. M. Shahariar Shibli

MaintNorm: A corpus and benchmark model for lexical normalisation and masking of industrial maintenance short text
Tyler Bikaun, Melinda Hodkiewicz and Wei Liu

Friday, March 22, 2024 (continued)

Correcting Challenging Finnish Learner Texts With Claude, GPT-3.5 and GPT-4 Large Language Models

Mathias Creutz
Department of Digital Humanities, University of Helsinki, Finland
mathias.creutz@helsinki.fi

Abstract

This paper studies the correction of challenging authentic Finnish learner texts at beginner level (CEFR A1). Three state-of-the-art large language models are compared, and it is shown that GPT-4 outperforms GPT-3.5, which in turn outperforms Claude v1 on this task. Additionally, ensemble models based on classifiers combining outputs of multiple single models are evaluated. The highest accuracy for an ensemble model is 84.3 %, whereas the best single model, which is a GPT-4 model, produces sentences that are fully correct 83.3 % of the time. In general, the different models perform on a continuum, where grammatical correctness, fluency and coherence go hand in hand.

1 Introduction

The motivation behind the present work is to help second-language (L2) learners express themselves fluently and idiomatically in a non-native language that they do not master very well. The problem can be studied through the automatic correction of challenging learner texts that contain numerous mistakes when it comes to inflection, spelling, word choice, word order and even low intelligibility overall. Previously, neural machine translation with different data augmentation techniques have been employed to solve this task (Sjöblom et al., 2021), but the advent of powerful large language models (LLMs) opens up new possibilities to tackle the problem.

Bryant et al. (2023) present an overview of the state of art in Grammatical Error Correction (GEC). The term *grammatical* is understood broadly and does not only refer to grammatical errors. However, GEC is typically seen as a *local* substitution task (Ye et al., 2023), where occasional mistakes are corrected in generally intelligible text. The survey covers methods and data sets (predominantly in English). The article was written before the breakthrough of GPT-3.5 and GPT-4, and observations regarding LLMs are therefore limited. Some small-scale experiments are mentioned (Wu et al., 2023; Coyne et al., 2023), concluding that LLMs tend to overcorrect for fluency, which causes them to underperform on datasets that were developed for minimal corrections (Fang et al., 2023). By contrast, Penteado and Perez (2023) find that LLMs outperform earlier methods on more challenging texts, typed in a hurry or containing slang, abbreviations, and neologisms.

The main goal of this paper is to study how well state-of-the-art large language models are capable of rephrasing beginner-level learner texts into idiomatic, correctly formulated texts. As advocated by Sakaguchi et al. (2016), the focus is not on the detection and correction of specific errors in isolation, but on the fluency and naturalness of entire correction hypotheses. As ensemble models have proven effective in earlier GEC tasks (Grundkiewicz and Junczys-Dowmunt, 2018; Li et al., 2019; Bryant et al., 2019), additional experiments are carried out, where multiple model outputs are combined.

2 Data

A subset of ICLFI, the International Corpus of Learner Finnish (Jantunen, 2011; Jantunen et al., 2013) is used as data for the experiments. [1] A random selection of 25 texts were selected for the study, all of them labeled with the lowest language proficiency level: CEFR A1.[2] The A1 level was chosen in order to obtain as challenging data as possible. Table 1 shows one text extracted from this data, with an approximate English translation. The total number of sentences in all 25 texts is 210.

Some English learner corpora, such as FCE (Yannakoudakis et al., 2011) and NUCLE (Dahlmeier

[1] Available online through the Language Bank of Finland: https://www.kielipankki.fi/corpora/iclfi/

[2] https://www.coe.int/en/web/common-european-framework-reference-languages

Proceedings of the Ninth Workshop on Noisy and User-generated Text (W-NUT 2024), pages 1–10
March 22, 2024

Minä lulee että, Anna on nyt niin erilainen kuin tavallisesti, koska hänellä on stressi. Anna ei ole aikaa puhumaan Jutan kanssa, koska korjata tule hänen kotiinsa. Annalla ei ole siihen jokin hyvä syy, koska pesukone on rikki, pesukone on siihen jokin hyvä syy. Minusta Anna on kateellinen, koska Juttasta Anssi on hauska mies.	I belives thatt, Anna is now so different than usually, because she is stressed. Anna is no time talking with Jutta, because repair come to her house. Anna has not some good reason for this, because the laundry machine is broken, the laundry machine is a good reason for that. I think Anna is jealous, because according Jutta Anssi is a fun guy.

Table 1: An example text from the ICLFI corpus (CEFR level A1). The Finnish text is on the left with an approximate English translation on the right. The intended meaning is not entirely clear, because one sentence contradicts itself.

et al., 2013) contain reference corrections that can be utilized for evaluation, but that is unfortunately not the case with the ICLFI corpus.[3] TopLing (University of Jyväskylä, 2016) is another Finnish learner corpus that lacks correction hypotheses. There used to exist an additional resource, the so-called YKI corpus based on Finnish national certificates of language proficiency exams (Yleiset kielitutkinnot), but it is no longer available because of copyright issues.

3 Models

Three different commercial LLM systems were tested in this study: Claude v1 by Anthropic[4], as well as GPT-3.5 (turbo) and GPT-4 by Open AI (OpenAI, 2023).[5] Claude may be an interesting complement to the GPT models, as it has been seen to outperform ChatGPT (GPT-3.5) in certain open-domain conversation tasks (Lin and Chen, 2023).

The LLMs were accessed through their APIs, Claude at the end of June and GPT-3.5 and GPT-4 at the end of July and beginning of August 2023. The models were prompted to reformulate the learner texts into fluent, impeccable Finnish language that contains no factual or grammatical errors. The exact prompts used can be found in Appendix A. Each prompt contained an entire text in order for the model to be able to exploit context across sentence boundaries.

LLMs are non-deterministic. The temperature parameter ranging between 0 and 1 regulates the randomness of the output. Low temperatures result in the most predictable result, whereas higher temperatures increase creativity.[6]

Each of the LLMs was tested on six different temperature values: 0.0, 0.1, ..., 0.5. Even with the lowest temperature of 0.0, the systems were not fully deterministic, and some variability remained in the output. Every configuration was run twice, because of the non-deterministic nature of the task. These runs were confirmed not to depend on the outcome of the previous run (see Appendix B). This resulted in 36 correction hypotheses for each of the 25 texts (3 LLMs times 6 temperature values times 2 runs each). In the following, these 36 setups will be referred to as *models* or *single models*.

4 Annotation

The 36 correction hypotheses produced by the LLMs for each of the 25 learner texts were manually tagged as correct or incorrect. The tagging was performed on the sentence level: either a sentence was fully correct or it was incorrect, considering the context of surrounding sentences.

The annotation was performed independently by two persons, the author of the paper and one of his colleagues. The annotators could see the full original text and the suggested corrections, sentence by sentence. When multiple models had produced the same sentence in the same context, it was sufficient to annotate that sentence only once. Theroretically, there would have been $36 * 210 = 7560$ sentences to annotate, but because of duplicates, the actual number was reduced to one fifth of that.

Initially, the annotators agreed in 83.9 % of the cases (type count, after sentence deduplication). This corresponds to 87.5 % of all generated sentences (token count). In a second round, the annotators discussed the results and decided which category to choose for the remaining cases. The main reasons for initial disagreement were minor errors that had gone unnoticed by either annotator, different levels of tolerance for the incorrect use of punctuation,[7] and confusion about the intended meaning of the original sentence.

[3] In fact, ICLFI has been automatically lemmatized and parsed, and some of the misspelled words have been corrected in the process, but this representation is not accurate enough to be used as a proper reference.

[4] `https://claudeai.pro/what-is-claude-v1/`

[5] `https://platform.openai.com/`

[6] `https://platform.openai.com/docs/guides/gpt/how-should-i-set-the-temperature-parameter`

[7] In the end, we decided not to be very strict about comma rules.

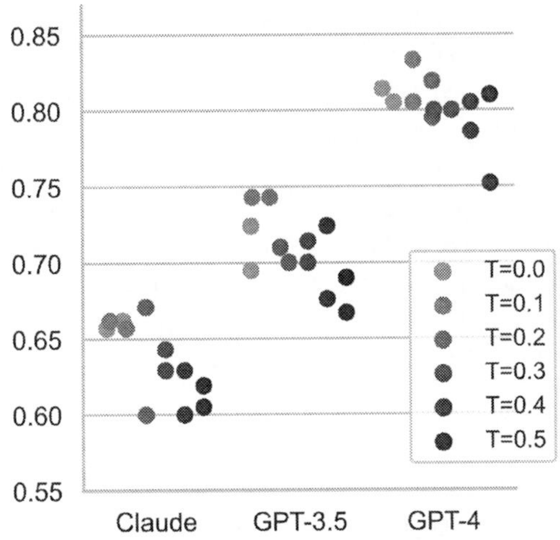

Figure 1: Accuracies of each of the 36 single models. Every model is represented by a dot, and the dots are grouped in "swarms" by LLM type. In every swarm, we progress from left to right as the temperature (T) rises, with higher temperatures rendered in darker color. The best model (GPT-4, $T = 0.1$, 1st run) reaches an accuracy of 0.833, which corresponds to 175 fully correct sentences out of 210 in the data.

5 Single Model Results

The accuracies of the 36 single models have been plotted in Figure 1. The results reveal two things: Firstly, there are clear differences in the performance levels of the LLMs. All GPT-4 models are better than all GPT-3.5 models, which are in turn better than all Claude models (with the exception of the one weakest GPT-3.5 model). Secondly, the temperature parameter works as expected. Conservative, predictable results are to be preferred in this correction task, and thus lower temperatures work better than higher temperatures. However, the best results are in general obtained for $T = 0.1$, not the lowest possible value $T = 0.0$.

In line with these findings, Coyne et al. (2023) observe that GPT-4 outperforms GPT-3.5 on English GEC data (Napoles et al., 2017; Bryant et al., 2019). They also confirm that a low temperature yields better performance in this task.

In previous work on Finnish GEC (Creutz and Sjöblom, 2019), an annotated sample of the (since then withdrawn) YKI corpus was used as test data. The full-sentence accuracy obtained for the best setup was 27.2 %, which falls far behind the accuracies in Figure 1. Direct comparisons cannot be made because of the different corpora used in the studies. However, the types and levels of the texts are very similar.

Hypotheses	Proposed by models											Label
	1	2	3	4	5	6	7	8	9	...	36	
How are you?	●		●		●	●						✓
How you are?											●	✗
How are things?				●				●				✓
What are you like?		●							●			✗
How old are you?							●					✗

Figure 2: Possible correction hypotheses for a fictive sentence *"How yuo are?"* (in English for illustration purposes). Among other things, we see that models 1, 3, 5 and 6 propose the first correction hypothesis *"How are you?"*, which is correct, whereas model 36 proposes *"How you are?"*, which is incorrect. From this example we get five data entries to train a supervised classification model. The inputs consist of 36-dimensional binary vectors, where every dimension corresponds to one of the single models and is zero or one depending on whether that model produced this particular hypothesis. The outputs are binary as well, indicating whether the hypothesis is correct or not.

6 Ensemble Models

The best single model produces 175 correct sentences out of 210 (83.3 %). However, if we look at all 36 models combined, there are only 7 sentences that all models get wrong. This suggests that by being very smart at combining sentences from different models, we could ideally reach an accuracy of $203/210$ (96.7 %).

In the following, we will study supervised learning of ensemble models that combine outputs from the single models. The simplifying assumption is made that sentences from different hypotheses can always be combined. For instance, the two partly correct texts *"Hi there! How's you?"* and *"Helo! How are you?"* can be combined coherently into *"Hi there! How are you?"*.

The problem is formulated as a classification task. For every input sentence, each of the 36 models has produced a correction hypothesis, but typically the number of unique hypotheses is lower than 36, because several models produce the same hypotheses. This is exploited by a classifier, which is trained to predict when a hypothesis is correct based on the subset of models that have proposed it, as illustrated in Figure 2.

As there is limited amount of data available, rather than setting aside a separate test set, cross-validation is used, such that every learner text in turn serves as the test set and the remaining 24 texts are used for training. In this way, test results are obtained for all 25 texts and direct comparisons can be made to the single model results (Figure 1). The feature extraction (Figure 2) produces 1532 vectors in total. As one text is left out in turn, on average 1470 vectors (24/25) are available for training.

6.1 Classifiers Used

The limited amount of data available calls for fairly simple classifiers with a small numbers of parameters to tune, in order to avoid overfitting.

Naive Bayes. (NLTK implementation, Bird et al., 2019) This classifier is not very sensitive to the size of the data set, because the training amounts to solving a closed-form expression. However, the underlying independence assumption may lead to the exaggeration of correlated features.

Maximum Entropy. This is logistic regression using the Maximum Entropy classifier of NLTK. Conditional independence is not assumed, but the lack of a closed-form solution may lead to suboptimal weights in the model.

Weighted Sum. This is a simplified, deterministic alternative to Maximum Entropy. A weight vector w of the same dimensionality as the binary correction hypothesis vectors x is estimated. During prediction, the hypothesis with the highest score s is selected: $s = w \cdot x$. The elements w_i of w correspond to the prominence of the ith model in the weighted sum and is proportional to the number of times that model has predicted a correct hypothesis, divided by the total number of models that predicted the same hypothesis. This mitigates the effect of correlated features.

N **Agreeing Models** An asymmetric decision tree is trained in order to explicitly model correlated features. The tree branches onto one side only ("`if` *condition 1* `then done else if` *condition 2* `then done ... else done`").

The conditions correspond to all combinations of 2 .. N models that are more accurate than the best single model when they are in agreement on what hypothesis to propose. These model combinations are sorted, most accurate first. The last fallback condition was originally the best single model, but was later replaced by the Naive Bayes classifier for better performance.

N values ranging from 2 to 5 have been tested. For higher values of N, all lower-order combinations of models are also included. The results for $N = 5$ turn out to be identical to those of $N = 4$.

For the pairs of models ($N = 2$), a minor variant ($N = 2^*$) was tested as well. In the basic case, the sorting order of the conditions is statically determined from the entire training set, whereas the extended version ($N = 2^*$) incrementally recalculates accuracies on the remainder of the training set, from which data points that triggered previous conditions in the chain have been removed.

6.2 Ensemble Model Results

If all single models are combined into ensemble models, only one of the resulting ensembles (N Agreeing Models with $N = 2^*$) outperforms the best single model (see Appendix C). The best ensemble obtains an accuracy of 0.838, compared to the best single model: 0.833. This is a rather insignificant improvement.

We have observed that the Claude models perform worst in the task and that low temperatures are to be preferred. By excluding the Claude models and temperatures above 0.3, the results in Figure 3 are obtained. Now, the advantage between the best ensemble model (Weighted Sum) and best single model is slightly larger (0.843 vs. 0.833). In other words, the sentence error rate is reduced by 6.0 %. This is the best result of all trials involving different combinations of single models. The theoretical upper bound on accuracy by an oracle model would be 0.967. None of the ensembles reach accuracies even close to that. Further analysis can be found in Appendix C.

Finding related work on ensemble models built on GPT-3.5 or GPT-4 is hard, and none of it addresses the GEC task. Work by Jiang et al. (2023), Yuan et al. (2023), Fu et al. (2023), Manakul et al. (2023), García-Díaz et al. (2023), and Portillo Wightman et al. (2023) relate to other NLP tasks, such as summarization, sentiment analysis and question answering. Tang et al. (2023) create ensembles of less advanced pre-trained language models (BART, BERT, GPT-2 etc.) for Chinese GEC, but fail to outperform the best single models.

7 Qualitative Evaluation

When the generated hypotheses were tagged as correct or incorrect, it was not known to the annotators which model had produced them. Therefore, no systematic qualitative evaluation of the differences between Claude, GPT-3.5 and GPT-4 is available.

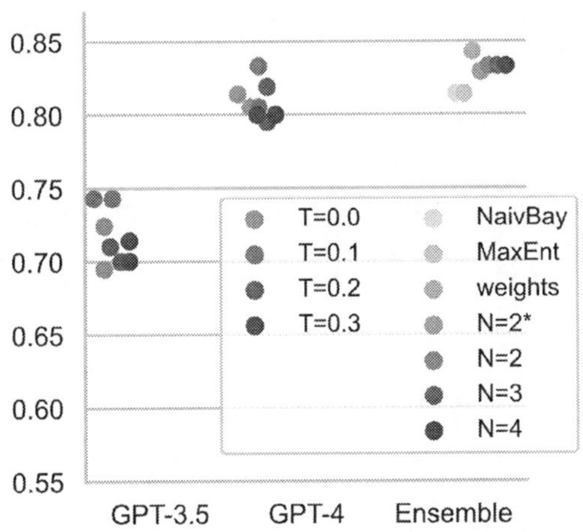

Figure 3: Ensemble models (in blue-green) created from a selection of single models (in red), based on GPT-3.5 and GPT-4 only ($T < 0.4$). The best ensemble model (Weighted Sum) obtains an accuracy of 0.843. Second best are the asymmetric decision trees $N = 2, 3, 4$ at 0.833, which is the same accuracy as for the best single model.

Nonetheless, it appears that the models perform on a continuum, where grammatical correctness, fluency and coherence go hand in hand.

In general, the Claude models most faithfully reproduce the original texts. However, this comes at the expense of not correcting all grammatical errors or resolving contradictions. The GPT models produce higher-quality output, but these models also reformulate the texts to a higher extent. Very few typos or grammar errors remain in their output. The GPT models may have a tendency to "over-correct" for fluency, but whether that is considered good or bad is subjective.

The best ensemble model fluently combines sentences from GPT-3.5 and GPT-4 output, but often fails to replace the trickiest parts that go wrong in the best single model with sentences that some less reliable single model actually got right.

A full example of a text that is corrected by each model type (Claude, GPT-3, GPT-4 and Ensemble) is shown in Appendix D.

8 Discussion and Conclusion

Finnish is a morphologically rich language that is considered hard to learn. This study has shown the capacity of state-of-the-art large language models to produce accurate correction hypotheses for challenging learner texts. Experiments could have been conducted on simpler, established data sets in other languages, but that would not have served the purpose. However, the lack of appropriate annotated data sets meant that a low-resource scenario was adopted, with a data set consisting of 210 sentences. As the output of every run had to be tagged manually and there were 36 runs, the number of sentences to tag was still rather high.

The annotation was performed using a binary scheme: Either a sentence was considered fully correct or incorrect. This obscures any differences between "almost correct" and "totally wrong". Whereas this may seem too coarse an analysis on the level of individual sentences, it is unlikely to make a large difference for the data set as a whole and the performance ranking of the models.

A verified gold-standard would allow for automatic, faster testing. There are typically multiple correct answers, however, and it is hardly possible to know all possible alternatives in advance.

The benefit of the ensemble models turned out to be limited. Alternative directions for improvement might involve few-shot chain-of-thought prompting and finetuning (Kwon et al., 2023; Fan et al., 2023).

9 Limitations

The present study is exploratory and the size of the data set is small (25 learner texts consisting of 210 sentences in total). This means that very fine-grained conclusions cannot be made, since some observed differences are not statistically significant. Nevertheless, the higher-level distinctions are statistical significant, such as the difference in performance between the different types of LLMs. Additionally, all individual test results are plotted as "swarms" in order to clearly visualize the magnitude of the variance between different setups.

A larger data set would have been preferred, but this would also have required a heavier annotation effort. The annotation could also have been performed differently. Initially, the two independent annotators were in agreement on the category of approximately 5/6 of the sentences. A joint decision then needed to be made for the remaining 1/6. This was a pragmatic decision suitable for an exploratory feasibility study. If the goal had been to create a solid gold-standard reference for wide public dissemination, more rigorous and time-consuming approaches could have been considered.

Some prompt engineering was performed qualitatively, but no systematic quantitative evaluation of the effect of changing the prompts was performed (see Appendix A).

A new version of Claude, Claude 2.0, has been published after the experiments were run. New experiments were not performed using Claude 2.0.

In this work, sentence accuracy is used as the evaluation metric. Analyzing the precision and recall of the corrections of specific error types is beyond the scope of this study. The aim is to look at the end result as a whole and investigate to what extent challenging learner texts can be reformulated into natural, correct, idiomatic language.

10 Ethical Considerations

The data set used in this study is a subset of the International Corpus of Learning Finnish (ICLFI). The corpus has been curated from authentic texts written by students of the Finnish language at international universities. The identities of the authors have nonetheless been protected. Names of people and places have been anonymized in the texts.

Large language models are trained on very large amounts of text data and may therefore learn harmful biases and prejudices that are reflected in some portions of the training data. Such tendencies have not been observed in the texts generated by the LLMs in this work.

Acknowledgments

I would like to express my sincere thanks and great appreciation to my colleague Mikko Aulamo for volunteering as an annotator of the data. I would also like to thank my colleagues Teemu Vahtola, Anssi Moisio and Jörg Tiedemann for valuable discussions and comments during the work on this paper. Likewise, I am very grateful to the reviewers of the manuscript for their insightful comments. This work has been supported by the *Behind the Words* project, funded by the Research Council of Finland 2021–2023.

References

Steven Bird, Ewan Klein, and Edward Loper. 2019. *Natural Language Processing with Python – Analyzing Text with the Natural Language Toolkit.*

Christopher Bryant, Mariano Felice, Øistein E. Andersen, and Ted Briscoe. 2019. The BEA-2019 shared task on grammatical error correction. In *Proceedings of the Fourteenth Workshop on Innovative Use of NLP for Building Educational Applications*, pages 52–75, Florence, Italy. Association for Computational Linguistics.

Christopher Bryant, Zheng Yuan, Muhammad Reza Qorib, Hannan Cao, Hwee Tou Ng, and Ted Briscoe. 2023. Grammatical Error Correction: A Survey of the State of the Art. *Computational Linguistics*, pages 1–59.

Steven Coyne, Keisuke Sakaguchi, Diana Galvan-Sosa, Michael Zock, and Kentaro Inui. 2023. Analyzing the performance of GPT-3.5 and GPT-4 in Grammatical Error Correction.

Mathias Creutz and Eetu Sjöblom. 2019. Toward automatic improvement of language produced by non-native language learners. In *Proceedings of the 8th Workshop on NLP for Computer Assisted Language Learning*, pages 20–30, Turku, Finland. LiU Electronic Press.

Daniel Dahlmeier, Hwee Tou Ng, and Siew Mei Wu. 2013. Building a large annotated corpus of learner English: The NUS corpus of learner English. In *Proceedings of the Eighth Workshop on Innovative Use of NLP for Building Educational Applications*, pages 22–31, Atlanta, Georgia. Association for Computational Linguistics.

Yaxin Fan, Feng Jiang, Peifeng Li, and Haizhou Li. 2023. GrammarGPT: Exploring open-source llms for native Chinese grammatical error correction with supervised fine-tuning.

Tao Fang, Shu Yang, Kaixin Lan, Derek F. Wong, Jinpeng Hu, Lidia S. Chao, and Yue Zhang. 2023. Is ChatGPT a highly fluent grammatical error correction system? A comprehensive evaluation.

Xingyu Fu, Sheng Zhang, Gukyeong Kwon, Pramuditha Perera, Henghui Zhu, Yuhao Zhang, Alexander Hanbo Li, William Yang Wang, Zhiguo Wang, Vittorio Castelli, Patrick Ng, Dan Roth, and Bing Xiang. 2023. Generate then select: Open-ended visual question answering guided by world knowledge. In *Findings of the Association for Computational Linguistics: ACL 2023*, pages 2333–2346, Toronto, Canada. Association for Computational Linguistics.

José Antonio García-Díaz, Camilo Caparros-laiz, Ángela Almela, Gema Alcaráz-Mármol, María José Marín-Pérez, and Rafael Valencia-García. 2023. UMUTeam at SemEval-2023 task 12: Ensemble learning of LLMs applied to sentiment analysis for low-resource African languages. In *Proceedings of the 17th International Workshop on Semantic Evaluation (SemEval-2023)*, pages 285–292, Toronto, Canada. Association for Computational Linguistics.

Roman Grundkiewicz and Marcin Junczys-Dowmunt. 2018. Near human-level performance in grammatical error correction with hybrid machine translation. In *Proceedings of the 2018 Conference of the North American Chapter of the Association for Computational Linguistics: Human Language Technologies, Volume 2 (Short Papers)*, pages 284–290, New Orleans, Louisiana. Association for Computational Linguistics.

Jarmo Jantunen. 2011. Kansainvälinen oppijansuomen korpus (ICLFI): typologia, taustamuuttujat ja annotointi. *Lähivõrdlusi. Lähivertailuja*, 21:86–105.

Jarmo Jantunen, Sisko Brunni, and University of Oulu, Department of Finnish Language. 2013. International Corpus of Learner Finnish.

Dongfu Jiang, Xiang Ren, and Bill Yuchen Lin. 2023. LLM-blender: Ensembling large language models with pairwise ranking and generative fusion. In *Proceedings of the 61st Annual Meeting of the Association for Computational Linguistics (Volume 1: Long Papers)*, pages 14165–14178, Toronto, Canada. Association for Computational Linguistics.

Sang Kwon, Gagan Bhatia, El Moatez Billah Nagoudi, and Muhammad Abdul-Mageed. 2023. Beyond English: Evaluating LLMs for Arabic grammatical error correction. In *Proceedings of ArabicNLP 2023*, pages 101–119, Singapore (Hybrid). Association for Computational Linguistics.

Ruobing Li, Chuan Wang, Yefei Zha, Yonghong Yu, Shiman Guo, Qiang Wang, Yang Liu, and Hui Lin. 2019. The LAIX systems in the BEA-2019 GEC shared task. In *Proceedings of the Fourteenth Workshop on Innovative Use of NLP for Building Educational Applications*, pages 159–167, Florence, Italy. Association for Computational Linguistics.

Yen-Ting Lin and Yun-Nung Chen. 2023. LLM-eval: Unified multi-dimensional automatic evaluation for open-domain conversations with large language models. In *Proceedings of the 5th Workshop on NLP for Conversational AI (NLP4ConvAI 2023)*, pages 47–58, Toronto, Canada. Association for Computational Linguistics.

Potsawee Manakul, Yassir Fathullah, Adian Liusie, Vyas Raina, Vatsal Raina, and Mark Gales. 2023. CUED at ProbSum 2023: Hierarchical ensemble of summarization models. In *The 22nd Workshop on Biomedical Natural Language Processing and BioNLP Shared Tasks*, pages 516–523, Toronto, Canada. Association for Computational Linguistics.

Courtney Napoles, Keisuke Sakaguchi, and Joel Tetreault. 2017. JFLEG: A fluency corpus and benchmark for grammatical error correction. In *Proceedings of the 15th Conference of the European Chapter of the Association for Computational Linguistics: Volume 2, Short Papers*, pages 229–234, Valencia, Spain. Association for Computational Linguistics.

OpenAI. 2023. GPT-4 technical report.

Maria Carolina Penteado and Fábio Perez. 2023. Evaluating GPT-3.5 and GPT-4 on grammatical error correction for Brazilian Portuguese.

Gwenyth Portillo Wightman, Alexandra Delucia, and Mark Dredze. 2023. Strength in numbers: Estimating confidence of large language models by prompt agreement. In *Proceedings of the 3rd Workshop on Trustworthy Natural Language Processing (TrustNLP 2023)*, pages 326–362, Toronto, Canada. Association for Computational Linguistics.

Keisuke Sakaguchi, Courtney Napoles, Matt Post, and Joel Tetreault. 2016. Reassessing the goals of grammatical error correction: Fluency instead of grammaticality. *Transactions of the Association for Computational Linguistics*, 4:169–182.

Eetu Sjöblom, Mathias Creutz, and Teemu Vahtola. 2021. Grammatical error generation based on translated fragments. In *Proceedings of the 23rd Nordic Conference on Computational Linguistics (NoDaLiDa)*, pages 398–403, Reykjavik, Iceland (Online). Linköping University Electronic Press, Sweden.

Chenming Tang, Xiuyu Wu, and Yunfang Wu. 2023. Are pre-trained language models useful for model ensemble in Chinese grammatical error correction? In *Proceedings of the 61st Annual Meeting of the Association for Computational Linguistics (Volume 2: Short Papers)*, pages 893–901, Toronto, Canada. Association for Computational Linguistics.

University of Jyväskylä. 2016. The Finnish Subcorpus of Topling - Paths in Second Language Acquisition.

Haoran Wu, Wenxuan Wang, Yuxuan Wan, Wenxiang Jiao, and Michael Lyu. 2023. ChatGPT or Grammarly? Evaluating ChatGPT on Grammatical Error Correction Benchmark.

Helen Yannakoudakis, Ted Briscoe, and Ben Medlock. 2011. A new dataset and method for automatically grading ESOL texts. In *Proceedings of the 49th Annual Meeting of the Association for Computational Linguistics: Human Language Technologies*, pages 180–189, Portland, Oregon, USA. Association for Computational Linguistics.

Jingheng Ye, Yinghui Li, Qingyu Zhou, Yangning Li, Shirong Ma, Hai-Tao Zheng, and Ying Shen. 2023. CLEME: Debiasing multi-reference evaluation for grammatical error correction.

Xingdi Yuan, Tong Wang, Yen-Hsiang Wang, Emery Fine, Rania Abdelghani, Hélène Sauzéon, and Pierre-Yves Oudeyer. 2023. Selecting better samples from pre-trained LLMs: A case study on question generation. In *Findings of the Association for Computational Linguistics: ACL 2023*, pages 12952–12965, Toronto, Canada. Association for Computational Linguistics.

Appendices

A Prompts

The following zero-shot prompt, written in Finnish, was utilized to ask GPT-3.5 and GPT-4 to produce corrected texts:

`Hei! Korjaisitko seuraavan tekstin siten, että siitä tulee sujuvaa, erinomaista suomen kieltä eikä sisällä asiavirheitä eikä kielioppivirheitä. Älä kirjoita ylimääräistä tekstiä. Pelkkä korjattu teksti riittää. Tekstin alku:\n <LEARNER TEXT GOES HERE>\n Teksti päättyy.`

In English the prompt reads: *Hi, could you please correct the following text in such a way that it becomes fluent, impeccable Finnish language and does not contain factual errors or grammar errors. Do not write superfluous text. Just the corrected text is enough. Start of the text:*\n <LEARNER TEXT GOES HERE> \n *Text ends.*

The same prompt was basically used for the Claude LLM as well, with the exception that Claude requires the use of the keywords "Human:" and "Assistant:" to mark the roles in the dialog:

`\n\nHuman: Hei! Korjaisitko seuraavan tekstin siten, että siitä tulee sujuvaa, erinomaista suomen kieltä eikä sisällä asiavirheitä eikä kielioppivirheitä. Älä kirjoita ylimääräistä tekstiä. Pelkkä korjattu teksti riittää.\n <LEARNER TEXT GOES HERE>\n\nAssistant:`

Some exploratory prompt engineering went into the design of the final prompt, but no quantitative evaluation was made. Specifically, it was observed that the LLMs tended to embed their answers in polite phrases to create the impression of a natural dialog. Therefore the prompt was modified to explicitly state that only the actual correction hypothesis was desired in the output.

B Random Fluctuation

For every learner text, 36 versions of corrected texts were obtained. Three LLMs were used with six temperature values each, and every such configuration was run twice. That is, every prompt was submitted twice to the same LLM with the same temperature.

As the LLMs are non-deterministic by nature, results are expected to be slightly different on every run. However, there should not be a systematic difference, such that better (or worse) results are consistently obtained the first (or second) time the same configuration is used. The accuracies produced by all single models are plotted in Figure 4, organized by runs (first or second).

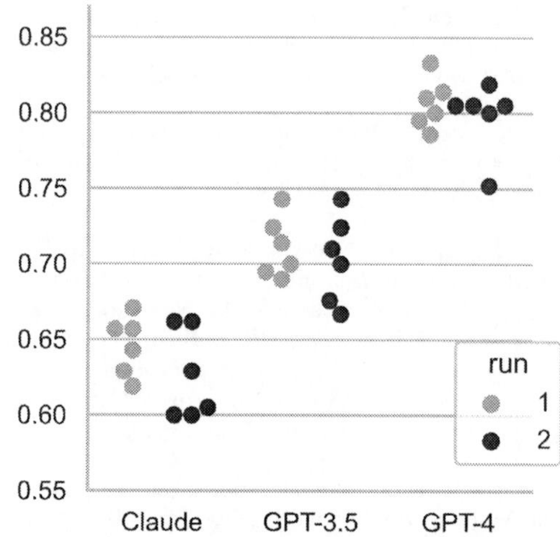

Figure 4: Accuracies obtained for all the single models. The data points are exactly the same as in Figure 1, but they have been grouped into "swarms" differently. Rather than using temperature as the categorizing feature, we now study whether the result was produced by running the configuration for the first or the second time. Thus, for every LLM, there are six dots in light color from running the prompts with six different temperatures for the first time, and six dots in dark color, from running the same setup again. If there is no systematic ordering effect, the averages from both runs should be approximately the same.

Statistical significance tests reject the hypothesis that the models are effected by the order of the runs. That is, the Claude, GPT-3.5 and GPT-4 models behave as expected in this respect.

C Further Analysis of Ensemble Models

Ensemble models based on all 36 single models were created. The accuracies obtained by the ensemble models are shown in Figure 5 together with the results from the individual single models. As discussed in Section 6.2, this is not the best possible result. A slightly better ensemble is obtained by using the Weighted Sum model and excluding all the Claude models and any models with temperatures above 0.3.

Claude + GPT-3.5? Inspired by the results from combining GPT-3.5 with GPT-4, can we benefit from combining GPT-3.5 with Claude as well? If,

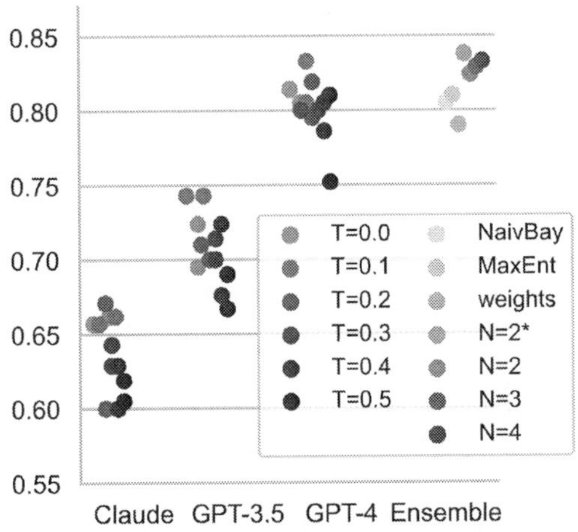

Figure 5: The single models (from Figure 1; in red) plotted together with the ensemble models (in blue-green). The best performing ensemble model is the asymmetric decision tree variant called $N = 2^*$, which attains an accuracy of 0.838. The model $N = 4$ performs on par with the best single model (accuracy 0.833), but the remaining ensemble models perform worse than the best single model.

for some reason, the best available LLM is not available, can this be compensated by using an ensemble of weaker LLMs? Unfortunately, this does not seem possible. The highest accuracy observed for an ensemble of GPT-3.5 and Claude models is 0.748. It is no better than an ensemble of GPT-3.5 models alone (accuracy: 0.752), and this setup outperforms none of the twelve single GPT-4 models.

The Naive Bayes and Maximum Entropy classifiers did not outperform the single models in the experiments. Possibly, the training sets were insufficient, or these classifiers simply failed to capture the correlations between features accurately. The Naive Bayes classifier did, however, prove useful as the fallback model in the decision-tree approach.

Further tests involved "standard", symmetric decision trees, using information gain as a splitting criterion for features. Their learning ability was poor on this task.

D Example Corrections

The differences between the different LLMs are illustrated in Table 2 using an example text. Models at temperature 0.1 have been selected as they are generally the strongest performing single models. Also the best ensemble model is included.

The text is challenging. In addition to spelling and grammar errors, it contains a contradiction. The Claude model most faithfully reproduces the original text, leaving some grammatical errors and a contradiction in the text.

The GPT models reformulate the text to a higher extent. No typos or grammar errors remain. However, these models are not able to resolve all factual errors. GPT-4 is more successful than GPT-3.5 at this, by simply dropping a part of a sentence that it cannot make sense of.

The ensemble model combines sentences from GPT-3.5 and GPT-4 without arriving at a fully correct text in this case.

These examples also highlight some challenges related to the annotation. Regarding the house being repaired when the laundry machine is broken, the original text is not clear. Apparently something needs to be fixed in the house because of the broken laundry machine, and therefore that sentence was annotated as correct. If Jutta thinks that Anssi is a fun guy, does that mean that they have fun together? The annotators found that to be the case. However, Anna is not jealous because she *herself* finds Anssi a fun guy, but because Jutta does. (Anna apparently also likes Anssi, but not necessarily because of him being fun.)

Original	
Minä lulee etttä, Anna on nyt niin erilainen kuin tavallisesti, koska hänellä on stressi. Anna ei ole aikaa puhumaan Jutan kanssa, koska korjata tule hänen kotiinsa. Annalla *ei ole siihen jokin hyvä syy*, koska pesukone on rikki, pesukone on siihen jokin hyvä syy. Minusta Anna on kateellinen, koska Juttasta Anssi on hauska mies.	I belives thatt, Anna is now so different than usually, because she is stressed. Anna is no time talking with Jutta, because repair come to her house. Anna *has not some good reason for this*, because the laundry machine is broken, the laundry machine is a good reason for that. I think Anna is jealous, because according Jutta Anssi is a fun guy.
Claude ($T = 0.1$)	
Minä luulen, että Anna on nyt niin erilainen kuin tavallisesti, koska hänellä on stressiä. Anna ei ole aikaa puhua Jutan kanssa, koska korjaaja tulee hänen kotiinsa. Annalla *ei ole siihen jotain hyvää syytä*, koska pesukone on rikki. Pesukone on siihen jokin hyvä syy. Minusta Anna on kateellinen, koska Juttasta Anssi on hauska mies.	I think that Anna is now so different than usual, because she is stressed. Anna is no time to talk to Jutta, because a repairman is coming to her house. Anna *does not have some good reason for this,* because the laundry machine is broken. The laundry machine is a good reason for that. I think Anna is jealous, because according Jutta Anssi is a fun guy.
GPT-3.5 ($T = 0.1$)	
Minä luulen, että Anna on nyt niin erilainen kuin tavallisesti, koska hänellä on stressiä. Annalla ei ole aikaa puhua Jutan kanssa, koska hänellä on korjaaja tulossa kotiinsa. Annalla *ei ole siihen mitään hyvää syytä*, koska pesukone on rikki. *Pesukoneella on siihen jokin hyvä syy.* Minusta Anna on kateellinen, koska Jutan ja Anssin välillä on hauskaa.	I think that Anna is now so different than usual, because she is stressed. Anna doesn't have time to talk to Jutta, because she will have a repairman come to her house. Anna *has no good reason for this*, because the laundry machine is broken. *The laundry machine has a good reason for that.* I think Anna is jealous, because Jutta and Anssi have fun together.
GPT-4 ($T = 0.1$)	
Minusta tuntuu, että Anna on nyt erilainen kuin tavallisesti, koska hän on stressaantunut. Anna ei ehdi jutella Jutan kanssa, koska hänen kotiaan ollaan korjaamassa. Annalla on hyvä syy tähän, sillä hänen pesukoneensa on rikki. Minusta Anna vaikuttaa kateelliselta, koska *hänestä* Anssi on hauska mies.	I think that Anna is now different than usual, because she is feeling stressed. Anna doesn't have time to talk to Jutta, because her house is being repaired. There is a good reason for this, because her laundry machine is broken. To me Anna seems jealous, because *she* thinks Anssi is a fun guy.
Ensemble (Weighted Sum policy based on GPT-3.5 and GPT-4 models only with $T < 0.4$)	
Minä luulen, että Anna on nyt niin erilainen kuin tavallisesti, koska hänellä on stressiä. Anna ei ehdi puhua Jutan kanssa, koska hänen kotiaan korjataan. Annalla *ei ole siihen mitään hyvää syytä*, koska pesukone on rikki. *Pesukoneella on siihen jokin hyvä syy.* Minusta Anna on kateellinen, koska Jutan ja Anssin välillä on hauskaa.	I think that Anna is now different than usual, because she is stressed. Anna doesn't have time to talk to Jutta, because her house is being repaired. Anna *has no good reason for this*, because the laundry machine is broken. *The laundry machine has a good reason for that.* I think Anna is jealous, because Jutta and Anssi have fun together.

Table 2: A learner text (from Table 1) with corrections suggested by a Claude, GPT-3.5, and GPT-4 model as well as an ensemble model. The Finnish text on the left is accompanied by an approximate English translation on the right. Spelling mistakes and grammatical errors have been underlined. Factual errors, such as contradictions and incorrect coreference are rendered in italics.

Context-aware Adversarial Attack on Named Entity Recognition

Shuguang Chen
University of Houston
schen52@uh.edu

Leonardo Neves
Snap Inc.
lneves@snap.com

Thamar Solorio
University of Houston
Mohamed bin Zayed University of Artificial Intelligence
tsolorio@uh.edu

Abstract

In recent years, large pre-trained language models (PLMs) have achieved remarkable performance on many natural language processing benchmarks. Despite their success, prior studies have shown that PLMs are vulnerable to attacks from adversarial examples. In this work, we focus on the named entity recognition task and study context-aware adversarial attack methods to examine the model's robustness. Specifically, we propose perturbing the most informative words for recognizing entities to create adversarial examples and investigate different candidate replacement methods to generate natural and plausible adversarial examples. Experiments and analyses show that our methods are more effective in deceiving the model into making wrong predictions than strong baselines.

1 Introduction

Existing methods for adversarial attacks mainly focus on text classification (Liang et al., 2018; Garg and Ramakrishnan, 2020), machine translation (Belinkov and Bisk, 2018; Cheng et al., 2019), reading comprehension (Jia and Liang, 2017; Wallace et al., 2019), etc. A slight perturbation to the input can deceive the model into making wrong predictions or leaking important information. Such adversarial attacks are widely used to identify potential vulnerabilities and audit the model robustness. However, in the context of named entity recognition (NER), these adversarial attack methods are inadequate since they are not customized for the labeling schemes in NER (Lin et al., 2021). This is especially problematic as the generated adversarial examples can be mislabeled.

Prior studies have proposed various context-aware attacks (i.e., perturb non-entity words) and entity attack (i.e., perturb only entity words) methods to address this issue. Despite their success, most existing methods randomly select words to

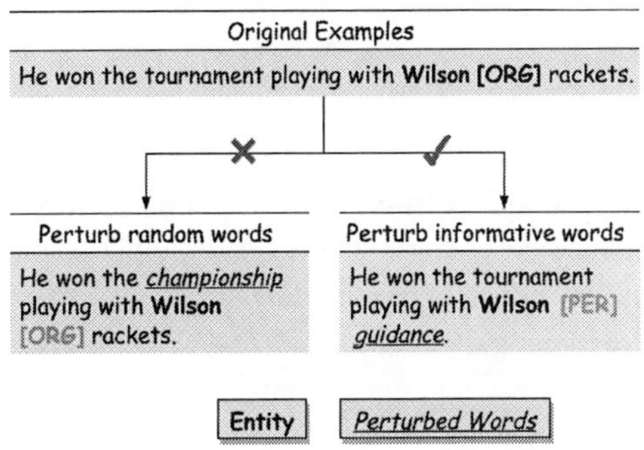

Figure 1: Comparison between adversarial attack with and without perturbing informative words.

perturb without taking the linguistic structure into consideration, limiting their effectiveness to consistently generate natural and coherent adversarial examples. Some words in a sentence are more informative than others in guiding the model to recognize named entities. For instance, in Figure 1, the word "rackets" can provide more information than the word "tournament" to infer the entity type of "Wilson". Perturbing such words can be effective in leading to more incorrect model predictions.

In this work, we explore the correlation between model vulnerability and informative words. We aim to conduct adversarial attacks by perturbing the informative words to expose the potential vulnerabilities of NER systems. To this end, we investigate different candidate selection methods to determine which words should be perturbed, including part-of-speech (POS) tagging, dependency parsing, chunking, and gradient attribution. To demonstrate the effectiveness of our proposed methods, we adapt two commonly-used candidate replacement approaches to replace the selected candidate words: synonym replacement (i.e., replace with a synonym) and masked language model replacement (i.e., replace with a candidate generated from a masked language model). We conduct experiments on three corpora and systematically evaluate our proposed methods

Proceedings of the Ninth Workshop on Noisy and User-generated Text (W-NUT 2024), pages 11–16
March 22, 2024 ©2024 Association for Computational Linguistics

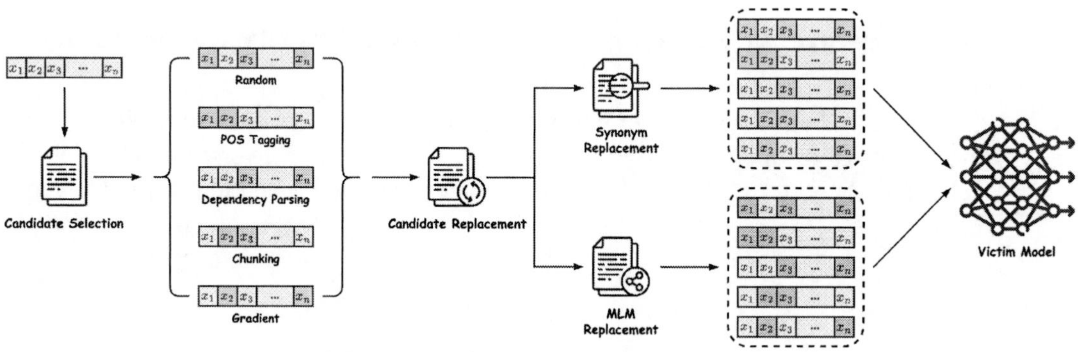

Figure 2: The pipeline of the proposed context-aware adversarial attack, including candidate selection to determine which words to perturb and candidate replacement for replacing candidate words.

with different metrics. Experimental results and analyses show that our proposed methods can effectively corrupt NER models.

In summary, our contributions are as follows:

1. We investigate different methods to perturb the most informative words for generating adversarial examples to attack NER systems.
2. Experiments and analyses show that the proposed methods are more effective than strong baselines in attacking models, posing a new challenge to existing NER systems.

2 Related Work

Adversarial attacks have been receiving increasing attention in the field of NER. Prior work in this research direction can be generally classified into two categories: i) context-aware attacks and ii) entity attacks. In the context-aware attacks, only the non-entity context words are modified. To achieve this, Lin et al. (2021) proposed to perturb the original context by sampling adversarial tokens via a masked-language model. Simoncini and Spanakis (2021) presented multiple modification methods to substitute, insert, swap, or delete characters and words. Wang et al. (2021) studied to create adversarial samples by concatenating different sentences into a single data point. For entity attacks, the entity words are modified while the non-entity context words are kept unchanged. In particular, Lin et al. (2021) exploited an external dictionary from Wikidata to find replacements for entity instances. Simoncini and Spanakis (2021) studied the use of the SCPNs (Iyyer et al., 2018) to generate candidate paraphrases as adversarial samples. Reich et al. (2022) proposed leveraging expert-guided heuristics to modify the entity tokens and their surrounding contexts, thereby altering their entity types as adversarial attacks. Wang et al. (2021) performed adversarial attacks by swapping words or manipulating characters.

3 Context-aware Adversarial Attack

In this work, we propose different methods to generate adversarial samples for the purpose of auditing the model robustness of NER systems. In the following sections, we describe the two main stages involved in this process: 1) candidate selection, which aims to determine which candidate words should be replaced; and 2) candidate replacement, which aims to find the best way to replace candidate words. The pipeline of adversarial data generation is shown in Figure 2.

3.1 Candidate Selection

To effectively attack the model, we consider perturbing the most informative words for recognizing entities. We investigate the following automated methods to select such words as candidates:

- **Random (RDM)**: select non-entity words at random from the sentence as candidate words.
- **POS tagging (PST)**: select semantic-rich non-entity words as candidate words based on their POS tags. Here, following Lin et al. (2021), we consider selecting adjectives, nouns, adverbs, and verbs.
- **Dependency parsing (DEP)**: select the non-entity words related to entity instances, including ascendants and descendants, as candidate words based on dependency parsing.
- **Chunking (CHK)**: select the non-entity words in the noun chunks that are close to entity instances as candidate words to preserve both semantic and syntactic coherence.
- **Gradient (GDT)**: select the non-entity words

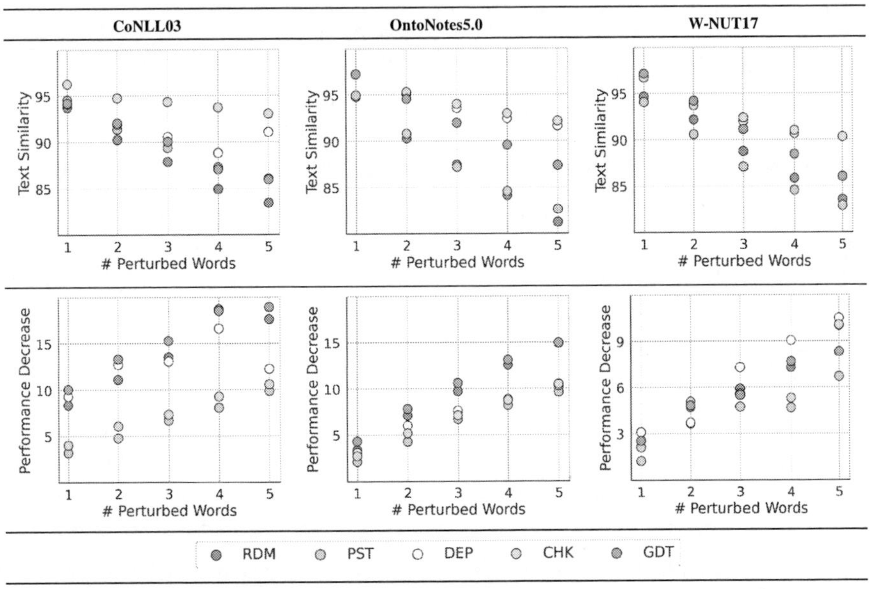

Table 1: Comparison between different candidate selection methods using synonym replacement. RDM, PST, DEP, CHK, GDT are short for random, POS tagging, dependency parsing, chunking, and gradient candidate selection, respectively. The x-axis denotes the number of perturbed words while the y-axis denotes the difference in F1 scores.

according to the integral of gradients. We use Integrated Hessians (Janizek et al., 2021) to determine the importance of non-entity words based on their feature interactions with entity instances, and select the words with higher importance scores to perturb.

To obtain linguistic features, including part-of-speech tags, dependency parsing, and chunking, for our proposed method, we use the statistical model from spaCy [1] to process text. Then we select the candidate words to perturb based on this information. For GDT, we use the gradient of the pre-trained $\text{BERT}_{\text{base}}$ model (Devlin et al., 2019) to determine the importance of each word.

3.2 Candidate Replacement

Perturbations in text at the character-level can be easily detected and defended by spell check and correction (Pruthi et al., 2019; Li et al., 2020). Therefore, we exclusively focus on the word-level perturbations in this work. Simply replacing a word with another one at random can lead to noisy data. For instance, in Figure 1, the label for "Wilson" is changed from *ORG* to *PER* by replacing "rackets" with "guidance", which has a conflict with its original gold label. Therefore, to keep original labels valid, we investigate the following two approaches to replace candidate words:

[1] https://github.com/explosion/spaCy

- **Synonym Replacement**: Using synonyms to replace candidate words as adversarial samples can guarantee the preservation of text semantics and make it hard to be perceived by human investigation. We use the WordNet (Miller, 1998) dictionary to find synonyms for candidate words, and then randomly select one of them as a replacement.
- **Masked Language Model Replacement**: The masked language model (MLM) attempts to predict the masked words in the given input sequence. In our work, we first create masks for candidate words, and then use a masked language model $\text{RoBERTa}_{\text{base}}$ (Liu et al., 2019) to generate a replacement based on the context. This approach is capable of preserving both semantics and syntax in the generated adversarial samples.

4 Experiments

In this section, we present the experimental setup and results. We systematically conduct experiments to evaluate our proposed methods on three corpora with different metrics and provide analyses to better understand their effectiveness.

4.1 Experiment Setup

Datasets We evaluate the proposed methods on three commonly-used corpora for NER tasks, in-

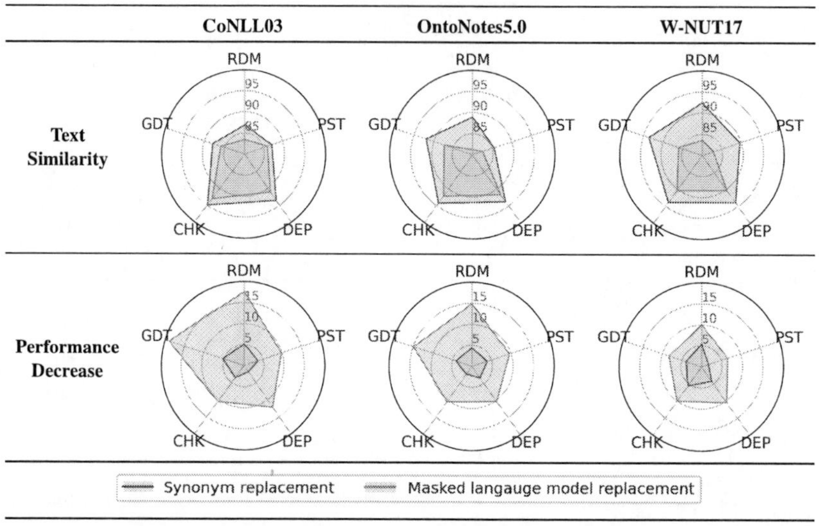

Table 2: Comparison between different candidate replacement methods when perturbing five words in each sentence. RDM, PST, DEP, CHK, GDT are short for random, POS tagging, dependency parsing, chunking, and gradient candidate selection, respectively.

cluding CoNLL03 (Tjong Kim Sang and De Meulder, 2003), OntoNotes5.0 (Pradhan et al., 2013), and W-NUT17 (Derczynski et al., 2017). The data statistics are summarized in Appendix A.

Victim Model The victim model consists of the $\text{BERT}_{\text{base}}$ (Devlin et al., 2019) as the base model and a linear layer as the classifier to assign NER tags. The details of hyper-parameters and fine-tuning are described in Appendix B.

Evaluation Metrics To examine the effectiveness of our proposed methods, we consider the following metrics for evaluation:

- **Textual Similarity (Sim.)**: cosine similarity between adversarial examples and the corresponding original examples using the Universal Sentence Encoder (Giorgi et al., 2021). A higher textual similarity score indicates that more semantics are preserved.
- **Performance Decrease (ΔPerf.)**: the difference in F1 scores between adversarial examples and their corresponding original examples. A higher performance decrease indicates that the model makes more mistakes.

4.2 Main Results

We compare candidate selection and replacement methods by perturbing the same number of words in the sentences. Below we present experimental results and summarize our findings:

Candidate Selection V.S. Metrics From the results in Table 1, we observe that the model performance decreases rapidly under adversarial attacks. When perturbing five words in the sentence, the F1 scores decrease by 10% ~20%. Among these attack methods, GDT and RDM are more effective at deceiving the model into making wrong predictions. When performing attacks with RDM, however, the text similarity is sacrificed in exchange for a greater performance decrease, which can potentially make adversarial examples easier to detect. Additionally, it is worth noting that DEP is also effective at a slight perturbation, although it can only result in a smaller performance decrease as we increase the number of perturbed words. In terms of textual similarity and performance decrease, PST is the least effective method in most cases.

Candidate Replacement V.S. Metrics The comparison between different candidate replacement methods is shown in Table 2. In general, compared to masked language model replacement, synonym replacement can achieve a higher textual similarity, indicating that more semantics are preserved in adversarial examples. However, its performance decrease is quite limited. At a slightly lower textual similarity, masked language model replacement leads to a much larger performance decrease. Besides, both replacement methods are relatively less effective on the W-NUT17 corpus. Compared to the text from CoNLL03 and OntoNotes5.0 which is long and formal, the text from W-NUT17 is short and noisy as it contains many misspellings and grammar errors. For this reason, the model cannot rely too heavily on context when making predictions, limiting the effectiveness of adversarial attacks on this corpus.

5 Conclusion

In this work, we study adversarial attacks to examine the model robustness using adversarial examples. We focus on the NER task and propose context-aware adversarial attack methods to perturb the most informative words for recognizing entities. Moreover, we investigate different candidate replacement methods for generating adversarial examples. We undertake experiments on three corpora and show that the proposed methods are more effective in attacking models than strong baselines.

Limitations

The proposed methods require linguistic knowledge (e.g., part-of-speech tags and dependency parsing) to processing the text. Most existing tools can automate this process for English. However, these tools may need to be extended to support other languages, especially for minority languages. Additionally, the proposed methods maybe not applicable with low computational resources or in real-time scenarios.

Acknowledgements

This work received partial support from the National Science Foundation under award number 1910192.

References

Yonatan Belinkov and Yonatan Bisk. 2018. Synthetic and natural noise both break neural machine translation. In *6th International Conference on Learning Representations, ICLR 2018, Vancouver, BC, Canada, April 30 - May 3, 2018, Conference Track Proceedings*. OpenReview.net.

Yong Cheng, Lu Jiang, and Wolfgang Macherey. 2019. Robust neural machine translation with doubly adversarial inputs. In *Proceedings of the 57th Annual Meeting of the Association for Computational Linguistics*, pages 4324–4333, Florence, Italy. Association for Computational Linguistics.

Leon Derczynski, Eric Nichols, Marieke van Erp, and Nut Limsopatham. 2017. Results of the WNUT2017 shared task on novel and emerging entity recognition. In *Proceedings of the 3rd Workshop on Noisy User-generated Text*, pages 140–147, Copenhagen, Denmark. Association for Computational Linguistics.

Jacob Devlin, Ming-Wei Chang, Kenton Lee, and Kristina Toutanova. 2019. BERT: Pre-training of deep bidirectional transformers for language understanding. In *Proceedings of the 2019 Conference of the North American Chapter of the Association for Computational Linguistics: Human Language Technologies, Volume 1 (Long and Short Papers)*, pages 4171–4186, Minneapolis, Minnesota. Association for Computational Linguistics.

Siddhant Garg and Goutham Ramakrishnan. 2020. BAE: BERT-based adversarial examples for text classification. In *Proceedings of the 2020 Conference on Empirical Methods in Natural Language Processing (EMNLP)*, pages 6174–6181, Online. Association for Computational Linguistics.

John Giorgi, Osvald Nitski, Bo Wang, and Gary Bader. 2021. DeCLUTR: Deep contrastive learning for unsupervised textual representations. In *Proceedings of the 59th Annual Meeting of the Association for Computational Linguistics and the 11th International Joint Conference on Natural Language Processing (Volume 1: Long Papers)*, pages 879–895, Online. Association for Computational Linguistics.

Mohit Iyyer, John Wieting, Kevin Gimpel, and Luke Zettlemoyer. 2018. Adversarial example generation with syntactically controlled paraphrase networks. In *Proceedings of the 2018 Conference of the North American Chapter of the Association for Computational Linguistics: Human Language Technologies, Volume 1 (Long Papers)*, pages 1875–1885, New Orleans, Louisiana. Association for Computational Linguistics.

Joseph D. Janizek, Pascal Sturmfels, and Su-In Lee. 2021. Explaining explanations: Axiomatic feature interactions for deep networks. *J. Mach. Learn. Res.*, 22:104:1–104:54.

Robin Jia and Percy Liang. 2017. Adversarial examples for evaluating reading comprehension systems. In *Proceedings of the 2017 Conference on Empirical Methods in Natural Language Processing*, pages 2021–2031, Copenhagen, Denmark. Association for Computational Linguistics.

Diederik P. Kingma and Jimmy Ba. 2015. Adam: A method for stochastic optimization. In *3rd International Conference on Learning Representations, ICLR 2015, San Diego, CA, USA, May 7-9, 2015, Conference Track Proceedings*.

Xiangci Li, Hairong Liu, and Liang Huang. 2020. Context-aware stand-alone neural spelling correction. In *Findings of the Association for Computational Linguistics: EMNLP 2020*, pages 407–414, Online. Association for Computational Linguistics.

Bin Liang, Hongcheng Li, Miaoqiang Su, Pan Bian, Xirong Li, and Wenchang Shi. 2018. Deep text classification can be fooled. In *Proceedings of the Twenty-Seventh International Joint Conference on Artificial Intelligence, IJCAI 2018, July 13-19, 2018, Stockholm, Sweden*, pages 4208–4215. ijcai.org.

Bill Yuchen Lin, Wenyang Gao, Jun Yan, Ryan Moreno, and Xiang Ren. 2021. RockNER: A simple method to create adversarial examples for evaluating the robustness of named entity recognition models. In *Proceedings of the 2021 Conference on Empirical Methods in Natural Language Processing*, pages 3728–3737, Online and Punta Cana, Dominican Republic. Association for Computational Linguistics.

Yinhan Liu, Myle Ott, Naman Goyal, Jingfei Du, Mandar Joshi, Danqi Chen, Omer Levy, Mike Lewis, Luke Zettlemoyer, and Veselin Stoyanov. 2019. Roberta: A robustly optimized BERT pretraining approach. *CoRR*, abs/1907.11692.

George A Miller. 1998. *WordNet: An electronic lexical database*. MIT press.

Sameer Pradhan, Alessandro Moschitti, Nianwen Xue, Hwee Tou Ng, Anders Björkelund, Olga Uryupina, Yuchen Zhang, and Zhi Zhong. 2013. Towards robust linguistic analysis using OntoNotes. In *Proceedings of the Seventeenth Conference on Computational Natural Language Learning*, pages 143–152, Sofia, Bulgaria. Association for Computational Linguistics.

Danish Pruthi, Bhuwan Dhingra, and Zachary C. Lipton. 2019. Combating adversarial misspellings with robust word recognition. In *Proceedings of the 57th Annual Meeting of the Association for Computational Linguistics*, pages 5582–5591, Florence, Italy. Association for Computational Linguistics.

Aaron Reich, Jiaao Chen, Aastha Agrawal, Yanzhe Zhang, and Diyi Yang. 2022. Leveraging expert guided adversarial augmentation for improving generalization in named entity recognition. In *Findings of the Association for Computational Linguistics: ACL 2022*, pages 1947–1955, Dublin, Ireland. Association for Computational Linguistics.

Walter Simoncini and Gerasimos Spanakis. 2021. SeqAttack: On adversarial attacks for named entity recognition. In *Proceedings of the 2021 Conference on Empirical Methods in Natural Language Processing: System Demonstrations*, pages 308–318, Online and Punta Cana, Dominican Republic. Association for Computational Linguistics.

Erik F. Tjong Kim Sang and Fien De Meulder. 2003. Introduction to the CoNLL-2003 shared task: Language-independent named entity recognition. In *Proceedings of the Seventh Conference on Natural Language Learning at HLT-NAACL 2003*, pages 142–147.

Eric Wallace, Shi Feng, Nikhil Kandpal, Matt Gardner, and Sameer Singh. 2019. Universal adversarial triggers for attacking and analyzing NLP. In *Proceedings of the 2019 Conference on Empirical Methods in Natural Language Processing and the 9th International Joint Conference on Natural Language Processing (EMNLP-IJCNLP)*, pages 2153–2162, Hong Kong, China. Association for Computational Linguistics.

Xiao Wang, Qin Liu, Tao Gui, Qi Zhang, Yicheng Zou, Xin Zhou, Jiacheng Ye, Yongxin Zhang, Rui Zheng, Zexiong Pang, Qinzhuo Wu, Zhengyan Li, Chong Zhang, Ruotian Ma, Zichu Fei, Ruijian Cai, Jun Zhao, Xingwu Hu, Zhiheng Yan, Yiding Tan, Yuan Hu, Qiyuan Bian, Zhihua Liu, Shan Qin, Bolin Zhu, Xiaoyu Xing, Jinlan Fu, Yue Zhang, Minlong Peng, Xiaoqing Zheng, Yaqian Zhou, Zhongyu Wei, Xipeng Qiu, and Xuanjing Huang. 2021. TextFlint: Unified multilingual robustness evaluation toolkit for natural language processing. In *Proceedings of the 59th Annual Meeting of the Association for Computational Linguistics and the 11th International Joint Conference on Natural Language Processing: System Demonstrations*, pages 347–355, Online. Association for Computational Linguistics.

A Data Statistics

Table 3 shows data statistics of the NER datasets we used in our experiments:

Split	CoNLL03	OntoNotes5.0	W-NUT17
Train	14,041	115,812	3,394
Validation	3,250	15,680	1,009
Test	3,453	12,217	1,287
Total	20,744	143,709	5,690

Table 3: Data Statistics of CoNLL03, OntoNotes5.0 and W-NUT17 corpus.

B Hyper-parameters and Fine-tuning

For the victim model, we use the $\text{BERT}_{\text{base}}$ (Devlin et al., 2019) without changing any hyper-parameters. The learning rate is set to 5e-5 and the training batch size is set to 8. We train the model using the Adam optimizer (Kingma and Ba, 2015) with a weight decay 0.01 for 10 epochs on CoNLL03 and OntoNotes5.0 data and 20 epochs on W-NUT17 data. For the hardware, we use 8 NVIDIA V100 GPUs with a memory of 24GB.

Effects of different types of noise in user-generated reviews on human and machine translations including ChatGPT

Maja Popović[1], **Ekaterina Lapshinova-Koltunski**[2], **Maarit Koponen**[3]
[1] ADAPT Centre, School of Computing, Dublin City University, Ireland
maja.popovic@adaptcentre.ie
[2] Language and Information Sciences, University of Hildesheim, Germany
lapshinovakoltun@uni-hildesheim.de
[3] School of Humanities, University of Eastern Finland
maarit.koponen@uef.fi

Abstract

This paper investigates effects of noisy source texts (containing spelling and grammar errors, informal words or expressions, etc.) on human and machine translations, namely whether the noisy phenomena are kept in the translations, corrected, or caused errors. The analysed data consists of English user reviews of Amazon products translated into Croatian, Russian and Finnish by professional translators, translation students, machine translation (MT) systems, and ChatGPT language model. The results show that overall, ChatGPT and professional translators mostly correct/standardise those parts, while students are often keeping them. Furthermore, MT systems are most prone to errors while ChatGPT is more robust, but notably less robust than human translators. Finally, some of the phenomena are particularly challenging both for MT systems and for ChatGPT, especially spelling errors and informal constructions.

1 Introduction

User-generated content (UGC) plays a great role in the information society as it facilitates fast information sharing. Therefore, translation of user-generated content is extremely important as it helps to make information accessible in other languages. There is a need for machine translation of UGC, as it facilitates cross-cultural communication by fast distribution of information across languages. Therefore, understanding problems in machine translation of user-generated reviews is important as most internet users trust the recommendations posted online, which means that their correct translation is essential. However, UGC input is still challenging for MT systems as it contains a considerable amount of noise including different types of grammar and spelling errors, emoticons and other symbols, as well as informal words and expressions including abbreviations (in this work, referred to as "noisy" or "non-standard" phenomena). The MT community has become aware of the existing problem: In WMT2022[1], the 'news' task was replaced by the 'general' task in order to include other, under-investigated, domains such as conversations, commercial product descriptions, as well as UGC (social media posts, user reviews, Kocmi et al., 2022). However, there is no clear understanding of what exactly challenges MT systems while translating UGC.

In addition, since such reviews are commonly translated automatically, we do not know how human translators would deal with such problems.

The novelty of our study is that we analyse translation of noisy phenomena in both human and machine translations. We perform our analysis on human, machine (MT) and large language model (specifically GPT3.5) translations for the three translation directions: English-Croatian, English-Finnish and English-Russian. We analyse user reviews of Amazon products which are not so noisy as social media posts, such as Reddit and Twitter data, but still contain numerous non-standard source phenomena. Our research questions include:

RQ1 Which types of noise are typical for the English user reviews at hand?

RQ2 What are the effects of those noisy phenomena onto different translations?

RQ3 Which noisy phenomena are particularly challenging for translation?

2 Related work

Although the issues of machine translation of user-generated content have been investigated in several works, many problems remain unsolved and understudied.

[1] https://www.statmt.org/wmt22/

Proceedings of the Ninth Workshop on Noisy and User-generated Text (W-NUT 2024), pages 17–30
March 22, 2024 ©2024 Association for Computational Linguistics

For instance, Roturier and Bensadoun (2011) looked into the impact of the source quality in online forums onto machine-generated translations. They evaluated several systems and came to a conclusion that especially spelling errors represent a problem. Misspelled words were also addressed by Gupta et al. (2021) who analysed user-generated reviews. Further problems that the authors focused on included ungrammatical constructions and colloquial expressions.

Another approach to improve performance is to use synthesized parallel data of UGC, as shown by Marie and Fujita (2020). Berard et al. (2019) suggested a number of strategies for dealing with non-standard issues such as emoticons, emojis and others. They included placeholders for rare characters, lowcasing and error detection and generation amongst others.

Interestingly, phrase-based statistical machine translation systems seemed to outperform the analysed attention-based neuronal ones when translating UGC, as stated by Rosales Núñez et al. (2019). Another study on phrase-based statistical machine translation (van der Wees et al., 2015) attempted to describe errors occurring in UGC and their impact on the MT output. The authors reported their observations on the effects showing that various types of UGC differed in error distributions which required diverse strategies for improvement.

This confirms observations by Baldwin et al. (2013) who showed that there were both differences and similarities in English social media text types lying on a continuum of similarity ranging from microblogs to collaboratively-authored content. This variation across UGC types points to the importance of analysis on different types of texts for a better understanding of the phenomena. Besides that, most of those studies were in pre-neural and pre-generative era, which means that the current system outputs may display different effects.

Their impact of various types of artificially created noise on the quality of both statistical and neural machine translation systems was examined by Khayrallah and Koehn (2018). They showed that neural machine translation was less robust to many types of noise than statistical machine translation. The impact of various user-generated content phenomena on translation performance was also analysed by Rosales Núñez et al. (2021) who used and annotated data set of UGC. The authors also showed that traditional models (e.g. strict zero-shot ones) could not handle certain phenomena such as unknown letters.

A data set to evaluate the output of MT was presented by Fujii et al. (2020). The annotated phenomena included proper nouns, abbreviations, colloquial expressions and words deviated from their canonical forms. The evaluation results showed that such phenomena, and specifically non-canonical forms, challenge MT systems, even the widely used off-the-shelf ones. The authors also claimed that the amount of training data was not that important in handling non-standard phenomena. There is a need in special treatment against such phenomena to further improve MT systems.

Our aim is not to assess or to improve the quality of a machine translation system, but rather to analyse the nature of the problems in the user-generated reviews and to examine their impact on human translations and MT outputs including ChatGTP in three different target languages. Our work is in this way similar to approaches that present benchmark data sets or annotated data. For instance, Michel and Neubig (2018) similarly examined different types of noise in a benchmark data set consisting of noisy comments on Reddit and their professional translations.

We focus on the analysis of Amazon product reviews, which were already addressed in (Popović et al., 2021). The authors compared product reviews with movie reviews, however, in terms of overall automatic and human scores. They also reported most frequent translation errors, but without mentioning the effects of the source texts. Popovic (2021) did address the latter in identifying an error type called "source error". However a detailed analysis of this error type was missing.

While there are many studies addressing source text errors or non-standard language use and their impact on machine translated texts, analyses of these phenomena in product review translation is still insufficient.

Furthermore, a better understanding of such phenomena in not only machine but also human translation is needed. To our knowledge, there has been no work involving human translation so far.

Moreover, no further studies known to us looked into translation of UGC with the help of ChatGPT. That is why we perform an analysis of effects of non-standard phenomena in multiple human and machine translations, including translations by ChatGPT, for three translation directions.

3 Data

For our analysis, we use the publicly available corpus DiHuTra[2] (Lapshinova-Koltunski et al., 2022). The corpus contains English Amazon product reviews and their translations into three languages, Croatian, Russian and Finnish, produced by two groups of translators: several professional translators and several students. The translators were only instructed to keep the given segmentation and not to use any MT system. They did not receive any guidelines about how to treat the noise and informality in the reviews. The reason for omitting such guidelines was to collect data on different ways translator respond to such features. Therefore, the corpus is suitable for exploring the subjectivity in translating UGC.

For Croatian MT outputs, we used the two best ranked outputs by human evaluation from the WMT 2022 shared task[3] (Kocmi et al., 2022). For Russian MT outputs, we used Google Translate[4] and DeepL Translator[5]. The Finnish MT outputs were produced using OPUS-MT (Tiedemann and Thottingal, 2020) pre-trained model (opus+bt-news-2020-03-21) and Google Translate[6]. ChatGPT[7] outputs for all target languages were generated using the publicly available GPT 3.5 version. Since human translators were given only simple instructions, a similar approach was used for ChatGPT as well, namely a simple prompt "translate into Croatian/Russian/Finnish".

The data set includes 196 Amazon reviews, fourteen from each of the fourteen products/topics, consisting of 1015 segments. The number of running words and vocabulary size for the source text and for each of the translations can be seen in Table 1.

text	running words	vocabulary
en source	15,236	3,155
hr prof	13,981	4,359
hr stud	13,931	4,446
hr mt1	13,467	4,309
hr mt2	13,465	4,247
hr gpt3.5	14,170	4,265
ru prof	14,217	4,414
ru stud	14,247	4,523
ru mt1	14,472	4,348
ru mt2	14,635	4,391
ru gpt3.5	15,015	4,397
fi prof	11,709	4,612
fi stud	12,274	4,665
fi mt1	11,977	4,461
fi mt2	11,988	4,421
fi gtp3.5	12,299	4,449

Table 1: Corpus statistics.

4 RQ1: Noisy phenomena in English user reviews

Overall analysis To address the first research question, we identify different types of noisy phenomena in the source text. Without using a predefined scheme for these phenomena, we started searching for errors, informal and non-standard parts of the source and identified these phenomena on the fly. In total, at least one phenomenon was found in 597 segments (58.8%), while the remaining 418 (41.2%) were clean.

The identified phenomena, as well as their distributions in source texts can be seen in Table 2 containing absolute number of occurrences, as well as the proportion against all identified phenomena. Table reveals that non-standard capitalisation is the most frequent one, followed by incorrect combinations of punctuation and space (pun+space), non-standard punctuation marks (punctuation), and spelling errors (spelling), missing pronouns (pronoun), and informal expressions and words (informal). Less common phenomena include missing or added spaces (space), incorrect morphological forms such as number, case, tense (form), missing articles (article), incorrect/non-standard structure such as combination and order of words (structure), format conversions (format), missing verbs (verb), added/repeated content (addition), symbols such as emoticons (symbol). There are several rare phenomena, namely missing prepositions (preposition), shortened versions of words (short), lexical errors (lexical), and conjunctions.

For the overall analysis of translations in Section 5.1, we consider all the phenomena, while the detailed analysis of effects of each phenomena in Section 5.2 includes only the most frequent ones (threshold of 50 occurrences). Although this thresh-

[2] http://hdl.handle.net/21.11119/0000-000A-1BA9-A

[3] https://www.statmt.org/wmt22/translation-task.html

[4] https://translate.google.com/, accessed in February 2023

[5] https://www.deepl.com/en/translator, accessed in August 2023

[6] accessed in December 2023

[7] https://chat.openai.com/, accessed in November 2023

phenomenon	occurrences	in %
capitalisation	225	27.3
pun+space	123	14.9
punctuation	109	13.2
spelling	84	10.2
pronoun	81	9.8
informal	53	6.4
space	26	3.2
form	25	3.0
article	19	2.3
structure	17	2.1
format	16	1.9
verb	14	1.7
addition	11	1.3
symbol	9	1.1
preposition	5	0.6
shortened	5	0.6
lexical	1	0.1
conjunction	1	0.1
total	824	

Table 2: Distribution of noisy phenomena in the source text (English user reviews).

old might sound somewhat arbitrary, we believe that the results of an in-depth analysis of the less frequent and especially rarely occurring phenomena would not be reliable. For the sake of completeness, we presents the analysis of these phenomena in Appendix.

Most frequent noisy phenomena Table 3 shows examples of the predominant types of noise:

capitalisation includes example 1) with several fully capitalised words[8], example 2) with one capitalised word. Example 3) shows the English pronoun *I* which does not impact the given target languages, but was included for completeness. Examples 4) and 5) show capitalisation errors in named entities, and example 6) an incorrectly capitalised adverb.

pun+space comprises various incorrect combinations of punctuation marks and spaces: in examples 7), 8) and 9) space is missing, in 10) and 11) the space is placed before the punctuation.

punctuation includes repeated question or exclamation marks (12), missing punctuation marks (13) and punctuation errors (14).

[8]Sometimes the entire review was written in capital letters.

spelling errors result in non-existing words (15) or homophones (16 and 17).

pronouns are often omitted in the reviews (18, 19): on one hand, it does not impact the given target languages due to their pro-drop character, on the other hand, this may cause verb errors related to person and number.

informal refers to informal usage of symbols (20), spelling (21) as well as words or expressions (22).

A number of segments contains more than one non-standard phenomenon (examples 23–27). In example 23), the pronoun *this* should be in plural (*these*), and the article and the pronoun are missing (*to test first* should be *to test the first one*).

Example 24) contains several capitalisation errors (*this* at the beginning of the sentence, *i*, and *MAc* instead of *MAC*), as well as one spelling error (*isnt*).

Example 25) illustrates a named entity with incorrect capitalisation (*sherlock*) and one with both incorrect capitalisation and spelling error (*homes* instead of *Holmes*).

All words in the sentence are fully capitalised in example 26), and one of them is also incorrectly spelled (*CLAPTION* instead of *Clapton*).

A pronoun is missing at the beginning of example 27) and a comma is missing after *case*. Moreover *love* is capitalised and repeated (*LOVE LOVE LOVE*).

5 Analysis of translations

In the next step, we address the second and the third research questions. We present the results on all target languages together, because the overall tendencies are similar. The detailed results for each target language separately can be found in Appendix.

5.1 Effects of source noise on translations (RQ2)

We start with annotating translations to determine the effects caused by the phenomena identified in Section 4 (RQ2). Each target language was covered by one annotator[9], native speaker of the corresponding language with expertise and experience in both human and machine translation.

[9]An exception is the English-Russian pair, where the annotations were cross-checked by the second annotator.

phenomenon		example
capitalisation	1)	**DO NOT BUY**!
	2)	This is **NOT** a good product!
	3)	**i** just received mine
	4)	Bill **gates**
	5)	Do not order on **AMAzon**!
	6)	Very **Cheaply** made product.
pun+space	7)	This is what I needed.It was in good condition
	8)	perfect size–not too big, not too small
	9)	didn't even try to use it...just packed it up
	10)	Exactly what I need .Easy to handle.
	11)	Absolutely love the case !!
punctuation	12)	Wonderful**!!!**
	13)	I love this book[] I bought it last year[]
	14)	batteries already dead**..**
spelling	15)	Heavenly **Hiway** Hymns
	16)	It does exactly what it's supposed **too**.
	17)	the phone says **its** charging
pronoun	18)	[] Have enjoyed it for years
	19)	[] Have not even introduced markers
informal	20)	Not worth the **$$**
	21)	I was **sooo** blessed
	22)	**Yay**!
form, art, pron, pun+space	23)	I bought 2 of **this** and tried to test [] first [] **...**
cap, cap spell, cap	24)	**this** is fake MAC, **i** just received mine and super upset to find out it **isnt** real **MAc**.
cap, spell&cap	25)	**sherlock** ***homes***
cap, cap&spell, cap, cap	26)	**NOT** ***CLAPTION*** **MUSIC VIDEO**!
pron, pun, informal&cap	27)	[] Don't know what I would do without this case[] ***LOVE LOVE LOVE*** it.

Table 3: Examples of the most prominent noisy phenomena in English user reviews: 1)–22) represent examples of single phenomenon in a segment, 23–27) represent multiple phenomena.

The annotators were given the following instructions: for each instance of a non-standard noisy phenomenon, assign:

- "y" (yes) if the phenomenon is kept in the translation
- "n" (no) if the phenomenon is corrected in the translation, or avoided by translating in a different way
- "e" (error) if the phenomenon caused a translation error of any type (mistranslation, omission, addition, grammar error, ...)

A phenomenon that was marked as "kept" might not be replicated in the translation in the exactly same form as in the target text. Rather, a slightly modified but still informal feature might be used by the translator (see e.g. the second example in Table 6). It should be noted that an informal feature being kept in the translation does not necessarily constitute an "error". It may be an intentional choice by the translator to aim for so-called dynamic equivalence (Nida, 1964) by creating a similar effect in the translation as in the source text. In other cases, however, source text may lead to issues that are considered translation errors. A detailed analysis of the types of error found in the translated versions is outside of the scope of this paper.

Table 4 displays the distribution of effects in different translations for all target languages together. It can be noted that the noisy sources are mostly corrected by ChatGPT (about 75%), followed by professional and student translators (60-70%), while MT systems correct only about a half. Furthermore,

	n	y	e
prof	68.8	29.3	1.9
stud	62.5	**34.9**	2.6
mt	51.9	**35.2**	**12.9**
gpt	**75.7**	19.8	4.5

Table 4: Distribution of effects of all source non-standard phenomena in different translations into all languages.

student translators keep a similar amount of noise as MT systems (35%), professionals keep about 30% while ChatGPT keeps only about 20%. As for errors, almost 13% of noisy parts translated by MT systems result in errors, while ChatGPT is much more robust with only 4.5% of errors, however notably less robust than human translators with about 2-3%.

5.2 Effects of individual noisy phenomena (RQ3)

We address the most frequent phenomena as mentioned in Section 4 above. Since the overall tendencies are similar for all languages, the proportions (in %) given in Table 5 are calculated on all target languages together, while the individual results are presented in Appendix.

We observe the following tendencies:

capitalisation is slightly more often kept than corrected in all types of translations with exception of ChatGPT which exhibits a reverse tendency. Furthermore, capitalisation causes rarely errors in human translations (1.3-1.6%), slightly more in ChatGPT (3.6%) and most often in MT, however less than 9%.

pun+space is almost always corrected by ChatGPT (97.5%) and frequently corrected by humans and MT. However, students keep it more often than professionals and MT systems. Less than 1% of them cause errors in human anc ChatGPT translations, and less than 3% in MT systems.

punctuation is very often corrected by ChatGTP (more than 90%) and more often corrected by professionals (58.4%) than by students (45%). Furthermore, students and MT systems keep them more often (50-60%) than professionals (40.4%) and ChatGTP (22.3%). The amount of errors in all translations is comparably slightly higher than for pun+space.

spelling is almost completely corrected by professionals and ChatGPT (over 90%) and slightly

phenomenon		n	y	e
capitalisation	prof	47.3	51.4	1.3
	stud	46.1	52.3	1.6
	mt	37.2	54.2	**8.7**
	gpt	56.4	40.0	**3.6**
pun+space	prof	75.6	23.6	0.8
	stud	64.8	**34.7**	0.5
	mt	69.9	27.2	**2.9**
	gpt	**97.5**	2.2	0.3
punctuation	prof	58.4	40.4	1.2
	stud	45.0	53.5	1.5
	mt	38.2	58.0	**3.8**
	gpt	**76.4**	**22.3**	1.2
spelling	prof	**90.9**	7.5	1.6
	stud	86.1	10.7	3.2
	mt	66.5	11.5	**22.0**
	gpt	**90.5**	2.0	**7.5**
pronoun	prof	**80.2**	18.5	1.2
	stud	76.5	21.8	1.6
	mt	75.9	10.4	**13.2**
	gpt	73.2	21.0	**5.6**
informal	prof	76.7	16.4	6.9
	stud	71.1	**20.1**	8.8
	mt	48.7	11.3	**39.9**
	gpt	74.2	13.2	**12.6**

Table 5: Effects of the most frequent source phenomena on different types of translations for all languages.

less by students (86.1%). In MT outputs, 22% of them cause errors, indicating that spelling errors are problematic for MT robustness. ChatGPT is less sensitive, but still 7.5% of them result in translation errors. Even student translators with 3.2% are notably more prone to errors than professionals.

pronoun Most of the missing pronouns do not have effect on human translations, but 13.2% of them cause errors in MT. ChatGPT is again more robust, with 5.6% of errors.

informal is often corrected by human translators and ChatGTP (about 75%). Also, students keep the informality at most (20.1%). Furthermore, almost 40% of informal constructions cause MT errors, and therefore, they should be taken into account for the MT robustness. ChatGPT is again more robust than MT systems, but still 12% of informal constructions result in translation errors.

All in all, spelling errors and informal parts represent the most prominent challenges both for MT systems and for ChatGTP, although ChatGPT is generally more robust to noise.

Other potential challenging types of noise, such as structure, space, form, verb (see Table 8 in Appendix) show the same tendencies, however they are rarely appearing in the analysed corpus so the results are not reliable and should be investigated further.

5.2.1 Examples of some specific effects

Table 6 illustrates three examples of noisy source texts and all their translations.

The **first example** contains one phenomenon only, i.e. added space (*a way* instead of *away*), which caused a mistranslation error in Croatian and Finnish MT outputs, literal translation of *give a way* in Russian MT outputs, and an omission in Russian students' translation. ChatGPT translated it correctly into all target languages.

The **second example** contains more phenomena: missing pronoun *I* at the beginning of the sentence, missing comma after *case*, and the fully capitalised informal expression *LOVE LOVE LOVE*. The missing pronoun has been kept in all translations, however, due to language properties it has an effect only on Russian translations by keeping the informal tone. The punctuation is added in some of translations, and it does not cause any errors in others. As for *LOVE LOVE LOVE*, capitalisation is kept in almost all translations except the one by Russian students. The informality is "corrected" only in the Croatian ChatGPT translation. In all other translations it is either kept (in all human translations and one Russian MT output) or caused errors (in the remaining MT outputs). The nature of errors is diverse: while in one Finnish and one Russian MT outputs this part is omitted, in the other Finnish output this part remained untranslated, and Croatian MT outputs contain incorrect disambiguation of the word *love*: an incorrect person of the verb *love* and the noun *love*. Keeping the informality is also diverse: Croatian students and Finnish professionals did not repeat the word three times, but introduced spaces/hyphens between the letters/syllables, while in the rest of the translations the three repetitions are kept. The Russian student, though, did not keep the capitalisation, and Russian ChatGPT used the word only once but added an adverb intensifying the meaning of the word. In fact, using the verb (*love*) three times should infer intensifying its meaning.

The **third example** is the most complex one, not only because of multiple phenomena but also because of ambiguity (mentioned in Section 4). Two phenomena are clear: the incorrect form of the pronoun *this* and the space before the punctuation mark ... in the end. While the incorrect form caused an error in Croatian and one of the Finnish MT outputs, the punctuation+space did not cause any, but was only kept in some of the translations.

However, the expression *to test first* is ambiguous since it can be interpreted in two ways: (a) *to test the first one*, or (b) *to test (one of) them first*. The annotator who identified the phenomena in the source language perceived the version (a) and therefore annotated the source as presented in Table 6. Further inspection revealed that different annotators as well as different translators had different interpretations. Croatian and Finnish professionals both read it as (b), and students read it as (a). Russian professionals, on the other hand, simply omitted the missing object, as did the two MT systems. In the version produced by ChatGPT, we observe the (a) reading in Croatian, the (b) reading in Russian, and the omission error in Finnish. As for annotators' interpretation, the Croatian one opted for (a) and therefore assigned an "e" to the professional translation, whereas the Finnish annotator perceived both (a) and (b) so they did not assign errors to any human translation. The Russian annotator also perceived the ambiguous reading including both (a) and (b). However, the object (*it* or *them* or *the first one*) is missing in the professional translation and in the two machine translations, so this case was tagged as an error. Although the translation by ChatGPT corresponds to the (b) reading, the annotator marked it as an error agreeing on the disambiguation as (a) suggested by the other annotators.

6 Conclusions

This work presents a detailed analysis of the effects of non-standard phenomena in source texts generated by users on both human and machine translations. While issues in machine-translated user-generated content has been already addressed and partly solved before, a better understanding of how to deal with non-standard language use in translation in general, also in human translation, is missing.

RQ1 Our results show that capitalisation, punctuation and space, spelling, missing pronouns, as well as informal usage of symbols and words belong to the most frequent noisy phenomena for Amazon product reviews written in English.

1) source	We just gave this game **a way** and kept our old one! (space)	
hr prof	Ovu smo igru proslijedili dalje i zadržali našu staru!	n
hr stud	Upravo smo vratili ovu igru i zadržali staru!!!	n
hr mt1	Upravo smo **poboljšali** ovu igru i zadržali našu staru!	e
hr mt2	Upravo smo **omogućili** ovu igru i zadržali našu staru!	e
hr gpt	Ovu novu igru smo samo poklonili i zadržali staru!	n
ru prof	Мы отдали эту игру, а себе оставили старую!	n
ru stud	В итоге мы [] играли в нашу старую игру!	e
ru mt1	Мы просто **дали этой игре дорогу** и сохранили старую!	e
ru mt2	Мы просто **дали этой игре дорогу** и сохранили нашу старую!	e
ru gpt	Мы просто подарили эту игру и сохранили нашу старую!	n
fi prof	Annoimme tämän pois ja pidimme vanhan versiomme!	n
fi stud	Me vain annoimme tämän pelin pois ja pidimme vanhan!	n
fi mt1	Me vain annoimme tälle pelille **keinon** ja pidimme vanhan!	e
fi mt2	Annoimme tälle pelille **tavan** ja säilytimme vanhan!	e
fi gpt	Juuri annoimme tämän pelin pois ja pidimme vanhan!	n

2) source	[] Don't know what I would do without this case[] ***LOVE LOVE LOVE*** it. (pronoun punctuation informal capitalisation)	
hr prof	Ne znam što bih bez ove maskice. VOLIM VOLIM VOLIM je.	n n y y
hr stud	Ne znam što bih bez ove maskice – O-BO-ŽA-VAM ju.	n n y y
hr mt1	Ne znam što bih bez ove kutije **VOLI VOLI VOLI to.**	n y e y
hr mt2	Ne znam što bih napravio bez ovog slučaja **LJUBAV LJUBAV LJUBAV to.**	n y e y
hr gpt	Ne znam što bih radio bez ovog slučaja, OBOŽAVAM ga.	n n n y
ru prof	Не знаю, что бы делала без него КРУТО КРУТО КРУТО.	y n y y
ru stud	Не знаю, что бы я делал без этого чехла. Очень, очень, очень доволен.	y n y n
ru mt1	Не знаю, что бы я делал без этого чехла ЛЮБЛЮ ЛЮБЛЮ ЛЮБЛЮ.	y n y y
ru mt2	Не знаю, что бы я делал без этого чехла. []	y n e e
ru gpt	Не знаю, что бы я делал без этого чехла. ОЧЕНЬ ЛЮБЛЮ его.	y n y y
fi prof	En tiedä mitä tekisin ilman tätä kuorta! R A K A S T A N.	n n y y
fi stud	En tiedä, mitä tekisin ilman tätä koteloa. RAKASTAN RAKASTAN RAKASTAN sitä.	n n y y
fi mt	En tiedä, mitä tekisin ilman tätä juttua. []	n n e e
fi mt2	En tiedä mitä tekisin ilman tätä tapausta **LOVE LOVE LOVE** sitä.	n y e y
fi gpt	En tiedä, mitä tekisin ilman tätä koteloa. RAKASTAN, RAKASTAN, RAKASTAN sitä.	n n y y

3) source	I bought 2 of **this** and tried to test [] first **[] ...** (form article pronoun pun+space)	
hr prof	Kupio sam 2 komada i **prvo** sam **ih** pokušao testirati ...	n e e y
hr stud	Kupio sam dva primjerka i pokušao isprobati jedan od njih...	n n n n
hr mt1	Kupio sam 2 od ovoga i **prvo** [] pokušao testirati ...	e e e y
hr mt2	Kupio sam 2 od ovoga i **prvo** [] pokušao testirati ...	e e e y
hr gpt	Kupio sam 2 ovakva proizvoda i pokušao testirati prvi...	n n n n
ru prof	Я купил 2 аккумлятора и решил проверить []...	n e y n
ru stud	Я приобрел две штуки этого зарядного устройства и решил испытать первое...	n n n n
ru mt1	Я купил 2 таких и попытался сначала протестировать []...	n e y n
ru mt2	Купил 2 штуки и попробовал сначала протестировать []...	n e y n
ru gpt	Купил 2 штуки и решил сначала протестировать **одну из них**...	n e y n
fi prof	Ostin kaksi tällaista ja yritin ensin testata yhtä ...	n n n y
fi stud	Ostin näitä kaksi ja kokeilin ensimmäistä...	n n n n
fi mt1	Ostin **tästä** kaksi ja yritin testata **ensin** [].	e e e n
fi mt2	Ostin 2 tätä ja yritin testata **ensin** [] ...	y e e y
fi gpt	Ostin 2 näitä ja päätin testata **ensin** []...	n e e n

Table 6: Examples of effects of different non-standard phenomena on translations; example 3 could be interpreted in two ways.

RQ2 In our data, these phenomena are mostly converted into a standard form by ChatGPT, followed by professional translators, while students and MT systems are often keeping them. Furthermore, MT systems often generate a translation error, while ChatGPT is more robust to the noise in the source text.

RQ3 Our further observation is that spelling errors (especially those resulting in an existing word) and informal constructions are particularly difficult for MT systems, as well as for ChatGPT although to a less extent. The results also indicate that incorrect or non-conventional structure as well as incorrect word forms also represent a potential challenge, however further work is needed in this direction since these types of noise are not sufficiently frequent in our data.

We believe that our results are of interest for both NLP and translation studies. On the one hand, our findings can help improving robustness of MT systems. On the other hand, the work should give an idea about the guidelines for human translators if human translations are needed for user-generated texts: translator guidelines should be clear on how and if source errors should be corrected in the resulting translation. Also, the findings could be helpful for guidelines for human evaluation of translated used-generated content - what should be considered as an error and what not.

Future work should further investigate the most prominent phenomena and their sub-types. Besides that, creating challenge test sets to better understand each phenomenon could be an asset. We also plan to look into the types of translation errors in more detail. Moreover, more noisy UGC (such as social media) should be analysed as well. Furthermore, we plan to extend the analysis on outputs produced by other large language models, as well as to explore different prompts.

Limitations

We investigate only one type of user-generated content, namely user reviews. This sub-domain is relatively clear compared to other noisy types such as social media posts, as it contains less non-standard texts. Therefore, some potentially problematic phenomena do not appear at all or not sufficiently often in the analysed corpus. However, most of the analysed phenomena appear in other types of UGC, too.

Also, we investigate only English as the source language. More source languages should be explored in future work.

The annotation of each translated text was carried out by a single evaluator with an exception for Russian, where problematic cases were discussed in a team of trained linguists.

While all source sentences were translated by each of the MT systems and ChatGPT, they were not translated by each of the individual translators, but only by each group of the translators.

Using different MT systems for different target languages can be a disadvantage, but on the other hand it introduces more diversity.

Ethics Statement

The data used in this study is derived from the corpus DiHuTra which is publicly available - the corpus is hosted by Fedora Commons Repository of the Saarland University (UdS) CLARIN-D centre[10]. The DiHuTra corpus is licensed under CCBY-NC-SA4.0. The translations collected in the corpus are all anonymised and do not contain any personal information. All the authors signed a consent agreement[11]. The corpus only contains the anonymised metadata on the experience, study program, age and gender of the translators who contributed to the data collection.

Acknowledgements

ADAPT, the SFI Research Centre for AI-Driven Digital Content Technology, is funded by Science Foundation Ireland through the SFI Research Centres Programme under Grant Agreement No. 13/RC/2106_P2. The Finnish subcorpus was supported by a Kopiosto grant awarded by the Finnish Association of Translators and Interpreters.

References

Timothy Baldwin, Paul Cook, Marco Lui, Andrew MacKinlay, and Li Wang. 2013. How noisy social media text, how diffrnt social media sources? In *Proceedings of the Sixth International Joint Conference on Natural Language Processing*, pages 356–364, Nagoya, Japan. Asian Federation of Natural Language Processing.

Alexandre Berard, Ioan Calapodescu, Marc Dymetman, Claude Roux, Jean-Luc Meunier, and Vassilina

[10]Persistent identifier `http://hdl.handle.net/21.11119/0000-000A-1BA9-A`

[11]The consent agreement form was made available by the corpus creators and can be viewed on the GitHub repository `https://github.com/katjakaterina/dihutra/blob/main/fortranslators/consent.pdf`

Nikoulina. 2019. Machine translation of restaurant reviews: New corpus for domain adaptation and robustness. In *Proceedings of the 3rd Workshop on Neural Generation and Translation*, pages 168–176, Hong Kong. Association for Computational Linguistics.

Ryo Fujii, Masato Mita, Kaori Abe, Kazuaki Hanawa, Makoto Morishita, Jun Suzuki, and Kentaro Inui. 2020. PheMT: A phenomenon-wise dataset for machine translation robustness on user-generated contents. In *Proceedings of the 28th International Conference on Computational Linguistics*, pages 5929–5943, Barcelona, Spain (Online). International Committee on Computational Linguistics.

Kamal Gupta, Soumya Chennabasavaraj, Nikesh Garera, and Asif Ekbal. 2021. Product review translation using phrase replacement and attention guided noise augmentation. In *Proceedings of Machine Translation Summit XVIII: Research Track*, pages 243–255, Virtual. Association for Machine Translation in the Americas.

Huda Khayrallah and Philipp Koehn. 2018. On the impact of various types of noise on neural machine translation. In *Proceedings of the 2nd Workshop on Neural Machine Translation and Generation*, pages 74–83, Melbourne, Australia. Association for Computational Linguistics.

Tom Kocmi, Rachel Bawden, Ondřej Bojar, Anton Dvorkovich, Christian Federmann, Mark Fishel, Thamme Gowda, Yvette Graham, Roman Grundkiewicz, Barry Haddow, Rebecca Knowles, Philipp Koehn, Christof Monz, Makoto Morishita, Masaaki Nagata, Toshiaki Nakazawa, Michal Novák, Martin Popel, and Maja Popović. 2022. Findings of the 2022 conference on machine translation (WMT22). In *Proceedings of the Seventh Conference on Machine Translation (WMT)*, pages 1–45, Abu Dhabi, United Arab Emirates (Hybrid). Association for Computational Linguistics.

Ekaterina Lapshinova-Koltunski, Maja Popović, and Maarit Koponen. 2022. DiHuTra: a parallel corpus to analyse differences between human translations. In *Proceedings of the 23rd Annual Conference of the European Association for Machine Translation*, pages 337–338, Ghent, Belgium. European Association for Machine Translation.

Benjamin Marie and Atsushi Fujita. 2020. Synthesizing parallel data of user-generated texts with zero-shot neural machine translation. *Transactions of the Association for Computational Linguistics*, 8:710–725.

Paul Michel and Graham Neubig. 2018. MTNT: A testbed for machine translation of noisy text. In *Proceedings of the 2018 Conference on Empirical Methods in Natural Language Processing*, pages 543–553, Brussels, Belgium. Association for Computational Linguistics.

Eugene Nida. 1964. *Toward a Science of Translating With Special Reference to Principles and Procedures Involved in Bible Translating*. Brill, Boston.

Maja Popovic. 2021. On nature and causes of observed MT errors. In *Proceedings of Machine Translation Summit XVIII: Research Track*, pages 163–175, Virtual. Association for Machine Translation in the Americas.

Maja Popović, Alberto Poncelas, Marija Brkic, and Andy Way. 2021. On machine translation of user reviews. In *Proceedings of the International Conference on Recent Advances in Natural Language Processing (RANLP 2021)*, pages 1109–1118, Held Online. INCOMA Ltd.

José Carlos Rosales Núñez, Djamé Seddah, and Guillaume Wisniewski. 2019. Comparison between NMT and PBSMT performance for translating noisy user-generated content. In *Proceedings of the 22nd Nordic Conference on Computational Linguistics*, pages 2–14, Turku, Finland. Linköping University Electronic Press.

José Carlos Rosales Núñez, Guillaume Wisniewski, and Djamé Seddah. 2021. Noisy UGC translation at the character level: Revisiting open-vocabulary capabilities and robustness of char-based models. In *Proceedings of the Seventh Workshop on Noisy User-generated Text (W-NUT 2021)*, pages 199–211, Online. Association for Computational Linguistics.

Johann Roturier and Anthony Bensadoun. 2011. Evaluation of MT systems to translate user generated content. In *Proceedings of Machine Translation Summit XIII: Papers*, Xiamen, China.

Jörg Tiedemann and Santhosh Thottingal. 2020. OPUS-MT – building open translation services for the world. In *Proceedings of the 22nd Annual Conference of the European Association for Machine Translation*, pages 479–480, Lisboa, Portugal. European Association for Machine Translation.

Marlies van der Wees, Arianna Bisazza, and Christof Monz. 2015. Five shades of noise: Analyzing machine translation errors in user-generated text. In *Proceedings of the Workshop on Noisy User-generated Text*, pages 28–37, Beijing, China. Association for Computational Linguistics.

A Appendix

A.1 Overall distribution of effects on each of the translations

(a) en-hr

	n		y		e	
prof	**604**	**73.3**	208	25.2	12	1.5
stud	553	67.1	255	31.0	16	1.9
mt1	437	53.0	309	37.5	**78**	**9.5**
mt2	435	52.8	302	36.6	**87**	**10.6**
gpt	**634**	**76.9**	**157**	**19.0**	33	4.0

(b) en-ru

	n		y		e	
prof	**538**	**65.3**	260	31.6	26	3.2
stud	506	61.4	285	34.6	33	4.0
mt1	474	57.5	288	35.0	**62**	**7.5**
mt2	511	62.0	263	31.9	**50**	**6.1**
gpt	**631**	**76.6**	**163**	**19.8**	30	3.6

(c) en-fi

	n		y		e	
prof	**558**	**67.7**	256	31.1	10	1.2
stud	486	59.0	322	39.1	16	1.9
mt1	332	40.3	274	33.2	**218**	**26.5**
mt2	376	45.6	306	37.1	**142**	**17.2**
gpt	**607**	**73.7**	**169**	**20.5**	48	5.8

Table 7: Distribution of effects of all noisy phenomena on each translation into each target language: (a) Croatian, (b) Russian, (c) Finnish.

A.2 Effects of less frequent types of noise on all target languages together

A.3 Effects of different types of noise on each of the translations

phenomenon		n	y	e
space (26)	prof	**78.2**	18.0	3.8
	stud	69.2	**26.9**	3.8
	mt	57.7	22.4	**19.9**
	gpt	73.1	21.8	**5.1**
form (25)	prof	93.3	6.7	0
	stud	**96.0**	2.7	1.3
	mt	76.0	6.0	**18.0**
	gpt	90.6	2.7	**6.7**
article (19)	prof	94.7	0	5.3
	stud	100	0	0
	mt	89.5	0.9	9.6
	gpt	94.7	0	5.3
structure (17)	prof	**90.2**	9.8	0
	stud	74.5	11.8	**13.7**
	mt	28.4	**32.4**	**39.2**
	gpt	68.6	17.7	**13.7**
format (16)	prof	75.0	18.8	6.2
	stud	37.5	47.9	14.6
	mt	41.7	45.8	12.5
	gpt	95.8	0	4.2
verb (14)	prof	85.7	11.9	2.4
	stud	78.6	21.4	0
	mt	61.9	25.0	**13.1**
	gpt	73.8	11.9	**14.3**
addition (11)	prof	81.8	12.1	6.1
	stud	78.8	18.2	3.0
	mt	77.3	9.1	13.6
	gpt	87.9	12.1	0
symbol (9)	prof	11.1	81.5	7.4
	stud	14.8	77.8	7.4
	mt	7.4	77.8	14.8
	gpt	14.8	81.5	3.7
preposition (5)	prof	93.3	6.7	0
	stud	93.3	6.7	0
	mt	76.7	6.6	16.7
	gpt	100	0	0
shortened (5)	prof	80.0	20.0	0
	stud	73.3	26.7	0
	mt	76.7	16.7	6.6
	gpt	86.7	13.3	0
lexical (1)	prof	100	0	0
	stud	100	0	0
	mt	83.3	0	16.7
	gpt	100	0	0
conjunction (1)	prof	100	0	0
	stud	66.7	33.3	0
	mt	33.3	50.0	16.7
	gpt	66.7	0	33.3

Table 8: Effects of less frequent (< 30 occurrences in source) source phenomena on different types of translations for all languages.

phenomenon	text	en-hr n	en-hr y	en-hr e	en-ru n	en-ru y	en-ru e	en-fi n	en-fi y	en-fi e
capitalisation	prof	109	114	2	100	119	6	110	114	1
(225)	stud	115	110	0	106	110	9	90	133	2
	mt1	80	138	7	91	118	16	85	94	**46**
	mt2	80	134	11	102	113	10	64	134	**27**
	gpt	**122**	96	7	137	**82**	6	122	**92**	11
pun+space	prof	98	25	0	91	30	2	90	32	1
(123)	stud	76	47	0	81	40	2	82	41	0
	mt1	87	36	0	105	18	0	46	67	10
	mt2	87	36	0	99	15	9	92	29	2
	gpt	**120**	2	1	**119**	4	0	**121**	2	0
punctuation	prof	70	38	1	57	49	3	64	45	0
(109)	stud	55	54	0	45	59	5	47	62	0
	mt1	26	82	1	48	57	4	55	45	9
	mt2	26	82	1	59	47	3	36	46	7
	gpt	**82**	25	2	**88**	20	1	**80**	28	1
spelling	prof	**82**	2	0	70	12	2	**77**	5	2
(84)	stud	**75**	8	1	66	13	5	**76**	6	2
	mt1	57	10	**17**	62	11	**11**	37	7	**40**
	mt2	56	10	**18**	71	10	3	52	10	**22**
	gpt	**78**	1	5	**77**	2	5	**73**	2	9
pronoun	prof	80	0	1	51	28	2	64	17	0
(81)	stud	78	2	1	49	30	2	59	21	1
	mt1	64	7	**10**	35	44	2	29	19	**33**
	mt2	65	6	**10**	41	37	3	37	22	**22**
	gpt	74	3	4	44	34	3	60	14	7
informal	prof	43	8	2	41	6	6	38	12	3
(53)	stud	37	10	6	41	8	4	35	14	4
	mt1	25	4	**24**	30	8	**15**	16	8	**29**
	mt2	24	3	**26**	34	7	**12**	26	6	**21**
	gpt	36	8	9	43	7	3	39	6	8

Table 9: Effects of the most prominent source phenomena with more than 50 occurrences on each of the translations.

		en-hr			en-ru			en-fi		
phenomenon	text	n	y	e	n	y	e	n	y	e
space	prof	20	5	1	21	3	2	20	6	0
(26)	stud	21	4	1	16	8	2	17	9	0
	mt1	16	5	**5**	17	4	**5**	13	6	**7**
	mt2	17	3	**6**	16	8	2	11	9	**6**
	gpt	20	5	1	19	6	1	18	6	2
form	prof	21	4	0	25	0	0	24	1	0
(25)	stud	24	1	0	24	0	1	24	1	0
	mt1	19	3	3	25	0	0	12	1	**12**
	mt2	18	4	3	24	0	1	16	1	**8**
	gpt	23	2	0	22	0	3	23	0	2
article	prof	18	0	1	18	0	1	18	0	1
(19)	stud	19	0	0	19	0	0	19	0	0
	mt1	18	0	1	16	1	2	17	0	2
	mt2	18	0	1	16	0	3	17	0	2
	gpt	19	0	0	17	0	2	18	0	1
structure	prof	16	1	0	14	3	0	16	1	0
(17)	stud	14	0	3	12	3	2	12	3	2
	mt1	3	9	5	8	6	3	2	2	**13**
	mt2	3	9	5	10	5	2	3	2	**12**
	gpt	8	6	3	15	0	2	12	3	2
format	prof	11	2	3	16	0	0	9	7	0
(16)	stud	5	8	3	13	2	1	0	13	3
	mt1	14	1	1	5	11	0	0	11	5
	mt2	14	1	1	3	13	0	4	7	5
	gpt	16	0	0	15	0	1	15	0	1
verb	prof	14	0	0	13	0	1	9	5	0
(14)	stud	13	1	0	14	0	0	6	8	0
	mt1	9	3	2	13	1	0	5	5	4
	mt2	8	4	2	13	1	0	4	7	3
	gpt	13	0	1	12	0	2	6	5	3
addition	prof	9	2	0	10	1	0	8	1	2
(11)	stud	9	2	0	9	2	0	8	2	1
	mt1	10	1	0	9	1	1	6	1	4
	mt2	10	1	0	10	1	0	6	1	4
	gpt	10	1	0	10	1	0	9	2	0

Table 10: Effects of the source phenomena with less than 50 and more than 10 occurrences on each of the translations

		en-hr			en-ru			en-fi		
phenomenon	text	n	y	e	n	y	e	n	y	e
symbol (9)	prof	2	6	1	1	7	1	0	9	0
	stud	2	6	1	2	7	0	0	8	1
	mt1	0	7	2	1	7	1	0	7	2
	mt2	0	6	3	3	6	0	0	9	0
	gpt	2	7	0	1	7	1	1	8	0
preposition (5)	prof	5	0	0	4	1	0	5	0	0
	stud	5	0	0	4	1	0	5	0	0
	mt1	4	1	0	4	0	1	4	0	1
	mt2	4	1	0	4	0	1	3	0	2
	gpt	5	0	0	5	0	0	5	0	0
shortened (5)	prof	4	1	0	4	1	0	4	1	0
	stud	3	2	0	4	1	0	4	1	0
	mt1	4	1	0	4	0	1	3	1	1
	mt2	4	1	0	5	0	0	3	2	0
	gpt	4	1	0	5	0	0	4	1	0
lexical (1)	prof	1	0	0	1	0	0	1	0	0
	stud	1	0	0	1	0	0	1	0	0
	mt1	1	0	0	1	0	0	1	0	0
	mt2	1	0	0	0	0	1	1	0	0
	gpt	1	0	0	1	0	0	1	0	0
conjunction (1)	prof	1	0	0	1	0	0	1	0	0
	stud	1	0	0	0	1	0	1	0	0
	mt1	0	1	0	0	1	0	0	0	1
	mt2	0	1	0	1	0	0	1	0	0
	gpt	1	0	0	1	0	0	0	0	1

Table 11: Effects of the source phenomena with less than 10 occurrences on each of the translations

Stanceosaurus 2.0: Classifying Stance Towards Russian and Spanish Misinformation

Anton Lavrouk, Ian Ligon, Tarek Naous, Jonathan Zheng, Alan Ritter, Wei Xu
College of Computing
Georgia Institute of Technology
{antonlavrouk, iligon3, tareknaous, jonathanqzheng}@gatech.edu; {alan.ritter, wei.xu}@cc.gatech.edu

Abstract

The Stanceosaurus corpus (Zheng et al., 2022) was designed to provide high-quality, annotated, 5-way stance data extracted from Twitter, suitable for analyzing cross-cultural and cross-lingual misinformation. In the Stanceosaurus 2.0 iteration, we extend this framework to encompass Russian and Spanish. The former is of current significance due to prevalent misinformation amid escalating tensions with the West and the violent incursion into Ukraine. The latter, meanwhile, represents an enormous community that has been largely overlooked on major social media platforms. By incorporating an additional 3,874 Spanish and Russian tweets over 41 misinformation claims, our objective is to support research focused on these issues. To demonstrate the value of this data, we employed zero-shot cross-lingual transfer on multilingual BERT, yielding results on par with the initial Stanceosaurus study with a macro F1 score of 43 for both languages. This underlines the viability of stance classification as an effective tool for identifying multicultural misinformation.

1 Introduction

Misinformation on social media is a highly multicultural phenomenon (Roozenbeek et al., 2020). In the ongoing Russia-Ukraine conflict, Russian-language misinformation and propaganda are important weapons used by both sides to influence the opinions of Internet users across the globe. Meanwhile, Spanish-language misinformation is surging unchecked through virtually every online community.[1] With these issues in mind, we seek to create a dataset that can help identify Spanish and Russian misinformation beyond a binary yes/no approach. We do this by expanding the Stanceosaurus dataset (Zheng et al., 2022) to include Spanish and Russian tweets annotated using a 5-way stance labeling schema (Gorrell et al. 2018, Schiller et al. 2021), thus creating *Stanceosaurus 2.0*. By fine-tuning multilingual BERT (Devlin et al., 2019), we experiment with zero-shot cross-lingual transfer, demonstrating the potential for *Stanceosaurus 2.0* to help drive forward misinformation research on Spanish and Russian. Furthermore, recent Twitter policies have made it clear that the site is moving away from account-based labeling of misinformation.[2] Our dataset presents the opportunity to identify potential misinformation on a per-tweet basis, allowing users to see relevant context for potentially misleading tweets. Some may argue that in recent times, Twitter (now X at the time of revision) has taken a far more "hands-off" approach to misinformation. While this may or may not be true, this dataset can be used on social media platforms that are different from Twitter/X. One can get around the tweet length limit by simply concatenating various tweets, etc. In the following sections, we discuss what exactly Russian and Spanish misinformation entail and why they are so important.

Russian Misinformation Misinformation and propaganda are crucial to Russian political warfare. Part of so-called "active measures", they are designed to "weaken the West [and] to drive wedges in the Western community alliances of all sorts, particularly NATO ..." (Alexander, 2017). When Russia launched a full-scale invasion of Ukraine in February of 2022,[3] both sides of the conflict engaged in hybrid warfare, putting an equal focus on the information front and global deception.[4] With propaganda machines in full force, the war in Ukraine has spawned many new misinformation claims. In this context, although a Russian stance dataset is present in Lozhnikov et al. (2018), it is limited, and our research aims to modernize

[1] The Guardian

[2] Twitter

[3] CNBC

[4] The Atlantic

Proceedings of the Ninth Workshop on Noisy and User-generated Text (W-NUT 2024), pages 31–43
March 22, 2024 ©2024 Association for Computational Linguistics

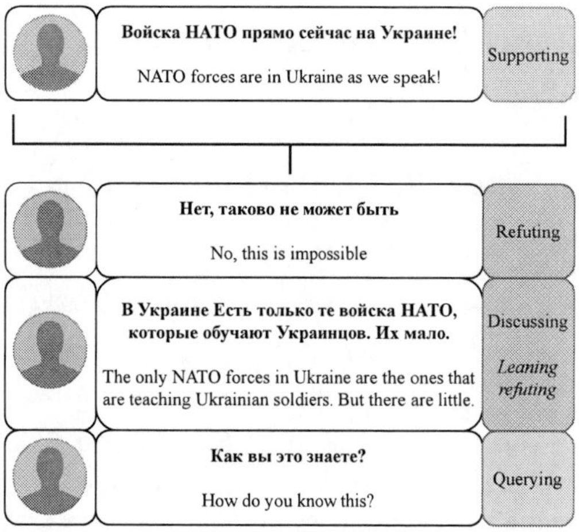

Figure 1: Example of a data point (tweet and context) in the Russian Stanceosaurus dataset. For the claim "NATO forces are currently fighting in Ukraine", we have an example tweet chain demonstrating various stances.

Russian stance data to include wartime misinformation. This is because Russian misinformation "then" and "now" are two different beasts. Potential feasibility for the idea of Russian Stanceosaurus can be seen via the findings in Park et al. (2022) which, among many interesting things, identified Twitter as a platform with a significant amount of Russian-language discussion regarding wartime events. The series of Solopova et al. (2023a) and Solopova et al. (2023b), which showcases great results on pro-Kremlin propaganda detection, also potentially implies feasibility of our stance-based approach.

Spanish Misinformation Misinformation is rampant in the Spanish-speaking world, surging through various online communities (Bonnevie et al., 2023). Despite being the fourth most spoken language in the world and an enormous medium for the spread of information worldwide both true and false, misinformation in Spanish is far more of a problem than in English[5]. This problem is further exacerbated when it is ignored; Facebook whistleblower Frances Haugen revealed an enormous disconnect between the proportion of users who speak Spanish and the amount of spending committed to anti-misinformation resources in this language[6]. Unsurprisingly, works such as Posadas-Durán et al. (2019) and Abonizio et al. (2020) attempt to help solve this crucial problem, particularly framing the problem as detecting fake news. These studies show that this kind of claim-based misinformation detection works quite well. Our approach was inspired by such studies. To our knowledge, there are two existing Spanish stance datasets. One is Zotova et al. (2020), a valuable but singular claim-limited collection of Spanish-language stance data. The other is Toledo-Ronen et al. (2020), which creates a wonderful Spanish stance dataset, but based on arguments and not misinformation claims. We aim to expand the set of Spanish misinformation via the five-way and three-way classification framework of Stanceosaurus.

[5]Washington Post

[6]The Guardian

2 Stanceosaurus 2.0: Details

In order to facilitate the study of Russian and Spanish misinformation, we have created a 5-way stance classification dataset in accordance with the guidelines established by Zheng et al. (2022). These stance categories are `Irrelevant`, `Supporting`, `Refuting`, `Querying`, and `Discussing`. The stance of a tweet is based on the misinformation claim it is discussing. An example of various misinformation claim related tweets and their stance categorization can be seen in Figure 1. Details on the five stance categories (and how they can be merged to 3 categories) are listed in appendix C.

2.1 Data Collection

Misinformation Claims We derived 18 examples of Russian-language misinformation, with 13 from the European Union initiative, *euvsdisinfo*, and manually translated them into Russian using a bilingual Russian/English speaker (both fluent). Despite criticism of fact-checking methodology (Giorio, 2018), euvsdisinfo is to our knowledge the best source of prominent misinformation which can be found on Russian-language Twitter, especially considering that there is no reliable Russian fact-checking website (this is the reason why we had to translate the claims to Russian). Nonetheless, to mitigate this bias, we supplemented these misinformation claims with 5 claims from the Western media. Again, the absence of claims from Russian sources or Russian-language fact-checking sites is notable. We re-iterate that identifying misinformation is challenging when Russian media is largely state controlled[7]. Any source that does fact-checking that might disagree with the state media would most likely get taken down or blocked by Roskomnadzor. Therefore,

[7]ForeignPolicy.com

for this study, we selected a ground truth based on western-leaning sources to assess Russian misinformation claims. For the Spanish corpus, we collected 23 misinformation claims from reputable Spanish-language fact-checking websites *Verificado*, *Chequeado*, *Newtral*, and *ChequeaBolivia*, including claims with various veracity ratings. The selection of both Spanish and Russian claims was guided by the volume of relevant Twitter discourse. The detailed Russian and Spanish claims are listed in Appendix A and B, respectively.

Tweet Collection & Reply Chains For both languages, we collect tweets using the Twitter API. Queries (Appendix A and B) are manually curated and iteratively refined in order to capture as many relevant tweets as possible while allowing for diversity in stance categories. This refinement was done by scraping data for a claim using a certain query, and then sampling 20 tweets and hand annotating them. Queries were then modified, and the process was repeated until a reasonably equal distribution of stances was achieved. Alongside tweets from queries, we also collect additional tweets for context, including those "above"(preceding) and "below"(following) in the reply chain. Similar to the original Stanceosaurus paper, context tweets were included to potentially help models make classification decisions. Annotation was done by sampling 50 tweets for each claim, adding up to 100 context tweets, which were then evaluated. These quantities were chosen based on the number of available annotators. All three annotators are college-educated students who are fluent in their respective languages. There were two annotators for Russian and one for Spanish. Future versions of this work will include another annotator for Spanish. The 5-class Cohen Kappa for the Russian data is 77.4. Reproducibility criteria for this process are discussed in Appendix D. A basic overview of corpus statistics is in Table 1. More detailed corpus statistics can be found in F. As mentioned in D, the dataset can be requested directly from the authors. Since the tweet ID's it contains can link tweets back to their authors, it is important that these tweets are used only for academic purposes, especially given that some of them present controversial political opinions.

2.2 Russian Corpus

Russian Twitter According to a Statista study (Statista, 2023a), only 5% of Russians surveyed reported using Twitter. This makes sense, as before this study, "Facebook, Instagram, and Twitter were all blocked by the Russian state in early March 2022 when the laws on antiwar activity came into force" (McCarthy et al., 2023). Thus, the only way to access Twitter in Russia is through a VPN. From this information, we gather that Russian speakers on Twitter either use a VPN, are native to another country where Russian is a common language, or live abroad. Acknowledging this is important, as it provides a population for the Twitter users that were sampled and presents a limitation of the data to be addressed with future work.

#tweets	Refute	Support	Irrel.	Query	Discuss	Total
Russian	119	332	999	50	407	1907
Spanish	270	302	1036	16	342	1966

Table 1: Corpus statistics of Stanceosaurus 2.0.

Code Switching There are instances of tweets that contain different languages. It is fairly common to see acronyms such as "HIMARS" and "NATO" being written in both English and Russian interchangeably. A brief analysis using regular expressions finds that tweets containing characters from the English alphabet make up about 12 percent of all tweets. Furthermore, sometimes the Russian language is phonetically written in the Latin alphabet. This poses a challenge when querying for relevant Tweets, which we addressed by accounting for as many code-switched variations as was reasonable. Furthermore, in the sampled reply chains, it was common to see the mixing of languages, especially between Russian and Ukrainian. Fortunately, since every single tweet was hand annotated by a fluent Russian speaker with proficient knowledge of Ukrainian, it was not difficult to differentiate between the two languages, as well as any other language that uses the Cyrillic alphabet.

Obscenities Due to the politically charged nature of the Russian misinformation claims, many tweets contain large amounts of cursing, which is known as *mat* (pronounced maht). It is argued that *mat* "is not merely an accumulation of obscenities, but rather constitutes a set of refined, complex structures", hinting at a "potentially limitless quantity of expressions" (Dreizin and Priestly, 1982). A cursory analysis indicates that around 10 percent of all Russian tweets collected contain some sort of obscenity. Context is key when trying to understand Russian obscenities, and this may prove to be quite confusing for a language model to interpret.

2.3 Spanish Corpus

Circumventing Filters Particularly when discussing the COVID-19 vaccine, many tweets include language that is most likely obscured to circumvent misinformation filters. When searching "vacuna" (Spanish for "vaccine"), Twitter sends users a warning to check federal websites for information related to the pandemic.[8] Accordingly, the queries had to be adjusted to include numerous alternative spellings for the word for vaccine (including 'vacuno', 'vacun@', 'vakuna', 'cacunados', 'v@cunad0s', 'kakuna', etc.).

Social Media Usage The decision to utilize Twitter for this corpus was driven by its accessible API and publicly shareable text-centric content for open and ethical NLP research. It is worth noting that within the Spanish-speaking realm, Twitter ranks behind Facebook, Instagram, and TikTok in terms of social media usage (Statista 2023b, StatCounter 2023). Additionally, more Hispanics use WhatsApp than any other race or ethnicity,[9] and significant volumes of misinformation spread on private channels such as WhatsApp[10] where misinformation detection is much more difficult and misinformation is less likely to be corrected by the public.

Code Switching Mixing Spanish and English together in a single tweet is common, particularly in Spanish-speaking communities in Northern Mexico and the USA. The spread of misinformation in bilingual communities is a unique challenge of particular importance in the United States, where more than one-third of all Hispanic adults self-identify as bilingual in English and Spanish (Pew, 2015).

3 Automatic Stance Detection Using Stanceosaurus 2.0

Zero-Shot Cross-Lingual Transfer In accordance with the original Stanceosaurus paper (Zheng et al., 2022), we conduct a zero-shot cross-lingual transfer experiment on our data. This entails training a model on the English Stanceosaurus dataset of 20,707 tweets and then evaluating it on the Russian and Spanish sets. We believe that this is the best way to evaluate Stanceosaurus 2.0 since we assume that there is little to no stance-based training data available for Russian and Spanish (something we observed during our research, and can be seen in Section 1 where we discuss related work). Also, various studies such as Pires et al. (2019) and Artetxe et al. (2020) have shown zero-shot cross-lingual transfer to be an effective approach in many languages, including Russian and Spanish.

Multilingual BERT Multilingual BERT (Devlin et al., 2019), or mBERT, has been shown to be very competitive in the zero-shot setting that we have described (Wu and Dredze 2019, Libovický et al. 2019). We believe that mBERT is a simple baseline that indicates the quality of our dataset and model performance. For our experiments, we follow the original Stanceosaurus paper (Zheng et al., 2022) and use the five stance label schema. To create model input, we format our strings using special tokens as follows: "[CLS] claim [SEP] text".

Loss Functions Similar to the original Stanceosaurus (Zheng et al., 2022), we examine three different loss functions: cross-entropy loss, weighted cross-entropy loss (Cui et al., 2019), and class-balanced focal loss (Baheti et al., 2021). While the cross-entropy loss is a baseline commonly used in classification tasks, we use weighted cross-entropy to modify this baseline to account for imbalanced classes by assigning more weights to classes with fewer samples. Class-balanced focal loss is an alternative method to account for imbalanced classes. It down-weights easy examples and focuses more on difficult ones (Cui et al., 2019).

Results The results of our experiments can be seen in Table 2. One can compare these results to English performance on BERT_{BASE} for unseen claims from the original Stanceosaurus paper (Zheng et al., 2022), as well as the same zero-shot cross-lingual transfer experiment on Hindi and Arabic. These extra experiments are also shown in 2, but they are clearly marked as the contribution of the authors of the original Stanceosaurus paper. Both Russian and Spanish datasets performed similarly to models for English to Hindi and English to Arabic transfer experiments in the original Stanceosaurus (Zheng et al., 2022). The weighted loss functions performed better overall, and both languages achieved an F1 score of around 43. Reproducibility criteria for our experiments can be seen in appendix E.

[8]This is no longer the case following recent changes to Twitter policy.

[9]Insider Intelligence

[10]Harvard Kennedy School

Russian (our contribution)

Loss	Precision	Recall	F1
CE	53.55±0.8	35.33±0.7	36.15±1.3
Weighted CE	44.38±0.2	42.84±0.5	42.09±0.1
CBFL	45.60±1.5	46.98±2.0	43.94±0.2

Spanish (our contribution)

Loss	Precision	Recall	F1
CE	50.26±1.9	40.86±0.7	41.81±1.0
Weighted CE	54.12±0.4	42.65±0.5	43.75±0.4
CBFL	51.26±2.2	44.15±0.9	43.83±1.0

Hindi (Zheng et al., 2022)

Loss	Precision	Recall	F1
CE	52.1±2.9	39.4±2.0	40.8±2.5
Weighted CE	55.0±4.2	42.4±1.4	44.3±1.8
CBFL	53.0±3.4	44.1±1.7	45.3±1.5

Arabic (Zheng et al., 2022)

Loss	Precision	Recall	F1
CE	44.8±4.0	40.1±2.5	40.0±2.0
Weighted CE	44.1±3.3	40.7±1.6	39.7±1.7
CBFL	46.1±2.6	44.7±1.1	43.1±0.2

English on BERT$_{BASE}$ (Zheng et al., 2022)

Loss	Precision	Recall	F1
CE	51.1±1.1	50.5±2.0	50.4±1.6
Weighted CE	50.5±1.9	52.7±1.1	51.3±1.3
CBFL	50.6±1.3	55.7±2.1	52.5±1.0

Table 2: Russian and Spanish experiments. Models are trained on English Stanceosaurus and then evaluated on either Russian or Spanish in our work. F1 is measured as macro F1. Results are taken as the average of 3 experiments, with error being one standard deviation. English, Arabic, and Hindi experiments are taken directly from Stanceosaurus (Zheng et al., 2022) as a comparison benchmark.

4 Conclusion

We introduce Stanceosaurus 2.0, an extension of the 5-way stance dataset Stanceosaurus (Zheng et al., 2022). Our dataset includes 18 Russian misinformation claims (1907 tweets) and 23 Spanish misinformation claims (1966 tweets). Our dataset is modern and up to date given the recent slough of misinformation and current events. It also contains Russian and Spanish, which as shown previously, are two languages in which misinformation thrives, and efforts to combat it are limited. Our zero-shot cross-lingual transfer experiments show that our dataset performs at similar levels to that of Hindi and Arabic in the original Stanceosaurus, with a macro F1 score of about 43. This means that there is potential to continue refining models and algorithms to create a somewhat reliable stance classifier using transformer-based models like mBERT. Future versions of this work will entail experiments on more models, as well as a second annotator for the Spanish version.

Limitations

The Veracity of Fact-Checked Claims One of the biggest limitations of our work is the fact that fact-checking is often not as black-and-white as it seems and is generally a practice that suffers from many limitations (Uscinski and Butler, 2013). It is very difficult to find objective truths that are verified to a degree of absolute precision for a work like this. This is doubly so for political-leaning claims, such as the claims in the Russian dataset.

Russian Misinformation Claims An unfortunate limitation of the Russian language is that there are no Russian fact-checking websites that would provide reasonably objective fact-checking, at least as far as we are aware. This is most likely due to the level of control that the Russian government has over the Russian internet (Polyakova and Meserole, 2019). This lack of resources means that Russian claims were hand-picked. This could introduce author bias, and may not be an accurate representation of the Russian internet, as claims were mostly all found on the heavily western-leaning website euvsdisinfo, as discussed in section 2.

Russian Twitter As mentioned in section 2.2, Twitter is not the most used social media, and this could introduce various biases into our data. Future work could involve the social media website VKontakte, which as mentioned earlier, is the most popular in Russia. However, some problems could arise due to state-owned entities being shareholders[11].

Spanish Twitter Likewise, Twitter is far from the most popular social media network in Latin America. More work should be done to analyze misinformation on Facebook and WhatsApp in the Hispanosphere. Despite favoring small-group communication, WhatsApp persists as a medium for rapid misinformation dissemination in Latin America (Nobre et al., 2022).

Spanish Queries As mentioned in section 2.3, numerous obstacles made it difficult to query for

[11]Reuters

relevant Tweets in Spanish. From properties inherent to the Spanish language like a highly inflectional morphology to broader social factors including the prevalence of code-mixing and filter circumvention, care had to be taken when querying Twitter's API to find relevant Tweets without biasing the data in any one direction (Pfaff, 1979). Future work might include broad queries to procure larger datasets that can then be manually cleaned to include more relevant Tweets.

Code Switching As mentioned in both sections 2.2 and 2.3, both languages experienced a decent amount of code-switching, whether it be in the context or the tweet itself. It has been shown before that dealing with code-switching is not an easy task (Winata et al., 2021). However, recently there has been a large number of code-switching datasets that have become available (Jose et al., 2020). Potential further research may include creating stance datasets exclusively on code-switched datasets.

Tweet Deletion A feature of the obscured version of the dataset (the version we plan on giving out in most cases) is that it only features tweet IDs. However, if someone deletes a tweet, that tweet will be gone from the obscured dataset. This maintains the user's right to remove their content without it still being a database. However, this may be an issue for researchers using this dataset a long time after the tweets were originally collected.

Ethics Statement

Working With Social Media Data Mining social media data from Twitter users without their consent is at best ethically problematic (Taylor and Pagliari, 2018). Unfortunately, this kind of data would not exist without this technique. However, our publicly available dataset only contains tweet IDs and does not include actual tweets and usernames. Furthermore, social media data can contain harmful biases towards certain groups, as moderating social media can be extremely difficult (Ganesh and Bright, 2020). We encourage a thorough review of the data and its context before deploying in a production environment.

Data Annotation We recognize that some of the tweets that have been annotated deal with sensitive topics and contain some hateful language, especially in the Russian dataset, given its political nature. We recognize that annotators need to be warned of this before they start annotating.

Propaganda Analysis An issue with analyzing propaganda and misinformation is that this analysis can potentially fall into the wrong hands. For example, using this dataset to analyze the effectiveness of Russian propaganda can inform the source of the propaganda exactly what they could improve on.

Acknowledgments

The authors would like to thank Dennis Pozhidaev for his help with data annotation and evaluation. This research is supported by the NSF (IIS-2052498) and IARPA via the HIATUS program (2022-22072200004). The views and conclusions contained herein are those of the authors and should not be interpreted as necessarily representing the official policies, either expressed or implied, of NSF, ODNI, IARPA, or the U.S. Government. The U.S. Government is authorized to reproduce and distribute reprints for governmental purposes notwithstanding any copyright annotation therein.

References

Hugo Queiroz Abonizio, Janaina Ignacio de Morais, Gabriel Marques Tavares, and Sylvio Barbon Junior. 2020. Language-independent fake news detection: English, portuguese, and spanish mutual features. *Future Internet*, 12(5).

Keith B. Alexander. 2017. Disinformation: A primer in russian active measures and influence campaigns. Prepared statement, United States Senate Select Committee on Intelligence.

Mikel Artetxe, Sebastian Ruder, and Dani Yogatama. 2020. On the cross-lingual transferability of monolingual representations. In *Proceedings of the 58th Annual Meeting of the Association for Computational Linguistics*. Association for Computational Linguistics.

Ashutosh Baheti, Maarten Sap, Alan Ritter, and Mark Riedl. 2021. Just say no: Analyzing the stance of neural dialogue generation in offensive contexts. In *Proceedings of the 2021 Conference on Empirical Methods in Natural Language Processing*, pages 4846–4862, Online and Punta Cana, Dominican Republic. Association for Computational Linguistics.

E Bonnevie, V Ricciulli, M Fields, and R O'Neill. 2023. Lessons learned from monitoring spanish-language vaccine misinformation during the covid-19 pandemic. *Public Health Rep*, 138(4):586–592. PMID: 37102367; PMCID: PMC10140774.

Yin Cui, Menglin Jia, Tsung-Yi Lin, Yang Song, and Serge Belongie. 2019. Class-balanced loss based on effective number of samples. In *Proceedings of the IEEE/CVF Conference on Computer Vision and Pattern Recognition (CVPR).*

Jacob Devlin, Ming-Wei Chang, Kenton Lee, and Kristina Toutanova. 2019. Bert: Pre-training of deep bidirectional transformers for language understanding.

F. Dreizin and T. Priestly. 1982. A systematic approach to russian obscene language. *Russ Linguist*, 6:233–249.

Bharath Ganesh and Jonathan Bright. 2020. Countering extremists on social media: Challenges for strategic communication and content moderation.

L. Giorio. 2018. *War on Propaganda or PRopaganda War?: A case study of fact-checking and (counter)propaganda in the EEAS project EUvsDisinfo.* Dissertation, Uppsala University, Jagiellonian University.

Genevieve Gorrell, Kalina Bontcheva, Leon Derczynski, Elena Kochkina, Maria Liakata, and Arkaitz Zubiaga. 2018. Rumoureval 2019: Determining rumour veracity and support for rumours.

Navya Jose, Bharathi Raja Chakravarthi, Shardul Suryawanshi, Elizabeth Sherly, and John P. McCrae. 2020. A survey of current datasets for code-switching research. In *2020 6th International Conference on Advanced Computing and Communication Systems (ICACCS)*, pages 136–141.

Jindřich Libovický, Rudolf Rosa, and Alexander Fraser. 2019. How language-neutral is multilingual bert?

Nikita Lozhnikov, Leon Derczynski, and Manuel Mazzara. 2018. Stance prediction for russian: Data and analysis.

Lauren A. McCarthy et al. 2023. Four months of "discrediting the military": Repressive law in wartime russia. *Demokratizatsiya: The Journal of Post-Soviet Democratization.*

Gabriel Peres Nobre, Carlos H.G. Ferreira, and Jussara M. Almeida. 2022. A hierarchical network-oriented analysis of user participation in misinformation spread on whatsapp. *Information Processing & Management*, 59(1):102757.

Chan Young Park, Julia Mendelsohn, Anjalie Field, and Yulia Tsvetkov. 2022. Challenges and opportunities in information manipulation detection: An examination of wartime russian media.

Pew. 2015. A majority of english-speaking hispanics in the u.s. are bilingual. Accessed: 2023-06-11.

Carol W. Pfaff. 1979. Constraints on language mixing: Intrasentential code-switching and borrowing in spanish/english. *Language*, 55(2):291–318.

Telmo Pires, Eva Schlinger, and Dan Garrette. 2019. How multilingual is multilingual bert?

Alina Polyakova and Chris Meserole. 2019. Exporting digital authoritarianism: The russian and chinese models. *Policy Brief, Democracy and Disorder Series*, pages 1–22.

Juan-Pablo Posadas-Durán et al. 2019. Detection of fake news in a new corpus for the spanish language. *Journal of Intelligent & Fuzzy Systems*, 36(5):4869–4876.

Jon Roozenbeek, Claudia R. Schneider, Sarah Dryhurst, John Kerr, Alexandra L. J. Freeman, Gabriel Recchia, Anne Marthe van der Bles, and Sander van der Linden. 2020. Susceptibility to misinformation about covid-19 around the world. *R. Soc. open sci.*, 7:201199.

B. Schiller, J. Daxenberger, and I. Gurevych. 2021. Stance detection benchmark: How robust is your stance detection? *Künstl Intell*, 35:329–341.

V. Solopova, OI. Popescu, C. Benzmüller, et al. 2023a. Automated multilingual detection of pro-kremlin propaganda in newspapers and telegram posts. *Datenbank Spektrum*, 23:5–14.

Veronika Solopova, Christoph Benzmüller, and Tim Landgraf. 2023b. The evolution of pro-kremlin propaganda from a machine learning and linguistics perspective. In *Proceedings of the Second Ukrainian Natural Language Processing Workshop (UNLP)*, pages 40–48, Dubrovnik, Croatia. Association for Computational Linguistics.

StatCounter. 2023. Social media stats spain. Accessed: June 11, 2023.

Statista. 2023a. Ranking of social media platforms in russia q3 2022, by user share. Accessed: 2023-05-26.

Statista. 2023b. Social media usage in latin america - statistics & facts. Accessed: June 11, 2023.

Joanna Taylor and Claudia Pagliari. 2018. Mining social media data: How are research sponsors and researchers addressing the ethical challenges? *Research Ethics*, 14(2):1–39.

Orith Toledo-Ronen, Matan Orbach, Yonatan Bilu, Artem Spector, and Noam Slonim. 2020. Multilingual argument mining: Datasets and analysis. In *Findings of the Association for Computational Linguistics: EMNLP 2020*, pages 303–317, Online. Association for Computational Linguistics.

Joseph E. Uscinski and Ryden W. Butler. 2013. The epistemology of fact checking. *Critical Review*, 25(2):162–180.

Genta Indra Winata, Samuel Cahyawijaya, Zihan Liu, Zhaojiang Lin, Andrea Madotto, and Pascale Fung. 2021. Are multilingual models effective in code-switching?

Shijie Wu and Mark Dredze. 2019. Beto, bentz, becas: The surprising cross-lingual effectiveness of bert.

Jonathan Zheng, Ashutosh Baheti, Tarek Naous, Wei Xu, and Alan Ritter. 2022. Stanceosaurus: Classifying stance towards multilingual misinformation.

Elena Zotova, Rodrigo Agerri, Manuel Nuñez, and German Rigau. 2020. Multilingual stance detection in tweets: The Catalonia independence corpus. In *Proceedings of the Twelfth Language Resources and Evaluation Conference*, pages 1368–1375, Marseille, France. European Language Resources Association.

A Russian Claims and Queries

Russian claims and queries can be found in figure 3.

B Spanish Claims and Queries

Spanish claims and queries can be found in figures 4 and 5.

C Stance Categorization

The following is a description of each stance:

- **Supporting:** Tweets that directly support the fact that a claim is true.
- **Refuting:** Tweets that refute the veracity of a claim.
- **Querying:** Questions the veracity of a claim.
- **Discussing:** Provides neutral information on the context or truth of a claim.
- **Irrelevant:** Not relevant to the given claim.

If a tweet is labeled as discussing, then to enable 3-way stance classification, the tweet is also given a leaning. The following is a description of each leaning:

- **Supporting:** The tweet has an indirect positive bias when discussing the claim.
- **Refuting:** The tweet has an indirect negative bias when discussing the claim.
- **Other:** The tweet does not have any sort of bias.

With this information, we can now construct our guidelines for 3-way stance categorization as well:

- **Supporting:** Merge supporting with discussing$_{supporting}$.
- **Refuting:** Merge refuting with discussing$_{refuting}$.
- **Other:** Merge irrelevant, querying, and discussing$_{other}$.

D Dataset Reproducibility Criteria

- Using the twitter API, up to 150 tweets were pulled for each claim using the queries listed in figures 3, 4, and 5. Context for each tweet was also retrieved. Context in this case means the entire reply chain from the root tweet down to the pulled tweet, as well as any immediate replies.
- Quality control was done by an extensive iteration of Twitter API queries. We aimed to make queries such that the distribution of stance categories was reasonably even, although this proved to be difficult with the "Querying" category.
- With these tweets in hand, up to 50 tweets were sampled for each claim for annotation. Context tweets were also annotated. Up to 50 parent context tweets were sampled and up to 50 context children tweets were sampled for each claim.
- Claims were annotated in accordance with details given in appendix C. Russian tweets were double annotated, while Spanish tweets currently only have a single annotator, but we are working to find another annotator at the moment.
- Tweets were pre-processed to remove duplicates using lexical similarity.
- The context chains were then reconstructed and formatted in json to match the original Stanceosaurus paper (Zheng et al., 2022).
- The dataset can be requested from the authors using the emails given in the paper. Since the data is potentially sensitive (tweets of political nature) we need to make sure that anyone who uses these tweets is doing so solely out of academic intent.

E Experiment Reproducibility Criteria

- **Model:** bert-base-multilingual-uncased
- **Computing Infrastructure:** 4 Nvidia Titan X GPUs. NVIDIA-SMI 460.84. Driver Version 460.84. CUDA version 11.2. Running on CentOS linux 7. Conda version 7. Package versions listed in `requirements.txt` file in code used.
- **Average Training Time:** Per experiment, around 40 minutes
- **Evaluation Metrics:** Best evaluation of the development set per training run
- **Number of Experiments:** Each row in 2 was

done 3 times. Results are the mean ± the standard deviation. Random seeds for the three runs were 10, 20, and 30.

- **Hyperparameters:** Hyperparameters were chosen based off of best performing hyper parameters in the original Stanceosaurus model, and then manually tuned.
  - **Learning Rate:** 3e-5
  - **Batch Size:** 8 per GPU, so 32 total
  - **Class Balanced Focal Loss:** Similar to the original paper, we tune β and γ between $[0.1, 1)$ and $[0.1, 1.1]$ respectively.
  - The rest are defaulted to what is used in the code. Run commands are included with code.
- Code zip file can be accessed upon request.

F Corpus Statistics

The distribution of labels and tweet types for Russian Spanish are shown in tables 3 and 4 respectively. A visual representation of the tweets (not context or replies) for Russian Spanish is shown in figures 2(a) and 2(b) respectively.

G Annotation Logistics

Annotators were American college students paid 18 dollars an hour. Each annotator was fluent in the language they were annotating. All annotators were recruited as people the authors directly knew. Verbally, annotators were told the scope of the paper and given the abstract.

H Use of AI assistants

AI assistants were used by the authors of this paper in order to proofread the paper. Occasionally, an AI assistant was asked to rephrase some text, just to generate some ideas on sentence flow. Work was never directly copied, and model output was used as inspiration.

	Refuting	Supporting	Irrelevant	Querying	$D_{supporting}$	$D_{refuting}$	D_{other}	Total
Tweets	109	315	149	39	77	169	41	899
Context	5	15	738	9	51	40	7	865
Replies	5	2	112	2	6	15	1	143
Total	119	332	999	50	134	224	49	1907

Table 3: Russian Corpus Statistics.

	Refuting	Supporting	Irrelevant	Querying	$D_{supporting}$	$D_{refuting}$	D_{other}	Total
Tweets	228	269	418	12	85	52	60	1124
Context	15	21	370	2	18	13	4	443
Replies	27	12	248	2	76	18	16	399
Total	270	302	1036	16	179	83	80	1966

Table 4: Spanish Corpus Statistics.

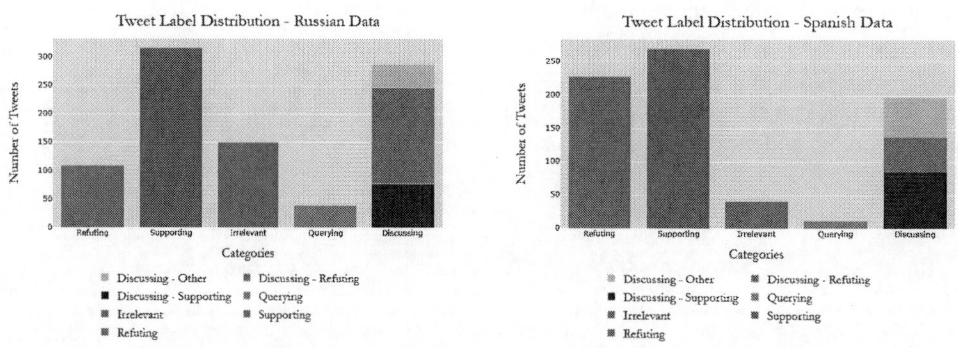

(a) (b)

Figure 2: Label distribution for tweets (by query, not context) in the (a) Russian dataset and (b) Spanish dataset.

Claim	Translation	Twitter API query
В Украине Воюют войска НАТО.	NATO forces are fighting against Russia in Ukraine.	("войска нато" OR "западные войска") ("в украине" OR "на украине") lang:ru -is:retweet
В украине есть лаборатории которые изготовлают биологическое оружие НАТО.	There are NATO bio-weapon labs in Ukraine.	"био лаборатории" OR "био-лаборатории" lang:ru -is:retweet
Буча – это Украинский фейк.	The Bucha massacre was faked by Ukraine.	буча (фейк OR fake) lang:ru -is:retweet
В Украинском правительстве заправляют нацисты	Nazism is prevalent in many facets of the Ukrainian government.	"нацизм в украине" OR "нацизм на украине" lang:ru -is:retweet
Геноцид Русскоязычных на Донбассе	There is a genocide of Russian speakers in the Donbas region of Ukraine	геноцид (русских OR русскоязычных) (украина OR украине) lang:ru -is:retweet
Украина – агрессор в войне	Ukraine is the aggressor in the 2022 Russo-Ukrainian war	"украина агрессор" lang:ru -is:retweet
В Украине запретили говорить на Русском языке.	Speaking the Russian language has been banned in Ukraine.	(запрет OR запретили) ("русского языка" OR "русский язык") lang:ru -is:retweet
НАТО хочет уничтожить Россию.	NATO wants to destroy Russia.	(НАТО OR запад) (уничтожить OR уничтожит) (Россию OR Россия) lang:ru -is:retweet
Украинцы сбили малазийский самолет MH17.	Ukrainian forces shot down MH17.	(Украина OR Украинцы) (MH17 OR MH-17 OR МН-17 OR МН17 OR МХ17 OR МХ-17 OR боинг) lang:ru -is:retweet
В Украине планируют строить концлагеря для русских	Ukraine is planning on building concentration camps for Russians/Russian speakers	"концлагеря для русских" OR "концлагеря для русскоязычных" lang:ru -is:retweet
Алексей Навальный мошенник.	Alexei Navalny is a fraudster.	"Навальный мошенник" OR "Навальный жулик" lang:ru -is:retweet
Запад не хочет мира	The west does not want peace (in Russia/Ukraine conflict)	запад не хочет мира lang:ru -is:retweet
Западные агенты подорвали газопровод Северный Поток.	Western agents (Anglo-Saxons according to Dimitry Medvedev) blew up the Nordstream pipeline.	ЦРУ северный поток lang:ru -is:retweet
Владимир Зеленский – наркоман	Volodimir Zelensky is addicted to drugs	зеленский наркоман lang:ru -is:retweet
США строят биолаборатории в странах бывшего СССР.	The US is fixing/organizing biolaboratories in ex-USSR countries	США биолаборатории lang:ru -is:retweet
Европа мерзнет без русского газа.	Europe is freezing without Russian natural Gas.	европа (мерзнет OR мёрзнет) lang:ru -is:retweet
Войска РФ только бьют по военным целям	The Russian Federation only targets military objects in its bombings and does not target civillians or civillian infrastructure	"только по военным целям" OR "только по военной инфраструктуре" lang:ru -is:retweet
Украина самая коррумпированная страна в мире/европе	Ukraine is the most corrupt country in the world/Europe	"Украина самая коррумпированная" lang:ru -is:retweet

Figure 3: Russian Claims and Queries

Claim	Translation	Twitter API query
No hay fracking en México	There's no fracking in Mexico	"hay fracking" mexico -"nueva mexico" lang:es
Broncho Vaxom previene COVID-19	Broncho Vaxom prevents COVID-19	broncho vaxom COVID AND (inhibe OR previene) lang:es
Los jóvenes están entre los sectores más afectados por la pandemia	Youth are one of the groups most heavily impacted by the pandemic	jovenes mas afectados pandemia lang:es
La Argentina es uno de los países latinoamericanos más retrasados en regímenes de licencias parentales	Argentina is further behind than most Latin American countries in terms of parental leave	argentina AND ("licencias parentales" OR "licencia parental") lang:es
Amber Heard ha plagiado un fragmento de la película 'El talento de Mr. Ripley' en el juicio frente a Johnny Depp	Amber Heard plagiarized the movie "The Talented Mr. Ripley" in her trial against Johnny Depp	Mr. Ripley lang:es
El brote de hepatitis infantil haya sido provocado por la vacuna contra la COVID-19 de Pfizer	The childhood Hepatitis rash has been caused by the Pfizer COVID-19 vaccine	(brote OR hepatitis) vacuna lang:es
Coca-Cola dejará de producir Mineragua y será reemplazada por Fanta Limón	Coca-Cola will stop producing Mineragua, which will be replaced by Fanta Limón	mineragua lang:es
El director ejecutivo de BioNTech no se vacunó contra el COVID-19	The CEO of BioNTech did not receive the COVID vaccine himself	ugur sahin lang:es
Estas imágenes de personas trans muestran a Salvador Ramos, autor de la masacre de Uvalde (Texas).	These images of a transgender person show Salvador Ramos, the Uvalde Texas school shooter.	("salvador ramos" OR uvalde OR tiroteo) (trans OR transexual OR genero OR transgenero OR transgenera) lang:es -filter:retweets
La viruela del mono está vinculada al grafeno y a las vacunas contra la COVID-19	Monkeypox is linked to graphene and the COVID-19 vaccine	(viruela OR virus OR viruel@) AND mono AND (vacuna OR vacunas OR pfizer OR moderna OR astrazeneca) lang:es -filter:retweets
Muchas de las personas transexuales eventualmente destransicionan	Many transgender people eventually detransition	destransicionar OR destransicion OR destransicionaron OR destransiciono OR destransiciona OR destransicionan lang:es -filter:retweets
Australia aprueba una ley que prohíbe cultivar tus propios alimentos	Australia approved a law that prohibits growing your own food	australia alimentos propios lang:es -filter:retweets
Australia retiró de circulación 50 millones de vacunas por dar positivo en pruebas de VIH	Australia recalled 50 million vaccine doses for making people test positive for HIV	(vacuna OR inyeccion OR vacunas OR inyecciones) positivo vih lang:es -filter:retweets since:2022-01-01
La viruela de mono es una enfermedad de transmisión sexual	Monkeypox is a sexually transmitted disease	(viruela OR viruelo OR viruel@) mono (sexual OR ets OR sex) lang:es -filter:retweets
Los perros domésticos pueden ser causa de la hepatitis atípica infantil	Domesticated dogs might be the cause of acute hepatitis in children	(perro OR perros) hepatitis lang:es -filter:retweets since:2022-03-01
Las vacunas aumentan el riesgo de muerto al entrar en contacto con el 5G	Vaccines increase the risk of death upon coming in contact with 5G	(vacuna OR vacunas) 5G lang:es -filter:retweets
Biden puso la Medalla de Honor al revés al condecorar a un veterano de guerra	Biden put the Medal of Honor on backwards while decorating a war veteran.	Biden medalla since:2022-07-01 lang:es -filter:retweets
El portavoz del Mundial de fútbol de Qatar advirtió que quien luzca la bandera LGTBI en la Copa del Mundo será arrestado con penas entre 7 y 11 años.	A spokesperson for the Qatar FIFA World Cup warned that anyone displaying the LGBT pride flag en the World Cup will be arrested with sentences between 7 and 11 years	(qatar OR catar) bandera lang:es -filter:retweets
La vicepresidenta electa de Colombia, Francia Márquez, posa delante de un grafiti que dice "hoy desayuné feto".	The vice president-elect of Colombia, Francia Márquez, poses beside graffiti which reads "today I ate a fetus for breakfast"	francia marquez (feto OR fetos) lang:es -filter:retweets
Hay evidencias de que la vacuna COVID-19 sea la causa del síndrome que afecta a Justin Bieber	There is evidence that the COVID-19 vaccine is the cause for Justin Bieber's Ramsay Hunt syndrome	bieber vacuna lang:es since:2022-05-01 -filter:retweets

Figure 4: Part 1 of Spanish Claims and Queries

Claim	Translation	Twitter API query
El 5G y la radiación inalámbrica producen efectos perjudiciales para la salud	5G and wireless radiation produce damaging effects for your health	(5G OR "radiacion inalambrica") (causa OR causan OR efecto OR efectos OR causaron OR causo OR causara OR causaran) lang:es -filter:retweets
Están usando fetos abortados en las vacunas contra el coronavirus	They are using aborted fetuses to produce the COVID vaccine	(feto OR fetos OR abortado OR abortados OR abortada OR abortadas) vacuna lang:es -filter:retweets
El director de Pfizer dijo que su objetivo es reducir la población mundial	The director of Pfizer said that their goal is to reduce the global population	pfizer (((reducir OR reduce OR reducen) AND poblacion) OR despoblacion OR sobrepoblacion) lang:es -filter:retweets

Figure 5: Part 2 of Spanish Claims and Queries

A Comparative Analysis of Noise Reduction Methods in Sentiment Analysis on Noisy Bangla Texts

Kazi Toufique Elahi, Tasnuva Binte Rahman, Shakil Shahriar, Samir Sarker, Md. Tanvir Rouf Shawon, G. M. Shahariar
Department of Computer Science and Engineering
Ahsanullah University of Science and Technology, Dhaka, Bangladesh
{ktoufiquee, tasnuvabinterahmansrishti, shakilshahriararnob, rohitsarker5, shawontanvir95, sshibli745}@gmail.com

Abstract

While Bangla is considered a language with limited resources, sentiment analysis has been a subject of extensive research in the literature. Nevertheless, there is a scarcity of exploration into sentiment analysis specifically in the realm of noisy Bangla texts. In this paper, we introduce a dataset (**NC-SentNoB**) that we annotated manually to identify ten different types of noise found in a pre-existing sentiment analysis dataset comprising of around 15K noisy Bangla texts. At first, given an input noisy text, we identify the noise type, addressing this as a multi-label classification task. Then, we introduce baseline noise reduction methods to alleviate noise prior to conducting sentiment analysis. Finally, we assess the performance of fine-tuned sentiment analysis models with both noisy and noise-reduced texts to make comparisons. The experimental findings indicate that the noise reduction methods utilized are not satisfactory, highlighting the need for more suitable noise reduction methods in future research endeavors. We have made the implementation and dataset presented in this paper publicly available[1].

Sentiment	Data	Noise
Neutral	**[B]** অনেক দিন ওয়েট করাইছেন সায়েম ভাই **[E]** *You kept me waiting for several days brother Sayem.*	Mixed Language Local Word
Positive	**[B]** আমি মাঝে মাঝে যাই খুব মানগত খাবার **[E]** *I occasionally visit, and the food is of high quality.*	Punctuation Error
Negative	**[B]** ভাই দয়াকরে খাবার নষ্ট করবেন্না **[E]** *Please don't waste food brother.*	Spacing Error Spelling Error

Table 1: Few examples from our **NC-SentNoB** dataset with sentiment on the leftmost column and noise types on the rightmost column. **B** represents the original text in Bangla and **E** represents the corresponding English translation.

1 Introduction

Sentiment analysis is the process of analyzing and categorizing the emotions or opinions expressed in textual content. This process holds considerable importance in evaluating public sentiments, analyzing social media posts, and assessing customer feedback. It contributes significantly to gaining insights into ongoing social media dynamics. There have been nearly 7000 papers published on this topic and 99% of the papers have appeared after 2004, making sentiment analysis one of the fastest-growing research areas (Mäntylä et al., 2018).

With the recent emergence of pre-trained language models (PLMs) (Devlin et al., 2018a; Liu et al., 2019; He et al., 2020; Raffel et al., 2020; Xue et al., 2020), there has been a notable enhancement in the sentiment analysis task. However, when confronted with increased textual noise, the performance of PLMs drops drastically (around 50%), primarily due to the inability of the tokenizer to handle misspelled words (Srivastava et al., 2020). This issue is less pronounced in English, where most typing tools and applications offer robust auto-correction systems. However, Bangla, despite being the seventh most spoken language with a minimum of 272.7 million speakers (Wikipedia, 2023), faces significant challenges due to the absence of an effective auto-correction system in digital devices and software. As a result, a considerable amount of text shared on social media platforms often exhibits diverse forms of noise, including informal language, regional words, spelling errors, typographic errors, punctuation errors, coined words, embedded metadata, a mixture of two or more lan-

[1] `https://github.com/ktoufiquee/A-Comparative-Analysis-of-Noise-Reduction-Methods-in-Sentiment-Analysis-on-Noisy-Bangla-Texts`

Proceedings of the Ninth Workshop on Noisy and User-generated Text (W-NUT 2024), pages 44–57
March 22, 2024

guages (code-mixed text), grammatical mistakes and so forth (Srivastava et al., 2020). For example, the sentence "না , মুই ওগো কিছু কই নাই , দুঃখু পাইবে" (*English: No, I did not tell them anything, they will get sad*) incorporates regional words like "মুই" ("আমি", *I*), "ওগো" ("ওদের", *them*), "কই" ("বলি", *tell*), "পাইবে" ("পাবে", *get*), alongside a spelling error "দুঃখু" ("দুঃখ", *sad*).

Recent investigations into Bangla sentiment analysis have primarily focused on Bangla texts, Romanized Bangla texts (Hassan et al., 2016), and social media comments (Chakraborty et al., 2022). However, there is a notable scarcity of research specifically addressing noisy Bangla texts, and the available datasets for such studies are limited. To address this gap, the **SentNoB** dataset (Islam et al., 2021) has been recently introduced, aiming to tackle challenges associated with sentiment analysis in noisy Bangla texts. Nevertheless, it is worth noting that this dataset lacks annotations for noise types present in the noisy texts and does not incorporate any noise reduction methods. The presence of noise significantly impacts the performance of models compared to their performance on noiseless text, which indicates a potential area for further research. To address these issues, we have made the following contributions:

- We present a dataset named **NC-SentNoB** (**N**oise **C**lassification on **SentNoB** dataset), designed for the identification of ten distinct types of noise found in approximately 15K noisy Bangla texts. Few sample instances are provided in Table 1.
- We employ machine learning, deep learning and fine-tune pre-trained transformer models to identify noise types in noisy Bangla texts (a multi-label classification task) and to perform sentiment analysis on both noisy and noise-reduced texts (a multi-class classification task).
- We conduct experiments with various techniques to reduce noise from Bangla texts including spell correction, back translation, paraphrasing and masking. To assess their effectiveness, we compare the performance of these methods against a set of 1000 random, noisy texts that have been manually corrected by annotators.
- We have made our dataset and codes openly accessible for further research in this field.

2 Related Works

Haque et al. (2023) integrated 42,036 samples from two publicly available Bangla datasets, achieving the highest accuracy (85.8%) in multi-class sentiment analysis with their proposed C-LSTM. Islam et al. (2020) introduced two manually tagged Bangla datasets, achieving 71% accuracy for binary classification and 60% for multi-class classification using BERT with GRU. Bhowmick and Jana (2021) outperformed the baseline model proposed by Islam et al. (2020), attaining a 95% accuracy on binary classification by fine-tuning `m-BERT` and `XLM-RoBERTa`. Samia et al. (2022) utilized `BERT`, `BiLSTM`, and `LSTM` for aspect-based sentiment analysis, where `BERT` performed best by achieving 95% in aspect detection and 77% sentiment classification. Hasan et al. (2023) fine-tuned transformer models where `BanglaBERT` surpassed other models with 86% accuracy and a macro F1-score of 0.82 in multi-class setting.

Bangla sentiment analysis has also been extended to address the challenges of noisy social media texts. One of the notable contributions is SentNoB, a dataset of over 15,000 social media comments developed by Islam et al. (2021). It was benchmarked by SVM with lexical features, neural networks, and pre-trained language models. The best micro-averaged F1-Score (0.646) was achieved by `SVM` with word and character n-grams. Hoq et al. (2021) added Twitter data to SentNoB and got 87.31% accuracy with multi-layer perceptrons. Islam et al. (2023) developed SentiGOLD, which is a balanced Bangla sentiment dataset consisting of 70,000 entries with five classes which utilized SentNoB for cross-dataset evaluation. It was benchmarked by `BiLSTM`, `HAN`, `BiLSTM`, `CNN with attention` and `BanglaBERT`. The best macro F1-Score (0.62) was achieved by fine-tuning `BanglaBERT`, which also got an F1-Score (0.61) on SentNoB during cross-dataset testing.

As for the correction of noisy texts, Koyama et al. (2021) performed a comparative analysis of grammatical error correction using back-translation models. It was observed that the transformer-based model achieved the highest score on the CoNLL-2014 dataset (Ng et al., 2014). Sun and Jiang (2019) employed a `BERT`-based masked language modeling for contextual noise reduction. This method involves sequentially masking and correcting each word in a sentence, starting from the left. They found that this noise reduction method significantly enhances performance in applications such as neural machine translation, natural language interfaces, and paraphrase detection in noisy texts.

3 Noise Identification

In this section, we first manually annotate all the instances from **SentNoB** dataset, categorizing them into **ten** separate noise categories. A single instance may fall into multiple noise categories. Then, we outline the process of noise identification, where the objective is to determine the type of noise present in a given noisy Bangla text. This task is framed as a multi-label classification task.

3.1 Existing Dataset

The **SentNoB** dataset (Islam et al., 2021) has a total of 15,728 noisy Bangla texts. While the dataset offers a collection of noisy Bangla texts, it lacks information regarding the specific types of noise present in these texts. The dataset is partitioned into three subsets: train (80%), test (10%), and validation (10%). Each text is categorized into one of three labels: *positive*, *neutral*, and *negative*. These labels represent the sentiment or tone expressed in each text.

3.2 Dataset Development

To the best of our knowledge, there is currently no dataset specifically designed for the purpose of identifying noise in Bangla texts. To address this gap, we expanded the SentNoB dataset to create a noise identification dataset named **NC-SentNoB** (**N**oise **C**lassification on **SentNoB** dataset), encompassing a total of 15,176 noisy texts. In the process, we eliminated 552 duplicate values present in the original dataset to enhance data integrity. We maintained the train-validation-test splitting ratio of the original dataset and the distribution of data in each partition is detailed in Table 2.

	Neutral	Positive	Negative
Train	2,767	4,948	4,318
Test	361	650	570
Validation	354	621	587
Total	3,482	6,219	5,475

Table 2: Data distribution in each partition.

3.3 Annotation

The primary idea behind developing the NC-SentNoB dataset was to categorize the noises available in the dataset. To do this, the authors thoroughly investigated the SentNoB dataset, determined ten categories, and defined rules for each noise type as the annotation guidelines. The details of each noise category are presented in Appendix C. We first invited seven native Bangla speakers to assist us with the annotating process. Next, we asked each participant to label 50 samples, from which we determined their trustworthiness score (Price et al., 2020). We used 10 samples out of the 50 as control samples and discovered that only four participants achieved the 90% trustworthiness score threshold. The degree of agreement across annotators is calculated using Fleiss' kappa score (Fleiss, 1971) to maintain the quality of the annotation. After computing the scores for four independent annotators, we found a reliable score of 0.69, indicating a substantial degree of agreement.

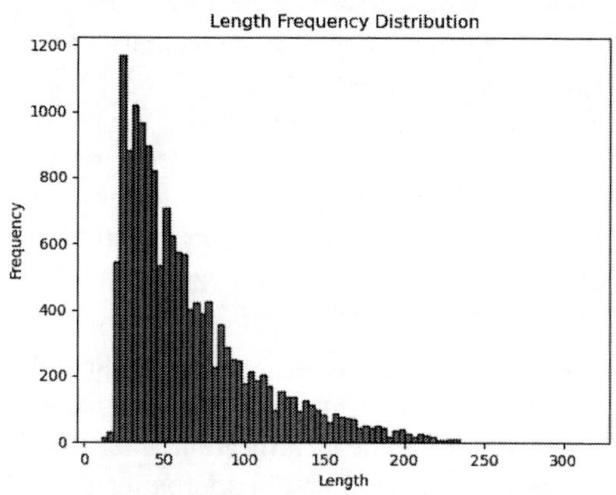

Figure 1: Length-Frequency distribution of Texts.

3.4 Dataset Statistics

It is evident from Table 2 that the dataset is imbalanced, with the number of texts in the *neutral* category significantly lower than those in both the *positive* and *negative* categories. In addition to the

Class	Instances	#Word/Instance
Local Word	2,084 (0.136%)	16.05
Word Misuse	661 (0.043%)	18.55
Context/Word Missing	550 (0.036%)	13.19
Wrong Serial	69 (0.005%)	15.30
Mixed Language	6,267 (0.410%)	17.91
Punctuation Error	5,988 (0.391%)	17.25
Spacing Error	2,456 (0.161%)	18.78
Spelling Error	5,817 (0.380%)	17.30
Coined Word	549 (0.036%)	15.45
Others	1,263 (0.083%)	16.52

Table 3: Statistics of **NC-SentNoB** per noise class.

class imbalance, the dataset also exhibits a wide

variation in the length of the texts. On an average, the texts have a length of 66 characters. The longest text is 314 characters, while the shortest text is only 11 characters long. Figure 1 shows the length frequency distribution of the texts over the whole dataset. Table 3 shows the statistics of different types of noise we found. This provides an insight into the most common noise of Bangla texts found on the dataset. The table shows that *Mixed Language* is the most common noise type, *Spelling Error* is the second most common, and *Wrong Serial* is the least common. Figure 2 indicates low correlation coefficients, suggesting a minimal linear association between noise categories. Notably, *Mixed Language* and *Spelling Error* have the least correlation at -0.12, implying a slight inverse relationship between these two types. This indicates if a sentence in the dataset contains an error of *Mixed Language*, it has a higher possibility of not having any *Spelling Error* and vice versa.

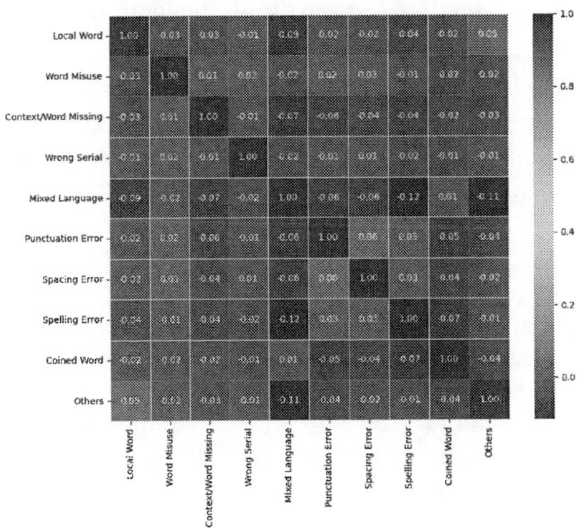

Figure 2: Heatmap of correlation coefficients among different noise types in **NC-SentNoB**.

3.5 Baselines

For noise identification, we implemented Support Vector Machine (SVM) (Cortes and Vapnik, 1995) (utilizing both character and word n-gram features), Bidirectional Long Short Term Memory (BiLSTM) (Hochreiter and Schmidhuber, 1997) network, and fine-tuned the pre-trained Bangla-BERT-Base (Sarker, 2020) model. The descriptions of the models can be found in Appendix A. The rationale behind the classification is to develop an automatic text pre-processing step that identifies different types of noise present in Bangla texts. We firmly believe that this pre-processing step will play a vital role in addressing challenges associated with noisy Bangla texts by aiding in the development of noise specific reduction methods.

3.6 Experimental Setup

SVM was implemented with a regularization parameter of 1. As for BiLSTM and Bangla-BERT-Base, Binary Cross-Entropy Loss was used. Both models were trained using the AdamW optimizer, with a learning rate of $1e-6$ for BiLSTM and $1e-5$ for Bangla-BERT-Base. The batch sizes were set at 256 for BiLSTM and 128 for Bangla-BERT-Base.

3.7 Results & Analysis

Table 4 presents the performance comparison of the implemented models on noise identification. Bangla-BERT-Base achieves the highest micro F1-score at 0.62, while SVM with character-level features secures the second-best score of 0.57. However, BiLSTM has the lowest micro F1-score of 0.24. The comparison between SVM with character-level

Model	Precision	Recall	F1-Score
SVM (C)	0.76	0.45	0.57
SVM (W)	0.64	0.38	0.48
SVM (C + W)	0.75	0.45	0.56
Bi-LSTM	0.36	0.18	0.24
Bangla-BERT-Base	0.73	0.54	**0.62**

Table 4: Performance comparison of different models on noise identification. **C** represents character level n-gram and **W** represents word level n-gram.

features and SVM with word-level features shows that the former attains a higher score. This suggests that character-level information is more crucial for noise identification. Implementing a similar character-level approach in neural network models and fine-tuning other pre-trained language models may improve the noise identification performance which we leave open for future work. Table 5 illustrates the performance of Bangla-BERT-Base on each type of noise. It can be seen that the model fails to classify instances of the *Wrong Serial* type. This is primarily due to the low amount of data available for this specific class in the dataset.

4 Sentiment Analysis

In this section, we outline the methodology employed for conducting sentiment analysis on the NC-SentNoB dataset. We employ a cost-sensitive learning objective to fine-tune seven pre-trained transformer models for the sentiment analysis task.

Class	Precision	Recall	F1-Score
Local Word	0.46	0.49	0.47
Word Misuse	0.65	0.16	0.25
Context/Word Missing	0.33	0.06	0.10
Wrong Serial	0.00	0.00	0.00
Mixed Language	0.75	0.85	0.80
Punctuation Error	0.83	0.54	0.65
Spacing Error	0.86	0.21	0.33
Spelling Error	0.64	0.55	0.59
Coined Word	0.82	0.89	0.86
Others	0.76	0.76	0.76

Table 5: Class-wise performance of **Bangla-BERT-Base** on noise identification task.

We conduct two distinct experiments: the first involves fine-tuning transformers on the noisy texts, while the second entails fine-tuning transformers after reducing noise from the original noisy texts.

4.1 Baselines

We utilized seven publicly available pre-trained transformer models: `Bangla-Bert-Base` (Sarker, 2020), `BanglaBERT` (Bhattacharjee et al., 2022a), `BanglaBERT Large` (Bhattacharjee et al., 2022a), `SahajBERT`[2], `Bangla-Electra`[3], `MuRIL` (Khanuja et al., 2021). The descriptions of the models can be found in Appendix A.

4.2 Cost-sensitive Learning

Cost-sensitive learning (Elkan, 2001) is a process of training where we can make the model prioritize samples from the minority class above those from the majority class by suggesting a manually established weight for every class label in the cost function that is being minimized. We adopted this method in the sentiment analysis task. In order to provide a more equitable and balanced model performance, we tried imposing larger costs to the classes that are in the minority in numbers due to the imbalance scenario in the NC-SentNoB dataset, as seen in Table 2. This was accomplished by providing class weights to the Cross-Entropy loss function used to train the models.

4.3 Experimental Setup

Cost-sensitive learning was incorporated by using class weights as a cost matrix into the Cross-Entropy loss function. The class weights were set at 1.4496 for *neutral*, 0.8106 for *positive*, and 0.9289 for *negative* classes. For fine-tuning, the AdamW optimizer was used with a learning rate of $1e-5$, betas set at (0.9, 0.9999), an epsilon value of $1e-9$, and a weight decay of 0.08. Due to resource constraints, batch size was set to 48 for `sahajBERT`, 32 for `BanglaBERT Large`, and 128 for the rest of the models.

Model	Precision	Recall	F1-Score
Bangla-BERT-Base	0.72	0.72	0.72
BanglaBERT	0.75	0.75	**0.75**
BanglaBERT Large	0.74	0.74	0.74
BanglaBERT Generator	0.72	0.72	0.72
sahajBERT	0.72	0.72	0.72
Bangla-Electra	0.68	0.68	0.68
MuRIL	0.73	0.73	0.73

Table 6: Performance of sentiment analysis models fine-tuned on noisy texts.

4.4 Experiment with noise

Table 6 illustrates the performance comparison of the seven fine-tuned models. `BanglaBERT` yields the highest scores across all evaluation metrics with a micro F1-score of 0.75. This result outperforms the highest micro F1-Score of 0.6461 with `SVM` previously reported by Islam et al. (2021). It is also noteworthy that all other models except `Bangla-Electra` have demonstrated results that are somewhat comparable with ranges between 0.72 and 0.75 in terms of micro F1-score.

4.5 Experiment by reducing noise

In this experiment, we first outline the noise reduction strategies utilized prior to sentiment analysis. We then randomly select 1000 noisy texts and manually correct them. We use these 1000 manually corrected texts as ground truth for measuring the performance of the noise reduction methods in terms of semantic similarity. To assess performance, we employ various established evaluation metrics.

Class	Instances
Local Word	132 (13.2%)
Word Misuse	32 (03.2%)
Context/Word Missing	39 (03.9%)
Wrong Serial	4 (00.4%)
Mixed Language	416 (41.6%)
Punctuation Error	323 (32.3%)
Spacing Error	133 (13.3%)
Spelling Error	376 (37.6%)
Coined Word	33 (03.3%)
Others	92 (09.2%)

Table 7: Statistics of noise types on manually corrected 1000 data.

[2]`https://huggingface.co/neuropark/sahajBERT`

[3]`https://huggingface.co/monsoon-nlp/bangla-electra`

4.5.1 Process of Noise Reduction

Complete elimination of noise from the noisy texts is impossible. However, our aim is to minimize noise to the greatest extent possible. This section details four distinct methods for reducing noise in noisy texts: back-translation, spelling correction, paraphrasing and replacing out of vocabulary (OOV) words with predictions generated by a masked language model (MLM). Additional details about the employed methods can be found in Appendix A.

(a) Back-translation. Back-translation serves as a method to correct various errors within a sentence. As pre-trained models have been trained on extensive corpora of noiseless sentences, they can generate a noiseless translated sentence when presented with a noisy sentence as input. Also, translating that sentence back into the original language may result in a corrected version. For this study, all input texts were initially translated into English and then into Bangla using back-translation. Two models were chosen for this purpose: Google Translate, a web service employing an RNN-based model and `BanglaT5` models pre-trained on the BanglaNMT English-Bangla and BanglaNMT Bangla-English dataset (Bhattacharjee et al., 2022b).

(b) Spelling Correction. For the noisy texts we are working with, correcting spelling errors can be a beneficial process as spelling errors can affect the tokenization process. To address this issue, we implemented a spell correction algorithm based on `Soundex` and `Levenshtein` distance. This algorithm replaces misspelled words with the closest matching words found in the Bangla dictionary[4]. However, as it is not context-based, there are instances where it fails to correct all spellings and may even introduce out-of-context words in the sentence.

(c) Paraphrasing. Paraphrasing involves changing the words of a sentence without altering its meaning. Similar to translation models, paraphrasing models have the potential to provide a noiseless paraphrased output when given a noisy input. For this study, we used the `BanglaT5` model pre-trained on the Bangla Paraphrase dataset (Akil et al., 2022). We observed the performance of the `BanglaT5` paraphrase model on some randomly selected noisy texts from our dataset and found that the model performs poorly when the input data contains misspelled words. To address this issue, we used the spelling corrector algorithm prior providing input to the model.

(d) Mask Prediction. To improve the quality of noisy texts and address out-of-vocabulary words, we replaced OOV words with <MASK> and used the predictions generated by a Masked Language Model (MLM). We also implemented random masking for replacement with each word having a 20% possibility of getting replaced by the MLM model. For both cases, we used `BanglaBERT Generator` (Kowsher et al., 2022) model.

4.5.2 Evaluation of Noise Reduction

We first use several well-known metrics to quantify the performance of the noise reduction techniques. The evaluation is performed based on 1000 manually corrected texts. The first four authors individually corrected 250 texts each, while the last two authors verified corrections for 500 texts each. We then compare and analyze the performance of the noise reduction methods.

Evaluation Metrics. To evaluate the noise reduction methods, we employed a range of metrics including BLEU, ROUGE-L, BERTScore, SBERT Score, BSTS, BERT-iBLEU, and Word Coverage (utilizing Word2Vec, FastText, and `Bangla-BERT-Base`). Additionally, we conducted human evaluations of the noise reduced sentences by native Bangla speakers. The detailed descriptions of the evaluation metrics along with the human evaluation procedure are presented in Appendix B.

Noise Reduction Performance. From the data presented in Table 8, it can be seen that the original noisy texts scored highest on BLEU and ROUGE-L, which is unsurprising since the ground truth sentences contain nearly identical words. This observation is further supported by the spell-corrected sentences, which also achieve a similar score due to having nearly identical words. Similarly, for BERTScore, SBERT Score, and BSTS, the scores are higher for noisy texts. This is primarily because of the nature of textual embeddings and the tokenization method used. As mentioned earlier, `BERT` uses WordPiece tokenization, which can result in identical words having the same token. Therefore, when comparing noisy texts with their corresponding ground truth sentences, many tokens are likely to match perfectly, leading to higher cosine similarity scores. However, although not having the

[4]https://github.com/MinhasKamal/BanglaDictionary

	BLEU	ROUGE-L	BERT Score	SBERT Score	BSTS	BERT -iBLEU	Word Coverage			Human Evaluation (%)
							Word2Vec	FastText	Bangla BERT	
Noisy Text	**65.77**	**79.71**	**93.21**	**88.32**	**93.67**	51.65	75.54	82.92	71.26	X
Google Translate	21.55	39.46	84.72	81.04	84.28	**80.93**	87.52	**89.01**	84.86	**37.90**
BanglaT5 Translate	16.57	32.09	81.30	75.27	82.15	80.12	**89.01**	87.52	85.66	21.10
Spell Correction (SC)	61.17	77.35	92.29	87.86	92.94	56.50	82.72	88.51	80.76	35.80
SC + Paraphrase	20.35	36.44	83.32	74.15	85.60	80.63	86.79	86.79	83.89	20.80
MLM (OOV)	60.99	76.44	90.72	86.90	91.82	56.60	88.51	82.27	87.18	26.80
MLM (Random)	44.17	70.00	90.76	85.26	93.45	68.93	86.41	88.35	**93.20**	10.40

Table 8: Performance comparison of different noise reduction methods

Before reduction	**[N]** আপনি তো হাত ধয়া ভুলে গেলেন ভাই **[C]** আপনি তো হাত ধোয়া ভুলে গেলেন ভাই **[E]** Brother you forgot to wash your hands.
After reduction	**[S]** আপনি তো হাত দয়া ভুলে গেলেন ভাই **[SP]** তুমি তোমার হাত-পায়রে দয়া ভুলে গেছ, ভাই। **[TG]** ভাই আপনি হাত ধুতে ভুলে গেছেন **[TM]** তুমি হাত ধরতে ভুলে গেছো **[MO]** আপনি তো হাত হারাতে ভুলে গেলেন ভাই **[MR]** আপনি তো হাত ধরতে ভুলে গেলেন ভাই

Table 9: Input and output of a single noisy text by the noise reduction methods. **N** denotes the original noisy text, **C** indicates the corrected text, and **E** represents English translation of the corrected text. **S**, **SP**, **TG**, **TM**, **MO**, and **MR** represent outputs of spelling correction, paraphrasing with spelling correction, back-translation using Google Translate, back-translation with T5 models, masked language modeling for out-of-vocabulary words, and random masked language modeling respectively. For each sentence, noisy words are marked with Red color, and noise reduced words are marked with Green color.

highest score, back-translation, paraphrasing, and mask prediction methods score above 80% in both BERTScore and BSTS, implying that they are semantically similar and the meaning of the sentences have not changed drastically. BERT-iBLEU score accounts for the presence of textually similar words by applying penalization while emphasizing semantic meaning, leading to Google Translate achieving the highest score in this metric. Moreover, the word coverage results show different methods scoring the highest instead of noisy texts. This is due to the generated words or sentences from these models having a higher possibility of being noiseless words from their respective vocabularies. All of the scores are based on the textual similarity of the ground truths and noise reduced sentences. Thus, we relied on human evaluation to select the best noise reduction method where 4 native Bangla speakers evaluated the sentences and discovered that the back-translation method utilizing Google Translate API was the most reliable in terms of maintaining contextual meaning. The input and output of each noise reduction method for a single noisy text are shown in table 9. Except for back-translation using Google Translate, all methods fail to rectify the spelling problem in the input. Most approaches change the meaning of the sentence by changing the noisy word.

4.5.3 Results & Analysis

We prioritized the human evaluation score based on the results of Table 8 and used back-translated data obtained from Google Translate to execute the sentiment analysis task by fine-tuning seven pre-trained transformer models. We applied the same noise reduction method on both the test and validation sets. We compared the sentiment analysis performance of the models fine-tuned on noisy and noiseless data presented in Tables 6 and 10. From Table 10, it can be seen that models fine-tuned on back-translated data only attain the highest F1-Score of 0.73. This outcome remains consistent across all models evaluated during our experimentation. The model fine-tuned on noisy data outperformed the same model fine-tuned on back-translated data. The reason for this disparity of performance is that, while back-translation can mitigate some sources of noise, it can also introduce

Model	Precision	Recall	F1-Score
Bangla-BERT-Base	0.69	0.69	0.69
BanglaBERT	0.72	0.72	0.72
BanglaBERT Large	0.73	0.73	**0.73**
BanglaBERT Generator	0.70	0.70	0.70
sahajBERT	0.70	0.70	0.70
Bangla-Electra	0.66	0.66	0.66
MuRIL	0.71	0.71	0.71

Table 10: Performance of sentiment analysis models fine-tuned on noise reduced texts (back-translation with google translate).

changes in the contextual meaning of the sentences (see Appendix D). Because of this, it had a score of 37.90% on human evaluation where our main priority of scoring was the contextual meaning of the sentence. We used the human evaluation score to achieve the best noise reduction strategy, although as shown in Table 8, other techniques scored well on several metrics as well. Nevertheless, it is worthwhile to explore alternative approaches beyond back-translation to determine whether a particular noise reduction method yields superior results in addressing specific types of noisy texts. Table 11 illustrates the class-wise results of our best-performing model - `BanglaBERT Large` on noise reduced data. It is clear from the table that the results are quite high for the positive and negative classes but the opposite for the neutral class. Few training data points might be the reason for this low performance in that particular class.

Class	Precision	Recall	F1-Score
Neutral	0.53	0.51	0.52
Positive	0.77	0.77	0.77
Negative	0.78	0.80	0.79
Micro	0.73	0.73	0.73
Macro	0.69	0.69	0.69
Weighted	0.72	0.73	0.72

Table 11: Class-wise performance of **BanglaBERT Large** on noise reduced texts (back-translation with google translate).

5 Limitations and Future Works

One obvious limitation is that none of the noise reduction methods we employed were able to correctly reduce noise from the noisy texts. As a result, fine-tuned models achieved a lower score in sentiment analysis than models fine-tuned on noisy texts. Another limitation is that we have not evaluated sentiment analysis by considering alternative noise reduction techniques other than back-translation by Google Translate. Although other noise reduction methods performed poorly in human evaluation, it would be interesting to study whether their performance in noise reduction correlates with the performance in sentiment analysis. Furthermore, the NC-SentNoB dataset contains only a very small number of *Wrong Serial* data instances. Other categories such as *Context/-Word Missing*, *Word Misuse*, and *Coined Word* are also underrepresented. In future, we would like to increase the data in these categories to tackle data imbalance, which may potentially enhance the performance of the transformer models. In addition, to combat noise coming from spelling variation and dialectal differences, we plan to incorporate text normalization methods i.e. character-level spell correction models (Farra et al., 2014; Zaky and Romadhony, 2019) and character-level Neural Machine Translation (NMT) models (Lee et al., 2017; Edman et al., 2023) for back-translation. We hypothesize that text normalization methods might be a viable solution due to their ability to comprehend context at character level. Finally, we will investigate noise-specific reduction techniques and report on the noise reduction approaches that demonstrate superior results in addressing particular types of noisy texts.

6 Conclusion

This study involves a comparison of various noise reduction techniques to assess their effectiveness in reducing noise within the NC-SentNoB dataset, which includes ten distinct types of noises. The results indicate that none of the noise reduction methods effectively reduce noise in the texts, leading to a lower F1-score compared to the sentiment analysis of noisy texts. This underscores the necessity for the development of noise-specific reduction techniques. We conducted a statistical analysis of our NC-SentNoB dataset and employed baseline models to identify the noises. However, the data imbalance adversely impacts the model performance suggesting potential enhancement upon addressing this imbalance.

References

Ajwad Akil, Najrin Sultana, Abhik Bhattacharjee, and Rifat Shahriyar. 2022. Banglaparaphrase: A high-quality bangla paraphrase dataset. *arXiv preprint arXiv:2210.05109*.

Abhik Bhattacharjee, Tahmid Hasan, Wasi Ahmad,

Kazi Samin Mubasshir, Md Saiful Islam, Anindya Iqbal, M. Sohel Rahman, and Rifat Shahriyar. 2022a. BanglaBERT: Language model pretraining and benchmarks for low-resource language understanding evaluation in Bangla. In *Findings of the Association for Computational Linguistics: NAACL 2022*, pages 1318–1327, Seattle, United States. Association for Computational Linguistics.

Abhik Bhattacharjee, Tahmid Hasan, Wasi Uddin Ahmad, and Rifat Shahriyar. 2022b. Banglanlg: Benchmarks and resources for evaluating low-resource natural language generation in bangla. *CoRR*, abs/2205.11081.

Anirban Bhowmick and Abhik Jana. 2021. Sentiment analysis for bengali using transformer based models. In *Proceedings of the 18th International Conference on Natural Language Processing (ICON)*, pages 481–486.

Partha Chakraborty, Farah Nawar, and Humayra Afrin Chowdhury. 2022. Sentiment analysis of bengali facebook data using classical and deep learning approaches. In *Innovation in Electrical Power Engineering, Communication, and Computing Technology: Proceedings of Second IEPCCT 2021*, pages 209–218. Springer.

Kevin Clark, Minh-Thang Luong, Quoc V Le, and Christopher D Manning. 2020. Electra: Pre-training text encoders as discriminators rather than generators. *arXiv preprint arXiv:2003.10555*.

Corinna Cortes and Vladimir Vapnik. 1995. Support-vector networks. *Machine learning*, 20:273–297.

Jacob Devlin, Ming-Wei Chang, Kenton Lee, and Kristina Toutanova. 2018a. Bert: Pre-training of deep bidirectional transformers for language understanding. *arXiv preprint arXiv:1810.04805*.

Jacob Devlin, Ming-Wei Chang, Kenton Lee, and Kristina Toutanova. 2018b. BERT: pre-training of deep bidirectional transformers for language understanding. *CoRR*, abs/1810.04805.

Lukas Edman, Antonio Toral, and Gertjan van Noord. 2023. Are character-level translations worth the wait? an extensive comparison of character-and subword-level models for machine translation. *arXiv preprint arXiv:2302.14220*.

Charles Elkan. 2001. The foundations of cost-sensitive learning. In *International joint conference on artificial intelligence*, volume 17, pages 973–978. Lawrence Erlbaum Associates Ltd.

Noura Farra, Nadi Tomeh, Alla Rozovskaya, and Nizar Habash. 2014. Generalized character-level spelling error correction. In *Proceedings of the 52nd Annual Meeting of the Association for Computational Linguistics (Volume 2: Short Papers)*, pages 161–167, Baltimore, Maryland. Association for Computational Linguistics.

Joseph L Fleiss. 1971. Measuring nominal scale agreement among many raters. *Psychological bulletin*, 76(5):378.

Rezaul Haque, Naimul Islam, Mayisha Tasneem, and Amit Kumar Das. 2023. Multi-class sentiment classification on bengali social media comments using machine learning. *International Journal of Cognitive Computing in Engineering*, 4:21–35.

Mahmud Hasan, Labiba Islam, Ismat Jahan, Sabrina Mannan Meem, and Rashedur M Rahman. 2023. Natural language processing and sentiment analysis on bangla social media comments on russia–ukraine war using transformers. *Vietnam Journal of Computer Science*, pages 1–28.

Asif Hassan, Mohammad Rashedul Amin, Abul Kalam Al Azad, and Nabeel Mohammed. 2016. Sentiment analysis on bangla and romanized bangla text using deep recurrent models. In *2016 International Workshop on Computational Intelligence (IWCI)*, pages 51–56. IEEE.

Pengcheng He, Xiaodong Liu, Jianfeng Gao, and Weizhu Chen. 2020. Deberta: Decoding-enhanced bert with disentangled attention. *arXiv preprint arXiv:2006.03654*.

Sepp Hochreiter and Jürgen Schmidhuber. 1997. Long short-term memory. *Neural computation*, 9(8):1735–1780.

Muntasir Hoq, Promila Haque, and Mohammed Nazim Uddin. 2021. Sentiment analysis of bangla language using deep learning approaches. In *International Conference on Computing Science, Communication and Security*, pages 140–151. Springer.

Khondoker Ittehadul Islam, Md Saiful Islam, and Md Ruhul Amin. 2020. Sentiment analysis in bengali via transfer learning using multi-lingual bert. In *2020 23rd International Conference on Computer and Information Technology (ICCIT)*, pages 1–5. IEEE.

Khondoker Ittehadul Islam, Sudipta Kar, Md Saiful Islam, and Mohammad Ruhul Amin. 2021. Sentnob: A dataset for analysing sentiment on noisy bangla texts. In *Findings of the Association for Computational Linguistics: EMNLP 2021*, pages 3265–3271.

Md Ekramul Islam, Labib Chowdhury, Faisal Ahamed Khan, Shazzad Hossain, Sourave Hossain, Mohammad Mamun Or Rashid, Nabeel Mohammed, and Mohammad Ruhul Amin. 2023. Sentigold: A large bangla gold standard multi-domain sentiment analysis dataset and its evaluation. *arXiv preprint arXiv:2306.06147*.

Simran Khanuja, Diksha Bansal, Sarvesh Mehtani, Savya Khosla, Atreyee Dey, Balaji Gopalan, Dilip Kumar Margam, Pooja Aggarwal, Rajiv Teja Nagipogu, Shachi Dave, Shruti Gupta, Subhash Chandra Bose Gali, Vish Subramanian, and Partha Talukdar. 2021. Muril: Multilingual representations for indian languages.

Md Kowsher, Abdullah As Sami, Nusrat Jahan Prottasha, Mohammad Shamsul Arefin, Pranab Kumar Dhar, and Takeshi Koshiba. 2022. Bangla-bert: transformer-based efficient model for transfer learning and language understanding. *IEEE Access*, 10:91855–91870.

Aomi Koyama, Kengo Hotate, Masahiro Kaneko, and Mamoru Komachi. 2021. Comparison of grammatical error correction using back-translation models. *arXiv preprint arXiv:2104.07848*.

Zhenzhong Lan, Mingda Chen, Sebastian Goodman, Kevin Gimpel, Piyush Sharma, and Radu Soricut. 2019. Albert: A lite bert for self-supervised learning of language representations. *arXiv preprint arXiv:1909.11942*.

Jason Lee, Kyunghyun Cho, and Thomas Hofmann. 2017. Fully character-level neural machine translation without explicit segmentation. *Transactions of the Association for Computational Linguistics*, 5:365–378.

Chin-Yew Lin. 2004. ROUGE: A package for automatic evaluation of summaries. In *Text Summarization Branches Out*, pages 74–81, Barcelona, Spain. Association for Computational Linguistics.

Yinhan Liu, Myle Ott, Naman Goyal, Jingfei Du, Mandar Joshi, Danqi Chen, Omer Levy, Mike Lewis, Luke Zettlemoyer, and Veselin Stoyanov. 2019. Roberta: A robustly optimized bert pretraining approach. *arXiv preprint arXiv:1907.11692*.

Mika V Mäntylä, Daniel Graziotin, and Miikka Kuutila. 2018. The evolution of sentiment analysis—a review of research topics, venues, and top cited papers. *Computer Science Review*, 27:16–32.

Hwee Tou Ng, Siew Mei Wu, Ted Briscoe, Christian Hadiwinoto, Raymond Hendy Susanto, and Christopher Bryant. 2014. The CoNLL-2014 shared task on grammatical error correction. In *Proceedings of the Eighteenth Conference on Computational Natural Language Learning: Shared Task*, pages 1–14, Baltimore, Maryland. Association for Computational Linguistics.

Tong Niu, Semih Yavuz, Yingbo Zhou, Nitish Shirish Keskar, Huan Wang, and Caiming Xiong. 2020. Unsupervised paraphrasing with pretrained language models. *arXiv preprint arXiv:2010.12885*.

Kishore Papineni, Salim Roukos, Todd Ward, and Wei-Jing Zhu. 2002. Bleu: a method for automatic evaluation of machine translation. In *Proceedings of the 40th Annual Meeting of the Association for Computational Linguistics*, pages 311–318, Philadelphia, Pennsylvania, USA. Association for Computational Linguistics.

David MW Powers. 2020. Evaluation: from precision, recall and f-measure to roc, informedness, markedness and correlation. *arXiv preprint arXiv:2010.16061*.

Ilan Price, Jordan Gifford-Moore, Jory Fleming, Saul Musker, Maayan Roichman, Guillaume Sylvain, Nithum Thain, Lucas Dixon, and Jeffrey Sorensen. 2020. Six attributes of unhealthy conversation. *arXiv preprint arXiv:2010.07410*.

Colin Raffel, Noam Shazeer, Adam Roberts, Katherine Lee, Sharan Narang, Michael Matena, Yanqi Zhou, Wei Li, and Peter J Liu. 2020. Exploring the limits of transfer learning with a unified text-to-text transformer. *The Journal of Machine Learning Research*, 21(1):5485–5551.

Nils Reimers and Iryna Gurevych. 2019. Sentence-bert: Sentence embeddings using siamese bert-networks. In *Proceedings of the 2019 Conference on Empirical Methods in Natural Language Processing*. Association for Computational Linguistics.

Moythry Manir Samia, Alimul Rajee, Md Rakib Hasan, Mohammad Omar Faruq, and Pintu Chandra Paul. 2022. Aspect-based sentiment analysis for bengali text using bidirectional encoder representations from transformers (bert). *International Journal of Advanced Computer Science and Applications*, 13(12).

Sagor Sarker. 2020. Banglabert: Bengali mask language model for bengali language understanding.

Sagor Sarker. 2021. Bnlp: Natural language processing toolkit for bengali language. *arXiv preprint arXiv:2102.00405*.

Md Shajalal and Masaki Aono. 2018. Semantic textual similarity in bengali text. In *2018 International Conference on Bangla Speech and Language Processing (ICBSLP)*, pages 1–5. IEEE.

Ankit Srivastava, Piyush Makhija, and Anuj Gupta. 2020. Noisy text data: Achilles' heel of bert. In *Proceedings of the Sixth Workshop on Noisy User-generated Text (W-NUT 2020)*, pages 16–21.

Yifu Sun and Haoming Jiang. 2019. Contextual text denoising with masked language models. *arXiv preprint arXiv:1910.14080*.

Wikipedia. 2023. List of languages by total number of speakers — Wikipedia, the free encyclopedia. `https://en.wikipedia.org/wiki/List_of_languages_by_total_number_of_speakers`. [Online; accessed 13-June-2023].

Linting Xue, Noah Constant, Adam Roberts, Mihir Kale, Rami Al-Rfou, Aditya Siddhant, Aditya Barua, and Colin Raffel. 2020. mt5: A massively multilingual pre-trained text-to-text transformer. *arXiv preprint arXiv:2010.11934*.

Damar Zaky and Ade Romadhony. 2019. An lstm-based spell checker for indonesian text. *2019 International Conference of Advanced Informatics: Concepts, Theory and Applications (ICAICTA)*, pages 1–6.

Tianyi Zhang, Varsha Kishore, Felix Wu, Kilian Q Weinberger, and Yoav Artzi. 2019. Bertscore: Evaluating text generation with bert. *arXiv preprint arXiv:1904.09675*.

Appendix

A Model Descriptions

A.1 Noise Identification

(a) SVM. Support Vector Machine (SVM) is designed to find a hyperplane in a high-dimensional space. This hyperplane separates data points of different classes while maximizing the margin between these classes. For feature extraction, the TF-IDF Vectorizer was employed, utilizing both a character analyzer and a word analyzer. These are represented as SVM (C) for the character analyzer and SVM (W) for the word analyzer, respectively, using n-grams in the range of 1 to 4. Additionally, a combination of both character and word n-gram features was tested, denoted as SVM (C + W).

(b) BiLSTM. BiLSTM captures long-range dependencies and contextual information among items in a sequence. It has two LSTM layers, one that reads the input sequence in a forward direction and the other in a reverse direction. The outputs of these two layers are then concatenated to produce a final output for each item in the sequence. Our BiLSTM implementation features an embedding size of 512, a hidden size of 110, and consists of 2 layers.

(c) Bangla-BERT-Base. A pretrained Bangla language model using mask language modeling objective (Sarker, 2020). It has the same architecture as the `bert-base-uncased` (Devlin et al., 2018b) model with an embedding size of 768 and a total parameter of 110M.

A.2 Noise Reduction

(a) BanglaT5. A sequence-to-sequence transformer model that has been pre-trained using the span corruption objective (Bhattacharjee et al., 2022b). It consists of 247 million parameters and has an embedding size of 768. For the implementation of the back-translation method, the BanglaT5 model, pre-trained on the BanglaNMT Bangla-English dataset (Bhattacharjee et al., 2022b), is used for Bangla to English translation. Conversely, for English to Bangla translation, the BanglaT5 model pre-trained on the BanglaNMT English-Bangla dataset (Bhattacharjee et al., 2022b) is utilized. Additionally, the paraphrasing model employed by us is also BanglaT5 model, which has been pre-trained on the BanglaParaphrase dataset (Akil et al., 2022).

(b) BanglaBERT Generator. This is an ELECTRA (Clark et al., 2020) generator that has been pre-trained using the Masked Language Modeling (MLM) objective, specifically on extensive Bangla corpora (Bhattacharjee et al., 2022a). It has an embedding size of 768 and consists of 110M parameters. This model has been employed to perform the MLM task on out-of-vocabulary words and to execute random MLM with each word having a 20% possibility of being masked.

A.3 Sentiment Analysis

(a) BanglaBERT. An ELECTRA (Clark et al., 2020) discriminator model pre-trained with the Replaced Token Detection (RTD) objective. It has an embedding size of 768 and a total of 110M parameters (Bhattacharjee et al., 2022a).

(b) BanglaBERT Large. A larger variant of BanglaBERT, with 335M parameters and an embedding size of 1024 (Bhattacharjee et al., 2022a).

(c) sahajBERT[5]. Pre-trained in Bangla language using Masked Language Modeling (MLM) and Sentence Order Prediction (SOP) objectives. It follows A Lite BERT (ALBERT) (Lan et al., 2019) architecture and has a total of 18M parameters and an embedding size of 128.

(d) Bangla-Electra[6]. Trained with ELECTRA-small (Clark et al., 2020) with an embedding size of 128 and a total of 14M parameters.

(e) MuRIL. A BERT model pre-trained on 17 Indian languages and their transliterated counterparts (Khanuja et al., 2021). It has 110M parameters and an embedding size of 768 for each token. The model is pre-trained on both monolingual and parallel segments.

B Performance Evaluation Metrics

B.1 Noise Reduction

(a) BLEU. Bi Lingual **E**valuation **U**nderstudy (Papineni et al., 2002) is a commonly used scoring method that measures the overlap between reference and candidate sentences, providing a similarity measurement.

(b) ROUGE-L. Recall-**O**riented **U**nderstudy for **G**isting **E**valuation - **L**ongest Common Subsequence (Lin, 2004) computes a similarity score by taking into account of longest common subsequences appearing in both reference and candidate sentences. Similar to the BLEU score, this scoring method does not provide much insight into

[5] `https://huggingface.co/neuropark/sahajBERT`

[6] `https://huggingface.co/monsoon-nlp/bangla-electra`

semantic measurements, only the similarity of overlapping words/sub-sequences.

(c) BERTScore. BERTScore (Zhang et al., 2019) uses the cosine similarity of contextual embedding of the token provided from a BERT-based model. For this, we used the `bert-score`[7] library, which uses a multilingual BERT for Bangla sentences.

(d) SBERT Score. For this method, we employed paraphrase-multilingual-MiniLM-L12-v2 (Reimers and Gurevych, 2019), a model that maps sentences and paragraphs to a 384 dimensional dense vector space. It supports more than 50 languages and employs cosine similarity to assess the similarity between the input text and the ground truth.

(e) BSTS. Bangla **S**emantic **T**extual **S**imilarity was first introduced by (Shajalal and Aono, 2018). It uses embeddings of Word2Vec to calculate the similarity between two sentences.

(f) BERT-iBLEU. The scoring method was originally proposed by (Niu et al., 2020), which combines BERT-Score and BLEU Score to measure the semantic similarity of sentences while penalizing for the presence of similar words. This scoring system is particularly suitable for our needs, as we intend to evaluate the method based on its ability to keep the semantic meaning intact while making necessary changes to reduce noises.

(g) Word Coverage. Pre-trained word embedding models like FastText (Sarker, 2021), and Word2Vec (Sarker, 2021) create a vocabulary on the corpus they are trained on. As they are trained on noiseless sources like Wikipedia articles, their vocabulary contains accurate words. By measuring the percentage of tokens of our data covered in their vocabulary, we can gain insight into what percentage of tokens were noise reduced properly. However, this method may not address all types of noises. Additionally, we also calculated word coverage using the vocabulary of Bangla-BERT-Base (Sarker, 2020).

(h) Human Evaluation. The output texts were evaluated by annotators by comparing them to the 1000 established ground truths. A noise reduced output was considered correct if it retained the same meaning as the ground truth and reduced at least some of the noise or complete noise from the original sentence. In essence, the score represents the proportion of accurate noise reduced data relative to the 1000 ground truth. The score can be defined as:

$$\text{Score (Human Evaluation)} = \frac{x}{T} * 100$$

Here, x = Accurately noise reduced data
T = Total number of data

B.2 Classification

For both classification tasks (noise and sentiment), we used micro precision, recall, and F1-score.

(a) Precision. Precision measures the accuracy of positive predictions, specifically how many of them are correct (true positives) (Powers, 2020). Alternatively known as True Positive Accuracy (TPA), it is calculated as:

$$\text{Precision} = \frac{TP}{TP + FP}$$

where TP indicates true positive and FP indicates false positive.

(b) Recall. Recall, or True Positive Rate (TPR), gauges the classifier's ability to accurately predict positive cases by determining how many of them it correctly identified out of all the positive cases in the dataset (Powers, 2020). It is defined as:

$$\text{Recall} = \frac{TP}{TP + FN}$$

where TP indicates true positive and FN indicates false negative.

(c) F1-Score. The F1-score is the harmonic mean of precision and recall, providing a balance between the two in cases where one may be more significant than the other. F1-score is defined as:

$$\text{F1-Score} = 2 \times \frac{\text{Precision} \times \text{Recall}}{\text{Precision} + \text{Recall}}$$

[7] https://pypi.org/project/bert-score/

C Types of Noise in NC-SentNoB

NC-SentNoB dataset contains labeled data for 10 types of noise. Table 12 illustrates the definition of each noise type annotators used for the annotation process. In case of **Punctuation Error**, an exception was made for sentences that end without a period "।" due to the nature of the data. If such instances were considered errors, the majority of the data would be labeled as having punctuation errors. This could lead to trained models predominantly focusing on this single type of error, rather than recognizing and learning from a broader range of punctuation errors.

Type	Definition	Example with Correction
Local Word	Any regional words even if there is a spelling error	**[N]** প্রশ্নের সাথে উত্তরের কোন মিল পাইলাম না **[C]** প্রশ্নের সাথে উত্তরের কোন মিল পেলাম না **[E]** I did not find any similarity between the question and the answer.
Word Misuse	Wrong use of words or unnecessary repetitions of words	**[N]** তাকে আইনের আওতায় শান্তি দেওয়া হোক **[C]** তাকে আইনের আওতায় শাস্তি দেওয়া হোক **[E]** He should be punished under the law.
Context/Word missing	Not enough information or missing words	**[N]** তিনি একমাএ পারেন এই মহাবিপদ □ পৃথিবীকে রক্ষা করতে **[C]** তিনি একমাত্র পারেন এই মহাবিপদ থেকে পৃথিবীকে রক্ষা করতে **[E]** He is the only one who can save the world from this catastrophe.
Wrong Serial	Wrong order of the words	**[N]** সারাদেশে অপরাধী খুঁজুন , আরো হয়ে হন্যে **[C]** আরো হন্যে হয়ে সারাদেশে অপরাধী খুঁজুন **[E]** Search for the criminal desperately.
Mixed Language	Words in another language. Foreign words that were adopted into the Bangla language over time are excluded from this type.	**[N]** ভাইরে এই নিউজটা সেরা নিইজ **[C]** ভাইরে, এই খবরটা সেরা খবর **[E]** Brother, this news is the best news.
Punctuation Error	Improper placement or missing punctuation. Sentences ending without "।" (দাঁড়ি) were excluded from this type.	**[N]** পরের পার্টগুলো কবে আসবে ভাই □ **[C]** পরের পর্বগুলো কবে আসবে ভাই? **[E]** When will the next episodes air brother?
Spacing Error	Improper use of white space	**[N]** পড়াশোনা টা চালিয়ে গেলে ভালো হতো **[C]** পড়াশোনাটা চালিয়ে গেলে ভালো হতো **[E]** It would be better to continue studying
Spelling Error	Words not following spelling of Bangla Academy Dictionary	**[N]** বাবিকে এত জাল খাওয়ানো ঠিক না **[C]** ভাবীকে এত ঝাল খাওয়ানো ঠিক না **[E]** It is not right to feed the sister-in-law so much spice.
Coined Word	Emoji, symbolic emoji, link	**[N]** আগে জানলে আপনার সাথে দেখা করতাম ♥ **[C]** ✗ **[E]** If I knew I would've met you earlier ♥
Others	Noises that do not fall into categories mentioned above.	**[N]** রদে কুত্তার বাচ্চাদের ফাঁসি চাই **[C]** ✗ **[E]** I want those sons of bitches hanged.

Table 12: Types of noise with the definition that was used to annotate the dataset. **N** represents the original noisy sentence, **C** represents the corrected sentence, and **E** represents the corresponding English translation. The types **Coined Word**, and **Others** do not have any correction as these types of noise are essential to the meaning of the sentence. For each example, noisy words of that particular type are marked with Red color, and their correction is marked with Green color.

D Failure Cases of Back-translation

To provide insight into the performance drop, we have illustrated examples where the back-translation method using Google Translate fails to adequately reduce noise in the input text in table 13. Moreover, it often alters or completely removes important contextual words, which possibly impacts the performance of sentiment analysis. Given a human evaluation score of 37.90%, it can be said that back-translation via Google Translate fails to effectively correct more than 50% of the 1000 manually corrected data.

Noisy data and corresponding Back-Translation	Observation
[N] এই জুয়ার টাকা পাপন পেত আমার মনে হয় **[C]** এই জুয়ার টাকা পাপন পেতো আমার মনে হয় **[E]** I think the gambling money went to Papan. **[B]** আমি মনে করি এই জুয়ার টাকা পরিশোধ করা হবে **[BE]** I think this gambling money will be repaid.	The input text contained only a spelling mistake, but the back-translation introduced new words, removed a named entity, and altered the sentence's meaning.
[N] ভাই খাবারের সাধ জেমনি হোক না কেন আপনার মুখে গেলে সেটা অম্রিত হয়ে যায় ধন্নবাদ **[C]** ভাই খাবারের স্বাদ যেমনি হোক না কেন আপনার মুখে গেলে সেটা অমৃত হয়ে যায়, ধন্যবাদ **[E]** Brother, whatever the taste of the food is, it becomes necter in your mouth, thanks. **[B]** ভাই, খাবারের স্বাদ যাই হোক না কেন, এটা আপনার মুখে আছে। **[BE]** Brother, whatever the taste of the food is, it's in your mouth.	The input text had multiple spelling mistakes and punctuation errors. The back-translation corrected one of these errors but changed the meaning of part of the sentence.
[N] এদের পিটের চামড়া তোলা হবে **[C]** এদের পিঠের চামড়া তোলা হবে **[E]** Their backs will be skinned. **[B]** তারা চামড়া হবে **[BE]** They will become skin.	The input text contained only a spelling mistake. However, the back-translation removed contextually important words, rendering the sentence meaningless.
[N] অ ামার মেছের সাথে এই হোটেল **[C]** আমার মেসের সাথে এই হোটেল **[E]** This hotel is with my hostel. **[B]** আমার জাল দিয়ে এই হোটেল **[BE]** This hotel with my net.	The back-translation altered a keyword in the sentence, which resulted in a loss of meaning.
[N] লিবুর সাতে কি আদা খেতে হবে □ **[C]** লেবুর সাথে কি আদা খেতে হবে? **[E]** Do I need to eat ginger with lemon? **[B]** আমি কি Libur Sate এ আদা খাওয়া উচিত? **[BE]** Should I eat ginger with Libur Sate?	The back-translation failed to correct a spelling mistake and converted the word into English, but it successfully added the missing punctuation.
[N] রানা দের মত ছেলেরা জাতে হারিয়ে না জায় **[C]** রানাদের মত ছেলেরা যাতে হারিয়ে না যায় **[E]** So that boys like Rana don't get lost. **[B]** রানার মতো ছেলেরা রেসে হেরে যায় না **[BE]** Boys like Rana do not lose in race.	The input sentence had spacing and spelling errors. The back-translation fixed the spacing issue but introduced mixed language, changing the sentence's meaning.

Table 13: Example scenarios where back-translation with google translate fails to reduce noise in the text. **N** represents the original noisy sentence, **C** represents the corrected sentence, **E** represents its English translation, **B** represents the result of back-translation, and **BE** represents the direct English translation of back-translated output. For each example, noisy words are marked with Red color and noise reduced words are marked with Green color.

Label Supervised Contrastive Learning for Imbalanced Text Classification in Euclidean and Hyperbolic Embedding Spaces

Baber Khalid, Shuyang Dai, Tara Taghavi, Sungjin Lee
Amazon Alexa, Bellevue, WA
{khababer,shuyadai,taghavit,sungjinl}@amazon.com

Abstract

Text classification is an important problem with a wide range of applications in NLP. However, naturally occurring data is imbalanced which can induce biases when training classification models. In this work, we introduce a novel contrastive learning (CL) approach to help with imbalanced text classification task. CL has an inherent structure which pushes similar data closer in embedding space and vice versa using data samples anchors. However, in traditional CL methods text embeddings are used as anchors, which are scattered over the embedding space. We propose a CL approach which learns key anchors in the form of label embeddings and uses them as anchors. This allows our approach to bring the embeddings closer to their labels in the embedding space and divide the embedding space between labels in a fairer manner. We also introduce a novel method to improve the interpretability of our approach in a multi-class classification scenario. This approach learns the inter-class relationships during training which provide insight into the model decisions. Since our approach is focused on dividing the embedding space between different labels we also experiment with hyperbolic embeddings since they have been proven successful in embedding hierarchical information. Our proposed method outperforms several state-of-the-art baselines by an average 11% F1. Our interpretable approach highlights key data relationships and our experiments with hyperbolic embeddings give us important insights for future investigations.

1 Introduction

A common way of approaching the text classification problem is training a model using pre-trained text embeddings as language features (Mikolov et al., 2013; Pennington et al., 2014; Devlin et al., 2018). These embeddings can be fine-tuned using the signals from an objective function to improve their efficacy for the classification task at hand.

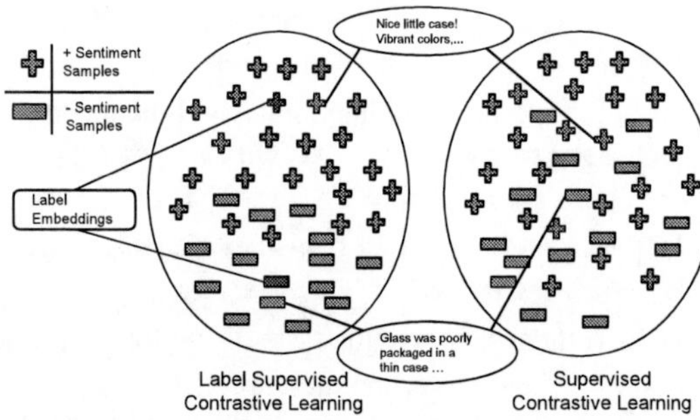

Figure 1: SCL can cause the embeddings for positive and negative sentiment text samples to be dispersed together in the embedding space (right illustration). Our approach in contrast utilizes the embedding space more effectively (left illustration). This is also shown in the form of Euclidean distance between embeddings of text samples of opposite sentiment. Our approach embeds these samples farther away from each than SCL in terms of Euclidean distance: *13.2* vs. *3.2*.

However, a common impediment to training a robust classifier is the fact that naturally occurring data is imbalanced. Since classifier predictions reflect the distribution of the training data, they can induce bias. There are many approaches proposed to address this issue, such as oversampling, undersampling, using weighted objective functions or using situation/domain specific methods to improve the robustness of classification models (Chawla et al., 2002a; Tahir et al., 2012). Our work focuses on introducing a novel algorithm to deal with the challenges of imbalanced data.

Recent research shows an increasing use of contrastive learning (CL) to solve different problems in areas of computer vision and NLP (Gao et al., 2021a; Hénaff et al., 2019; Jaiswal et al., 2021). In this work, we explore CL to address the problem of imbalanced text classification. In general, CL uses anchors to embed similar samples closer in the embedding space while pushing dissimilar examples away. Unsupervised CL (Tian et al., 2019) tries to contrast a data sample, called anchor, with every

Proceedings of the Ninth Workshop on Noisy and User-generated Text (W-NUT 2024), pages 58–67
March 22, 2024

sample in the batch while supervised CL (SCL) (Khosla et al., 2020a) tries to utilize label information and embed samples from the same class as the anchor closer to each other. However, these CL approaches rely on utilizing data embeddings as anchors which are scattered over the embedding space. We hypothesize that label embeddings, representing a label category in the embedding space, can be utilized as key anchors in CL. This allows a model to embed data samples closer to their category representations and results in a model learning better embedding representations for the data. We present an illustration in the figure 1 where we compare how SCL divides embedding space in comparison to our approach utilizing label embeddings in a binary classification task. This shows that our approach is able to achiever better class separation between data belong to different labels. This is highlighted by the fact that distance between a positive and negative text embedding pair is larger when our approach is utilized in comparison to the SCL.

Our proposed approach uses two embedding modules 1) a self-attention layer to embed text and 2) an embedding layer for labels. These are fine-tuned using label supervised CL (LSCL). We also experiment with hyperbolic embeddings, where pre-trained model (e.g. BERT), provides representations with hyperbolic structure (Chen et al., 2021). Our approach of treating the classification task as learning to minimize the distance between data samples and their label embeddings is akin to embedding hierarchy between labels and their corresponding data and this is a strength of hyperbolic spaces. We show that our approach outperforms several SOTA and CL baselines in both Euclidean and hyperbolic spaces. Finally, we also try to improve the interpretability of our model by proposing a modification to our approach which allows it to represent inter-class relationships in an intuitive manner for a multi-class classification task. Section 2 of our work talks about related works and section 3 and 4 talk about CL and our approach. Section 5 talks about our approach in hyperbolic spaces while sections 6, 7 talk about our experiment setup and evaluation work which are followed by limitations and conclusion.

2 Related Work

Data imbalance is a common problem and classification literature has adopted a variety of approaches to deal with the biases it might introduce. One of these ways is oversampling of less frequent data. SMOTE is the first minority oversampling method (Chawla et al., 2002b). Iglesias et al. (2013) presents a hidden markov model which generates data from minority distribution. Other works focus on the use of oversampling on the basis of sample difficulty (Tian et al., 2021). Song et al. (2016) combines the SMOTE technique with a K-Means based undersampling algorithm to try and improve classifier performance on an imabalanced dataset. Some methods undersample the majority class samples to create a balanced data distribution for the training process. Smith et al. (2013); Anand et al. (2010) both present methods which use a notion of sample difficulty to undersample the majority class samples.

Some works rely on weighing the objective function to deal with data imbalance. The idea is to increase the loss contribution for the minority classes during the training. Cao et al. (2019); Chen et al. (2016); Park et al. (2021) each presents a different way of weighing the label-specific loss.

There is a third class of works which tries to introduce novel algorithms focused on the data imbalance problem. These methods avoid inducing biases that might arise because of distribution changes in data. An example is (Gao et al., 2021c) which introduces a convolution based algorithm to handle the class imbalance problem in data. Our work fits in this category as we explore the use of label-supervised CL to address this problem. Another example is Díaz-Vico et al. (2018), which uses cost-sensitive learning to regularize the posterior distributions for a given sample. This relies on domain specific information which can be hard to obtain in realistic scenarios (Krawczyk, 2016).

Lately, contrastive learning is being used in a variety of tasks due to its effective utilization of embedding space. Kang et al. (2021) present KCL which is a variation of SCL algorithm (Khosla et al., 2020b) and explores the use of contrastive learning for learning balanced embedding spaces in the area of computer vision. Lopez-Martin et al. (2022); Zhang et al. (2022) present label-centered variations of CL methods but do not explore the data-imbalance effects or the effect of computational spaces on the model performance.

Hyperbolic spaces are becoming well-known for their superiority in embedding hierarchical information like WordNet graphs (Nickel and Kiela, 2017,

2018). This is because of their natural hierarchical structure. We view the classification task as a sub-class of hierarchical problem where a label embedding represents a category and each data sample is near to its label embedding. This is why we try to assess the performance of our model in the hyperbolic space as well. Another motivation for our work comes from Chen et al. (2021), which show that BERT embeddings contain hyperbolic structure between tokens by probing BERT embedding in hyperbolic spaces.

3 Contrastive Learning Overview

Contrastive learning tries to embed similar samples closer in the embedding space by trying to make the samples closer to their anchors. Formally, CL can be expressed as (Tian et al., 2019; Khosla et al., 2020b):

3.1 Contrastive Learning

We can define $\{(t_1, y_1), (t_2, y_2), ..., (t_N, y_N)\} = D$ as a dataset consisting of a set of text $t_i = \{w_{i1}, w_{i2}, .., w_{is_n}\}$ and label pairs y_i, where s_n is the length of the text sample t_i and w_ij is the token representation corresponding to the jth token in the text sample t_i. Given an embedding representation x_i for the text sample t_i, we can define contrastive learning objective L for mini-batches $B_k \subset D$ of size b_n as:

$$\frac{-1}{b_n} \sum_{x_i \in X_k} log \frac{exp(sim(x_i, x_i^+))}{\sum_{x_j \in \{x_i^+\} \cup A(i)} exp(sim(x_i, x_j))} \tag{1}$$

where sim is a similarity function (usually the dot product), $A(i) = \{x_j | x_j \neq x_i, x_j \in X_k\}$, X_k is set of text representations in the mini-batch B_k and x_i^+ is an augmented representation of the text sample t_i. This objective causes a model to learn embedding for x_i which are closer to its augmentation and pushes it away from other examples in the mini-batch.

4 Proposed Approach

We propose a supervised CL approach which uses label embeddings as anchors and causes the model to learn representations which are closer to their respective label representations or key anchors in the embedding space. An architecture diagram for our approach, Label Supervised Contrastive Learning (LSCL), is presented in the figure 2 and its formulation L_{LSCL} is given as follows:

$$L_{LSCL} = \frac{1}{b_n} \sum_{x_i \in X_k} -log \frac{exp(sim(x_i, l_i))}{\sum_{l_j \in L} exp(sim(x_i, l_j))} \tag{2}$$

where L is the set of all label representations. This approach embeds the text samples closer to their label embeddings in the embedding space. Labels for each text embedding can be predicted by choosing the label whose embedding is closest.

4.0.1 Increasing Interpretability Through Learning Inter-Class Relationships

In a multi-class classification scenario, sometimes label categories are related to each other, e.g. emotions *love* and *joy* are likely to be expressed in similar ways in many cases. In such cases it is hard to interpret how model embedded certain text samples in certain parts of the embedding space. Considering this we modify our approach to learn interpretable inter-class relationships, in form of a weight matrix, so these could be used to highlight the reasoning behind model decisions. This variation L_{LSCL-W} can be formulated as follows:

$$\frac{-1}{b_n} \sum_{x_i \in X_k} log \frac{exp(sim(x_i, l_i))}{\sum_{l_j \in L - l_i} w_{ij} exp(sim(x_i, l_j))} \tag{3}$$

where $w_{ij} \in W^{|L|*|L|}$ is a weight matrix we learn during the training process and $w_{ij} = 1$ when $i = j$. A problem here is that a learning method would just take the weight matrix W to zero. To prevent that, we add a Shanon Entropy (Shannon, 1948) regularization term to the objective which ensure that there is a relative difference in the magnitude of weights so the new objective L'_{LSCL-W} becomes:

$$\begin{aligned} L'_{LSCL-W} &= L_{LSCL-W} + \lambda H(W_i) \\ H(W_i) &= - \sum_{w_{ij} \in W_i} w_{ij} log(w_{ij}) \end{aligned} \tag{4}$$

where w_{ij} is the relation between labels l_i and l_j. The greater the weight the more difficult to separate data belonging to these two labels which is why the model assigns a higher weight to the contrastive weight of these labels. The λ is a term between 0 and 1 to control the contribution of entropy objective. W is not symmetric because of the data imbalance.

4.0.2 How Our Approach Helps with Data Imbalance

Our approach tries to bring the data samples in the closer to their respective labels and push the other

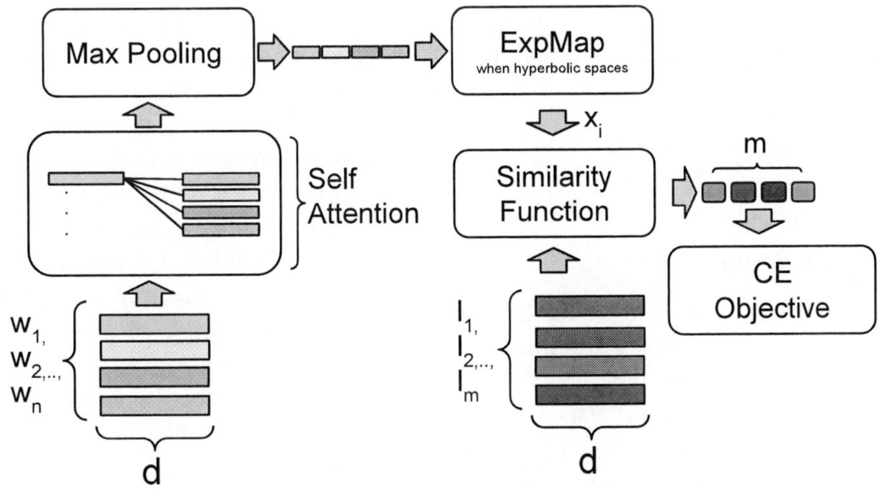

Figure 2: A batch of utterances is passed through a self-attention encoder to obtain text embeddings. These embeddings may be passed through an exponential map function to obtain embeddings in hyperbolic plane. Label embeddings are obtained by passing the input labels through a label embedding layer. These label embeddings are used as anchors in the CL objective which outputs loss signals for fine-tuning both the text encoder and label embedding layer together.

label embeddings away. This creates a push-pull effect for data samples w.r.t to the label embeddings. Both of these effects help improve the model performance. The data samples belonging to the majority class help improve the performance for the minority classes in this way as these samples push the minority label embeddings away as well while trying to get close to the their respective label embeddings.

5 Generalization to Multiple Computational Spaces

Hyperbolic models show great promise for embedding hierarchical or graph structures (Nickel and Kiela, 2017, 2018). Our CL approach treats the classification problem as a hierarchical task by trying to learn the embedding regions for their respective labels. In addition, Chen et al. (2021) shows that pre-trained text embedding contain hyperbolic structure. Due to these reasons we explore the effect of hyperbolic embeddings on our approach and show that these models perform competitively to their Euclidean counterparts and outperform all the baselines.

5.1 Manifold Centric Label Embeddings

We wanted to make use of the information encoded in the pre-trained textual representations and they are usually trained in Euclidean space. Due to this reason, we make use of hyperbolic exponential map to obtain hyperbolic textual embeddings. However, label embeddings need not have any such restriction so we embed the labels in a manifold specific representation space. This entails that hyperbolic versions of our approach embed labels directly in the hypberbolic space so there is no need to use exponential map to obtain label embeddings.

5.2 Notion of Similarity

Contrastive learning uses a measure of similarity to embed similar examples closer to each other in a higher dimensional space. We generalize the notion of similarity between two vectors h and h' across Euclidean and hyperbolic manifolds, in an intuitive manner, as follows:

$$sim_{manifold}(h, h') = -d_{manifold}(h, h') \tag{5}$$

where $d_{manifold}$ represents the manifold specific distance function.

5.2.1 Vector Similarity in Euclidean Space

Following the formulation specified above the similarity function can be defined as:

$$sim_{eucl}(h, h') = -\sum_{i<=d} \sqrt{(h_i - h'_i)^2} \tag{6}$$

5.2.2 Vector Similarity in Hyperbolic Space

For our hyperbolic model variation, we use *Lorentz* formulation of Riemannian Manifolds because (Nickel and Kiela, 2018) suggests that *Loretnz* formulation of hyperbolic space is numerically stable compared to the *Poincare'* formulation. The similarity function for the hyperbolic variation is thus given as:

$$sim_{lorentz}(h, h') = -arcosh(- < h, h' >_L)$$
$$< h, h' >_L = -h_0 h'_0 + \sum_{1<=d} h_i h'_i \quad (7)$$

6 Experiment Setup

We conduct experiments to compare the performance of our approach on two classification tasks with several baselines. In addition, we conduct experiments to compare the performance of our approach between hyperbolic and Euclidean embeddings. We rely on 256 dimensional variation of BERT (Turc et al., 2019) to obtain the seed embeddings for our text encoder.

6.1 Datasets

We rely on two datasets for the purpose of our evaluation: 1) Amazon Reviews Sentiment Classification (Keung et al., 2020) 2) Twitter Emotion Classification dataset[1]. We create a binary sentiment classification task from the former by splitting the the review ratings into positive and negative classes. Reviews with rating greater >=4 are categorized as positive and reviews with rating <=2 are considered negative. We induce a data imbalance of 9:1 for positive and negative classes respectively to obtain an imbalanced dataset containing a total of 15000 reviews.

Twitter emotion dataset is a multi-class data with six emotions: sadness, joy, love, anger, fear, surprise, contains a total of 20000 tweets and is naturally imbalanced. Class ratios for both datasets are given in the tables 1 and 2.

6.2 Model Parameters

Figure 2 shows the architecture of the text encoder we use for CL. We utilize a self-attention layer to embed the text embeddings. When we need to obtain the hyperbolic embeddings we utilize the exponential map operation to project the euclidean embeddings into the hyperbolic space. We seed our text embedding layer with BERT embeddings which improves the training time of the model during fine-tuning with CL. The right side of the architecture diagram shows the label embeddings which are used to computer similarity with the text emebddings. These embeddings are fine-tuned using the LSCL training objective shown in the section 4. We use a prefix of E or H to indicate whether the model utilizes euclidean embeddings or hyperbolic ones respectively.

When using euclidean embeddings we fine-tune our model using the Adam optimizer (Kingma and Ba, 2014) while we use Reimannian SGD[2] to optimize the hyperbolic weights as it relies on the exponential map to update the weights using Reimannian gradients. Inspired from (Gao et al., 2021b), we use a dropout layer (*rate: 0.1*) to obtain the augmented representations when needed. We use a learning rate of 10^{-3} for Adam and a learning rate of 10^{-1} for Reimannian optimizer with a batch size of 64.

6.3 Baselines

We compare our proposed approach with several baselines. We divide the baselines in two groups: 1) SOTA baselines – baselines designed to help with data imbalance in classification task; and 2) CL baselines – baselines utilzing other versions of contrastive.

6.3.1 Baselines for Imbalanced Classification

We use the following baselines to indicate the advantages of using a label-supervised CL approach to deal with the problem of class imbalance in a classification task.

SetConv: Gao et al. (2021c) presents a convolution based method to learn better representations for the minority class samples. It utilizes a minority class representative as anchor to learn kernel weights during the training process.

GILE: Pappas and Henderson (2019) uses joint embeddings obtained using a dimension-wise product of text and label embeddings. Their approach uses a fully-connected layer to score these joint embeddings and makes use of binary cross-entropy objective to train the model.

BertGCN: Lin et al. (2021) treats the textual data as a graph of token and document representations. The graph encodes token-level information using measures like tf-idf and documents using BERT representations. The approach utilizes a graph convolution operation to obtain a vector representation for a given text document.

6.3.2 Contrastive Learning Baselines

We utilize the following CL approaches to highlight the advantages of utilizing our CL approach in a

[1]https://huggingface.co/datasets/emotion

[2]https://github.com/facebookresearch/poincare-embeddings

classification task.

K-Contrastive Learning: Kang et al. (2021) presents KCL, a variation of supervised contrastive learning in the domain of computer vision which learns balanced features spaces. Instead of using batch data samples as positive and negative anchors their approach samples k samples for each class from training data.

Supervised Contrastive Learning: SCL (Khosla et al., 2020a) is a CL approach which tries to contrast data samples from one class with data samples belonging to other classes while trying to bring the data samples from same classes closer to each other. As highlighted by the results presented below, this is a poor choice for imbalanced classification as skew in data distribution will create a bias in favor of majority class data when the model tries to bring samples from same class together.

7 Performance Analysis

We evaluate the performance of our approach on two tasks: binary sentiment classification and multi-class emotion classification. Both tasks highlight different aspects of our approach as a binary classification task with sufficient disparity in labels might be easier than a multi-class classification task which requires a model to learn inter-class relationships. For all our experiments, we measure the overall performance of a model using macro F1 score average because it equally weighs the model performance of the minority classes; hence reflects effect of data imbalance. Our key insights are:

- Our proposed CL approach is able to outperform the baselines in both computational spaces as shown in the tables 1 and 2).
- Euclidean version of our approach achieves the best overall performance as shown in the tables 1 and 2.
- We can improve model-decision interpretability by learning inter-class relationship weights. This is highlighted in the figure 4.
- Visualizing our approach in a 2-dimensional setting shows that hyperbolic version of our approach divides the embedding space fairly in the binary setting. This is highlighted in the figure 3.

7.1 Baseline Performance Comparison

We compare the performance of our approach with several contrastive learning and SOTA baselines

Model	Macro F1	Positive Class F1	Negative Class F1
Class Ratios		0.9	0.1
SOTA Baselines			
SetConv	0.682	0.888	0.476
GILE	0.706	0.951	0.462
BertGCN	0.702	0.948	0.455
Contrastive Learning Baselines			
SCL	0.594	0.95	0.237
KCL(k=5)	0.646	0.944	0.346
Our Approach			
HLSCL	0.72	0.930	0.511
ELSCL	**0.779**	**0.959**	**0.6**

Table 1: This table shows the per class F1 scores achieved by our model and their corresponding macro averages on Amazon Reviews Sentiment classification task. We show the results of both hyperbolic and euclidean models. The bold numbers represent the best performing model.

as stated in the section 6.3. In short, our approach outperforms the best SOTA baseline by a margin of 7% and 14% in the tasks of binary sentiment classification and multi-class emotion classification, respectively. These results are shown in the tables 1 and 2 respectively. In addition our approach does not sacrifice the majority class performance for a gain in minority class performance. This can be observed in both the binary and multi-class classification settings as our model consistently outperforms all the baselines in both overall and per-class performance, as highlighted in the table 1.

In the multi-class classification setting, the best performing baseline for the minority emotion *surprise* is BertGCN with a macro F1 of 38%. Our approach utilizing hyperbolic embeddings outperforms BertGCN by 7% in the minor class while achieving better performance in the majority classes – sadness and joy, as shown in the table 2.

Comparing the performance of our approach with CL baselines in the tables 1 and 2, specially SCL, shows the our approach to CL outperforms the other approaches in the task of imbalanced text classification.

7.2 Performance Comparison Among Computational Spaces

As described earlier, our formulation of the classification problem inspires us to test the performance of hyperbolic space embeddings in the tasks of binary and multi-class text classification tasks. In both cases, euclidean embeddings are better at embedding the text samples in the hidden space. However, hyperbolic variant of our approach still

Model	Macro F1	Sadness	Joy	Love	Anger	Fear	Surprise
Class Ratios		0.292	0.335	0.0815	0.135	0.121	0.0357
SOTA Baselines							
SetConv	0.361	0.425	0.469	0.297	0.314	0.378	0.283
GILE	0.401	0.607	0.675	0.242	0.42	0.325	0.138
BertGCN	0.554	0.712	0.778	0.330	0.571	0.55	0.383
Contrastive Learning Baselines							
SCL	0.285	0.555	0.646	0.0523	0.213	0.243	0.0
KCL(k=5)	0.299	0.508	0.63	0.0971	0.219	0.295	0.047
Our Approach							
HLSCL	0.621	0.757	0.774	0.553	0.597	0.595	0.451
ELSCL	**0.695**	**0.793**	**0.836**	**0.611**	**0.704**	**0.637**	**0.591**

Table 2: This table shows the per class and macro F1 scores achieved by our model on the task of emotion classification. We present both the hyperbolic and euclidean versions of our approach. The best performance numbers have been made bold.

outperforms all the baselines. This is evident from the results in the tables 1 and 2. In the case, of binary classification task, the highest performance difference between models in both spaces is minor, approximately 2% macro F1 score, but this difference increases in the case of multi-class sentiment classification task to approximately 8% macro F1. This shows that Euclidean models are better at the task of imbalanced classification even though hyperbolic models are effective classifiers.

7.3 Analyzing Embedding Space

We train our approach in both euclidean and hyperbolic spaces with 2-dimensional embeddings to visualize how our approach divides the embedding space. We find that hyperbolic variation of our approach divides the space more fairly between the minority and majority class in the binary classification case. This is interesting and may require further investigation in future work, as we fail to observe such a result when it comes to the multi-classification task. This could be because of data characteristics or may point to an innate trait of hyperbolic embeddings.

7.4 Interpreting Model Decisions Using Inter-Class Relationships

As described in the section 4, we proposed an approach to make model decisions interpretable by learning the inter-class relationships in the form of weights between 0 and 1. We train a model with the weighted variation of our approach and results highlight that model tries to distance embeddings which belong to similar emotions more than those belonging to different ones. This is apparent by looking at the weights in the figure 4 which shows that relationship weight between the positive labels *love* and *joy* (0.540) is higher in contrast to the weight between opposite ones *joy* and *sadness* (0.186). Similarly, weight between correlated emotions like *anger* and *surprise* (0.447) is higher than between emotions which are not correlated like *anger* and *love* (0.0558). The is interesting as this shows that model is capturing the fact that some emotions even though not similar are correlated. Another interesting insight is that the relationship between non-opposite categories like *anger* and *surprise* or *surprise* and *joy* are comparatively higher. This may point to an interesting characteristic of the data and alludes the fact that text expressing surprise can both be positive or negative. These results highlight that, along with improving interpretability, our approach can be utilized to highlight data specific characteristics and relationships. These may be used in data modeling or adopting data specific approaches for implementing practical solutions.

8 Limitations and Future Work

Our current approach is limited by the architecture of the label embedding layer. In our current implementation the label embeddings are obtained using a simple embedding which is fine-tuned during training along with text embedding module. In future works, we should experiment with more sophisticated ways to obtain label embeddings to check if we can improve our approach further.

Our approach, specially with hyperbolic embeddings, may have applications in hierarchical classification tasks where classes have a hierarchy and relationships between data samples and their classes are more complex. Such a task may be able to better utilize the natural structure of hyperbolic plane more effectively. In addition, our hyperbolic models fall behind in performance to their Euclidean

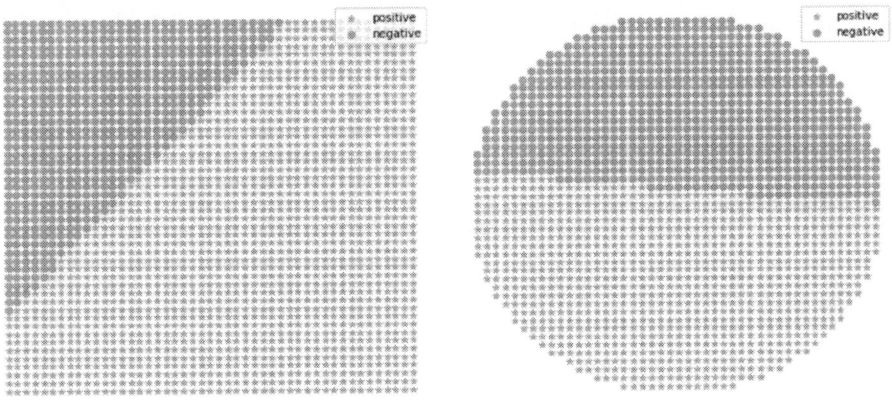

Figure 3: Space division by the 2-dimensional variation of our approach with negative text-samples. The figure shows how our approach divides the embedding space when trained with hyperbolic vs. euclidean embeddings. Rectangular space shows the normalized euclidean space while the circular shows a hyperbolic disk of poincare radius=1.

	Sadness	Joy	Love	Anger	Fear	Surprise
Sadness	--	0.0285	0.1939	0.436	0.1273	0.2144
Joy	0.1855	--	0.1708	0.399	0.0375	0.2072
Love	0.1398	0.5399	--	0.1284	0.1027	0.0893
Anger	0.1142	0.2254	0.0558	--	0.157	0.4475
Fear	0.3165	0.2517	0.1144	0.1889	--	0.1284
Surprise	0.1326	0.5381	0.0569	0.0683	0.204	--

Figure 4: Cells with darker red colors represent that model learns to separate these pairs more.

counterparts so more investigation is needed into how can hyperbolic spaces be used to learn effective classifiers.

Another significant limitation of our approach, lie in the problem formulation. One powerful aspect of CL approaches is that they do not need label information. However, we rely on the presence of label information in the corpus to learn label embeddings. This may not always be possible. In the future, we may be able to combine our approach with traditional CL approaches. This will involve dividing the embedding space during pre-training in the first phase. Using the results from this pre-training, we may be able to obtain key anchors by averaging out the embeddings in a region. These key anchors may then be used in an approach similar to ours to reduce noise in the CL training and better split the embedding space between different distributions in the data.

Finally, weighted variation of our CL objective is successful in quantifying relationship between class pairs. This provides additional insight into how our model is making decisions and improves interpretability. It even helps decipher information which is not obvious without a detailed look at data, like relationship between correlated emotions. However, it does not help in improving the performance. Investigation into how this information can be used to learn better classifiers is another possible venue for future work. Similarly, using this information to design data specific solutions for deployment may offer another avenue for future research.

9 Conclusion

We present a novel CL approach which uses label embeddings as anchors for the task of imbalanced text classification in both the binary and multi-class classification settings. Our approach outperforms several baselines by a margin of 7% in the binary classification task and a margin of 15% in the multi-class classification task. In addition, we extend our approach to hyperbolic spaces, show its effectiveness in the task of imbalanced data classification. We also conduct a study of how our approach utilizes embedding space and show that it may be worth for future investigation that hyperbolic models divide the embedding space in a fairer manner than euclidean couterparts. Finally, we present a interpretable variation of our approach for multi-class classification which helps us draw important conclusions about data relationships.

References

Ashish Anand, Ganesan Pugalenthi, Gary Fogel, and Ponnuthurai Suganthan. 2010. An approach for classification of highly imbalanced data using weighting and undersampling. *Amino acids*, 39:1385–91.

Kaidi Cao, Colin Wei, Adrien Gaidon, Nikos Arechiga,

and Tengyu Ma. 2019. Learning imbalanced datasets with label-distribution-aware margin loss. In *Advances in Neural Information Processing Systems*, volume 32. Curran Associates, Inc.

N. V. Chawla, K. W. Bowyer, L. O. Hall, and W. P. Kegelmeyer. 2002a. SMOTE: Synthetic minority over-sampling technique. *Journal of Artificial Intelligence Research*, 16:321–357.

Nitesh V. Chawla, Kevin W. Bowyer, Lawrence O. Hall, and W. Philip Kegelmeyer. 2002b. Smote: Synthetic minority over-sampling technique. *J. Artif. Int. Res.*, 16(1):321–357.

Boli Chen, Yao Fu, Guangwei Xu, Pengjun Xie, Chuanqi Tan, Mosha Chen, and Liping Jing. 2021. Probing BERT in hyperbolic spaces. *CoRR*, abs/2104.03869.

Kewen Chen, Zuping Zhang, Jun Long, and Hao Zhang. 2016. Turning from tf-idf to tf-igm for term weighting in text classification. *Expert Systems with Applications*, 66:245–260.

Jacob Devlin, Ming-Wei Chang, Kenton Lee, and Kristina Toutanova. 2018. Bert: Pre-training of deep bidirectional transformers for language understanding.

David Díaz-Vico, Aníbal R. Figueiras-Vidal, and José R. Dorronsoro. 2018. Deep mlps for imbalanced classification. In *2018 International Joint Conference on Neural Networks (IJCNN)*, pages 1–7.

Tianyu Gao, Xingcheng Yao, and Danqi Chen. 2021a. Simcse: Simple contrastive learning of sentence embeddings.

Tianyu Gao, Xingcheng Yao, and Danqi Chen. 2021b. SimCSE: Simple contrastive learning of sentence embeddings. In *Proceedings of the 2021 Conference on Empirical Methods in Natural Language Processing*, pages 6894–6910, Online and Punta Cana, Dominican Republic. Association for Computational Linguistics.

Yang Gao, Yi-Fan Li, Yu Lin, Charu Aggarwal, and Latifur Khan. 2021c. Setconv: A new approach for learning from imbalanced data.

Olivier J. Hénaff, Aravind Srinivas, Jeffrey De Fauw, Ali Razavi, Carl Doersch, S. M. Ali Eslami, and Aaron van den Oord. 2019. Data-efficient image recognition with contrastive predictive coding.

E.L. Iglesias, A. Seara Vieira, and L. Borrajo. 2013. An hmm-based over-sampling technique to improve text classification. *Expert Systems with Applications*, 40(18):7184–7192.

Ashish Jaiswal, Ashwin Ramesh Babu, Mohammad Zaki Zadeh, Debapriya Banerjee, and Fillia Makedon. 2021. A survey on contrastive self-supervised learning. *Technologies*, 9(1).

Bingyi Kang, Yu Li, Sa Xie, Zehuan Yuan, and Jiashi Feng. 2021. Exploring balanced feature spaces for representation learning. In *International Conference on Learning Representations*.

Phillip Keung, Yichao Lu, György Szarvas, and Noah A. Smith. 2020. The multilingual amazon reviews corpus. In *Proceedings of the 2020 Conference on Empirical Methods in Natural Language Processing*.

Prannay Khosla, Piotr Teterwak, Chen Wang, Aaron Sarna, Yonglong Tian, Phillip Isola, Aaron Maschinot, Ce Liu, and Dilip Krishnan. 2020a. Supervised contrastive learning.

Prannay Khosla, Piotr Teterwak, Chen Wang, Aaron Sarna, Yonglong Tian, Phillip Isola, Aaron Maschinot, Ce Liu, and Dilip Krishnan. 2020b. Supervised contrastive learning. *CoRR*, abs/2004.11362.

Diederik P. Kingma and Jimmy Ba. 2014. Adam: A method for stochastic optimization.

Bartosz Krawczyk. 2016. Learning from imbalanced data: Open challenges and future directions. *Progress in Artificial Intelligence*, 5.

Yuxiao Lin, Yuxian Meng, Xiaofei Sun, Qinghong Han, Kun Kuang, Jiwei Li, and Fei Wu. 2021. BertGCN: Transductive text classification by combining GNN and BERT. In *Findings of the Association for Computational Linguistics: ACL-IJCNLP 2021*, pages 1456–1462, Online. Association for Computational Linguistics.

Manuel Lopez-Martin, Antonio Sanchez-Esguevillas, Juan Ignacio Arribas, and Belen Carro. 2022. Supervised contrastive learning over prototype-label embeddings for network intrusion detection. *Information Fusion*, 79:200–228.

Tomas Mikolov, Kai Chen, Greg Corrado, and Jeffrey Dean. 2013. Efficient estimation of word representations in vector space.

Maximilian Nickel and Douwe Kiela. 2017. Poincaré embeddings for learning hierarchical representations. *CoRR*, abs/1705.08039.

Maximilian Nickel and Douwe Kiela. 2018. Learning continuous hierarchies in the lorentz model of hyperbolic geometry. *CoRR*, abs/1806.03417.

Nikolaos Pappas and James Henderson. 2019. GILE: A generalized input-label embedding for text classification. *Transactions of the Association for Computational Linguistics*, 7:139–155.

Seulki Park, Jongin Lim, Younghan Jeon, and Jin Young Choi. 2021. Influence-balanced loss for imbalanced visual classification. In *Proceedings of the IEEE/CVF International Conference on Computer Vision (ICCV)*, pages 735–744.

Jeffrey Pennington, Richard Socher, and Christopher Manning. 2014. GloVe: Global vectors for word representation. In *Proceedings of the 2014 Conference on Empirical Methods in Natural Language Processing (EMNLP)*, pages 1532–1543, Doha, Qatar. Association for Computational Linguistics.

C. E. Shannon. 1948. A mathematical theory of communication. *Bell System Technical Journal*, 27(3):379–423.

Michael R. Smith, Tony R. Martinez, and Christophe G. Giraud-Carrier. 2013. An instance level analysis of data complexity. *Machine Learning*, 95:225–256.

Jia Song, Xianglin Huang, Sijun Qin, and Qing Song. 2016. A bi-directional sampling based on k-means method for imbalance text classification. In *2016 IEEE/ACIS 15th International Conference on Computer and Information Science (ICIS)*, pages 1–5.

Muhammad Atif Tahir, Josef Kittler, and Fei Yan. 2012. Inverse random under sampling for class imbalance problem and its application to multi-label classification. *Pattern Recognition*, 45(10):3738–3750.

Jiachen Tian, Shizhan Chen, Xiaowang Zhang, Zhiyong Feng, Deyi Xiong, Shaojuan Wu, and Chunliu Dou. 2021. Re-embedding difficult samples via mutual information constrained semantically oversampling for imbalanced text classification. In *Proceedings of the 2021 Conference on Empirical Methods in Natural Language Processing*, pages 3148–3161, Online and Punta Cana, Dominican Republic. Association for Computational Linguistics.

Yonglong Tian, Dilip Krishnan, and Phillip Isola. 2019. Contrastive multiview coding.

Iulia Turc, Ming-Wei Chang, Kenton Lee, and Kristina Toutanova. 2019. Well-read students learn better: On the importance of pre-training compact models. *arXiv preprint arXiv:1908.08962v2*.

Zhenyu Zhang, Yuming Zhao, Meng Chen, and Xiaodong He. 2022. Label anchored contrastive learning for language understanding. In *Proceedings of the 2022 Conference of the North American Chapter of the Association for Computational Linguistics: Human Language Technologies*, pages 1437–1449, Seattle, United States. Association for Computational Linguistics.

MaintNorm: A corpus and benchmark model for lexical normalisation and masking of industrial maintenance short text

Tyler Bikaun, Melinda Hodkiewicz, Wei Liu
The University of Western Australia
tyler.bikaun@research.uwa.edu.au

Abstract

Maintenance short texts are invaluable unstructured data sources, serving as a diagnostic and prognostic window into the operational health and status of physical assets. These user-generated texts, created during routine or ad-hoc maintenance activities, offer insights into equipment performance, potential failure points, and maintenance needs. However, the use of information captured in these texts is hindered by inherent challenges: the prevalence of engineering jargon, domain-specific vernacular, random spelling errors without identifiable patterns, and the absence of standard grammatical structures. To transform these texts into accessible and analysable data, we introduce the MaintNorm dataset, the first resource specifically tailored for the lexical normalisation task of maintenance short texts. Comprising 12,000 examples, this dataset enables the efficient processing and interpretation of these texts. We demonstrate the utility of MaintNorm by training a lexical normalisation model as a sequence-to-sequence learning task with two learning objectives, namely, enhancing the quality of the texts and masking segments to obscure sensitive information to anonymise data. Our benchmark model demonstrates a universal error reduction rate of 95.8%. The dataset and benchmark outcomes are made available to the public under the MIT license.[1]

1 Introduction

Industrial user-generated content, such as maintenance work order (MWO) records, logbooks, and incident reports, constitutes a rich repository of data. This data is pivotal for applications in predictive maintenance, safety analysis, process optimisation, and product life cycle management (Brundage et al., 2021). Specifically, in the maintenance sector, MWO short texts (MST) are instrumental in documenting the condition of assets and the maintenance activities performed, as well as informing the design of maintenance strategies. These texts, typically authored by technicians, serve as critical input for future maintenance endeavours. Furthermore, reliability engineers scrutinise these historical records to gain a deeper understanding of equipment failure modes (Lee et al., 2023), enhance root cause analysis (Valcamonico et al., 2024), and develop key performance indicators such as mean-time-to-failure and remaining useful life (Lukens et al., 2019; Bikaun and Hodkiewicz, 2021).

A	AN426 REPLACE BROKEN ALT BOLT **<id> replace broken alternator bolt** R/H Steering Cyl Pin & Brg **right hand steering cylinder pin and bearing**
B	air con belt u/s **air conditioner belt unserviceable** 1000H Mech Insp Carry Roll No 2 RH DN9817 **<num> hour mechanical inspection carry roller number <num> right hand <id>**
C	ZH6907 C/out pos 2 tyre **<id> change out position <num> tyre** Left cab aircon e/leakage flt **left cabin air conditioner electrical leakage fault**

Table 1: User-Generated maintenance short texts for heavy mobile equipment across three companies, with **bold** blue text indicating normalised and masked forms.

Consider Table 1, which showcases examples of MSTs from various companies. These texts, often characterised by technical jargon, domain-specific vernacular, and frequent linguistic inaccuracies, pose significant challenges regarding data quality and processing efficiency (Hodkiewicz and Ho, 2016; Brundage et al., 2021). The resultant ambiguity and lack of standardisation impede effective pattern recognition and trend analysis, impacting maintenance decision-making.

MSTs frequently contain sensitive information, ranging from equipment identifiers to personnel names, raising confidentiality concerns (Brundage

[1]https:github.com/nlp-tlp/maintnorm

Proceedings of the Ninth Workshop on Noisy and User-generated Text (W-NUT 2024), pages 68–78
March 22, 2024 ©2024 Association for Computational Linguistics

et al., 2021). Consequently, there is a scarcity of publicly available industrial (as opposed to governmental) raw MST datasets, with limited examples like MaintNet comprising 7,000 MSTs, and a dataset on excavators with 5,486 MSTs.[2,3] Industrial companies' hesitation to release data, driven by concerns over identification (Sikorska et al., 2020) and a lack of appropriate anonymisation tools, significantly hamper the advancement of technical language models in this critical commercial sector.

Lexical normalisation, the process of transforming non-standard words and phrases into their standard forms (Han and Baldwin, 2011), provides a promising solution for addressing the issue of poor text quality in MSTs. While there has been extensive research on the lexical normalisation of social media texts (Baldwin et al., 2015; van der Goot et al., 2021), industrial maintenance texts have not received similar attention. Currently, state-of-the-art lexical normalisation has been achieved by formulating it as a sequence-to-sequence learning task whereby a sequence with potentially non-canonical (noisy) tokens is transduced into a sequence of canonical (clean) tokens (Samuel and Straka, 2021).

This paper addresses the need to enhance the quality of MST data and simultaneously de-identify sensitive information through a sequence-to-sequence learning approach. Our annotated corpora and model are designed to generate high-quality, normalised sequences with strategically masked segments to obscure sensitive or semantically redundant information. This is particularly crucial in knowledge elicitation for tasks such as information extraction annotation, which rely on domain expertise due to the tacit knowledge needed for interpreting these short texts, whom have limited time resources.

This paper's primary contributions are threefold:

- We introduce the first publicly available annotated corpus for lexical normalisation and masking of maintenance short texts,
- We systematically characterise the lexical noise present in maintenance short texts, and
- We demonstrate the efficacy of sequence-to-sequence language modelling in performing lexical normalisation and masking as a unified task using a structured encoding scheme.

2 Background and Related Work

Lexical normalisation, an important task in natural language processing, involves converting non-standard or informal language—such as abbreviations, colloquialisms, and misspellings—into a more standard form. This process is especially pertinent in the context of MSTs, where the prevalence of informal language poses unique challenges (Brundage et al., 2021). Lexical normalisation, as defined by Han and Baldwin (2011), aims to systematically transform non-standard words to their standard equivalents, thereby enhancing readability and facilitating more effective processing for a range of downstream natural language processing applications.

MSTs are key information sources in asset-intensive organisations. Numerous studies, such as those by Hodkiewicz and Ho (2016), Saetia et al. (2019), Gao et al. (2020), and Akhbardeh et al. (2020), have explored the unique lexical challenges these texts present. These works have primarily focused on enhancing MST quality for downstream tasks, employing methods ranging from heuristic approaches to normalisation dictionaries and distance-matching algorithms such as Levenshein (Levenshtein et al., 1966). However, these approaches often lack robustness and adaptability in broader maintenance contexts. Moreover, the confidentiality concerns associated with MSTs remain challenging to address, resulting in a scarcity of publicly available datasets, as highlighted by Akhbardeh et al. (2020) and Brundage et al. (2021).

In contrast to work on MSTs, the field of lexical normalisation has evolved significantly over time. Early insights into the challenges and methodologies were provided by foundational studies like those of Han and Baldwin (2011) and Baldwin et al. (2015). The work of van der Goot et al. (2021) expanded these insights to multilingual normalisation, demonstrating the task's complexity across different languages. The task of lexical normalisation has witnessed a paradigm shift from non-sequence-to-sequence models, such as *MoNoise* by van der Goot (2019), to more sophisticated sequence-to-sequence models (Samuel and Straka, 2021). This transition, highlighted in the work of Lourentzou et al. (2019), marks a critical juncture in the history of lexical normalisation.

[2]MaintNet Large Technical Database

[3]Prognostics Data Library: Excavator MWOs

The formulation of lexical normalisation as a sequence-to-sequence learning task has led to the use of pre-trained knowledge representations as explored by Muller et al. (2019), and the joint normalisation and masking of e-commerce dialogues by Nguyen and Cavallari (2020). More recently, the Shared Task on Multilingual Lexical Normalization (van der Goot et al., 2021) saw the extensive application of sequence-to-sequence learning predominately through Transformer-based models leveraging pre-trained language models such as (Samuel and Straka, 2021)'s state-of-the-art token-by-token normalisation using ByT5 (Xue et al., 2022) which represents the cutting-edge in the field.

The convergence of these developments in MSTs and lexical normalisation underscores the necessity for adaptable, robust models capable of managing the complexities of maintenance texts. Our research aims to leverage state-of-the-art techniques to improve the lexical quality of MSTs, focusing on joint normalisation and masking to enhance both readability and confidentiality.

3 Data Description

The MaintNorm dataset comprises 12,000 MSTs sourced from three major Australian mining companies.[4] These texts pertain to heavy mobile equipment (HME) – machinery used for operations like excavation, material handling, and earth transportation, including but not limited to haul trucks, dozers, excavators, water trucks, and drill machines. The content of these texts encompasses both routine and ad-hoc maintenance tasks, both planned and executed, as well as insights into the condition of the HME systems and their individual components. Table 1 provides examples sampled from each company.

3.1 Selection

To create the MaintNorm dataset, maintenance texts were randomly selected from a comprehensive repository belonging to the three participating organisations. Each organisation contributed 4,000 texts, ensuring equal representation. The primary objective of this diverse collection is to investigate the feasibility of developing a normalisation and masking model that can effectively operate across different organisational contexts for a given asset type. This approach also helps to discern whether specific models, attuned to the unique linguistic characteristics of each organisation, yield superior results. Detailed corpus statistics, including average text length, vocabulary size, and total token count for each company, are presented in Table 2.

3.2 Preprocessing

The preprocessing of the MaintNorm corpus was minimal to preserve the raw characteristics of the texts, the texts only underwent basic tokenisation based on whitespace prior to annotation.

3.3 Annotation

Annotation is performed by the first author due to resource constraints. The annotator is experienced with lexical normalisation and industrial maintenance. The annotation tool LexiClean (Bikaun et al., 2021) was used for all lexical normalisation and masking. An overview of the annotated corpora is presented in Table 5. Similar to Han and Baldwin (2011), the following guidelines were used in the annotation process:

Spelling corrections. Canonical forms are adopted to rectify spelling discrepancies within the corpus, such as omissions, redundancies, or incorrect characters. For example, abbreviations like 'eng' are converted to their full form 'engine'.

True casing. The dataset is standardised using true casing, where inappropriate capitalisation is corrected. For instance, 'REPLACE ENGINE' is modified to 'replace engine', except for proper nouns that retain capitalisation, e.g., 'UL123 tele-remote' to 'UL123 Tele-Remote'. Acronyms are cased according to their standard usage.

Abbreviation expansion. Maintenance text abbreviations are expanded to their full lexical forms to facilitate uniformity and clarity. For instance, 'c/o' becomes 'change out'.

Concatenation and tokenisation. Incorrectly concatenated multi-word expressions are separated (e.g., 'repair/replace' to 'repair / replace', '250hr' to '250 hour'), enhancing the granularity for downstream tasks such as information extraction.

Token masking. In addition to normalisation, token-level entity masks (tags) were applied to text spans using the scheme in Table 4. The use of token-level entity tags is twofold. First, due to confidentiality concerns, the texts have been preprocessed to obfuscate any identifiers about assets, or-

[4]We use A, B, and C to refer to these companies to ensure their privacy.

Company	Length ($\mu \pm \sigma$)	Vocab Size	Tokens	Modified	Norm Only	Mask Only
A	5.2 (1.2)	2,561	20,944	-	-	-
	5.4 (1.3) (↑ 3%)	1,106 (↓ 57%)	21,591 (↑ 3%)	3,998	115	45
B	5.5 (1.4)	3,100	21,919	-	-	-
	6.2 (1.8) (↑ 13%)	1,360 (↓ 56%)	24,690 (↑ 13%)	3,946	192	321
C	5.1 (1.5)	4,168	20,559	-	-	-
	5.5 (1.8) (↑ 7%)	2,048 (↓ 51%)	22,114 (↑ 7%)	3,431	1,879	150
A+B+C	5.3 (1.4)	7,612	63,422	-	-	-
	5.7 (1.7) (↑ 8%)	2,872 (↓ 62%)	68,395 (↑ 8%)	11,375	2,116	586

Table 2: Summary of MaintNorm corpus statistics: This table displays statistics for 4,000 texts from each company, focusing on heavy mobile equipment. It includes token-based text length and vocabulary size. Greyed rows represent post-normalisation and masking statistics. Changes due to normalisation and masking are indicated by arrows and percentages (↑/↓ X%). The right-hand section of the table delineates the text transformations, categorising them as *Modified* for texts undergoing normalisation or masking, *Norm Only* for texts exclusively normalised, and *Mask Only* for texts solely subjected to masking.

N	M	Example
1	1	Single word normalisation, e.g., 'eng' to 'engine'.
1	> 1	Single to multi-word normalisation, e.g., 'c/o' to 'change out'.
1	0	Removal of superfluous characters, e.g., 'T' in 'replace engine T' where 'T' is erroneous.
> 1	1	Concatenation of fragmented words, e.g., 'eng ine' to 'engine'.
> 1	> 1	Combining fragmented words into multi-word normalisations, e.g., 'eng ineoi l' to 'engine oil'.

Table 3: Examples of N:M normalisation transformations in the MaintNorm dataset.

Mask	Description
<id>	Asset identifiers e.g. *ENG001, rd1286*
<sensitive>	Sensitive organisation-specific information such as proprietary systems, third-party contractors, names of personnel, etc.
<num>	Numerical digits e.g. *8, 7001223*
<date>	Numerical and phrase representations of dates e.g. *10/10/2023, 8th Dec*

Table 4: MaintNorm token masking scheme used for privacy preservation and redundancy removal.

ganisations, personnel, etc, using token-level masking, which was applied in the annotation process. Second, tags such as <num> and <date> reduce the semantic duplication of texts for downstream annotation tasks such as information extraction as maintenance short texts can be generated in very similar fashions such as 'replace pump 1' and 'replace pump 2', here the semantics is the same but there is redundancy when annotating for other tasks. Hence, it is desirable to normalise texts like these to a unified form such as 'replace pump <num>', which represents this structure generally.

3.4 Post-processing and Obfuscation

Two steps were performed post-annotation to ensure the texts were suitable for model training and public release. First, all token-level entity masks were used to mask the respective tokens, e.g. an <id> entity masks on the "PU001" in "replace PU001" would subsequently convert the text into "replace <id>". This process was performed for all masking tokens. Simultaneously, we ensure that masked tokens are obfuscated before public release. We do this by mapping over each text and identifying any masked tokens, which we map to an arbitrary representation of the same semantic type. For example, for <id>, we copy the alphanumerical and cased structure of the original identifier. For <date> and <num>, we copy the structure but permutate it. For <sensitive>, we detect the n-gram size and correspondingly impute a non-sensitive value. These actions ensure that the dataset captures the original essence of the task whilst maintaining a level of desensitisation to allow public release of the dataset.

3.5 Dataset Split

For the purpose of evaluating the generalisation of lexical normalisation and masking within our dataset, we divided it into training, development, and testing sets. Adhering to the conventional split ratio of 80/10/10, our dataset is segmented into 3,200 training texts and 400 texts each for development and testing. Furthermore, we organised the data into distinct company-specific segments (A, B, C) and an aggregated dataset (A+B+C). This segmentation strategy aims to investigate whether the

		A	B	C	A+B+C
Normalisation Operations	Char. addition	3,022	4,704	2,781	10,507
	Char. removal	191	939	247	1,377
	Char. rearrangement	145	118	233	358
	Char. replacement	209	508	231	950
	Token expansion	662	2,264	1,281	4,207
	Token removal	194	97	195	486
	Titled cased	69	118	97	284
	Partial casing added	8	6	9	23
	All casing removed	13,826	9,214	7,098	30,138
	All casing added	4	29	36	69
	No change	1,978	7,187	10,173	19,338
Norm. Transforms	1:1	17,898	12,233	8,694	38,825
	1:N	662	2,264	1,281	4,207
	N:1	194	97	195	486
	N:M	2	4	2	8
	N:0	7	15	6	28
Masking Ops.	<id>	4,055	3,916	1,116	9,087
	<sensitive>	44	25	155	224
	<num>	573	1,349	847	2,769
	<date>	9	2	49	60

Table 5: Summary of the normalisation and masking operations applied to maintenance short texts for each organisation and combined. Tokens can have multiple normalisation operations performed upon them; for example "tlerEMOTE" which is normalised to "Tele-Remote" would have the operations character addition ("tleremote" → "tele-rEMOTE"), all casing removed ("tele-rEMOTE" → "tele-remote") and title casing ("tele-remote" → "Tele-Remote"), representing a 1 : 1 normalisation transformation ("tlerEMOTE" → "Tele-Remote"). *Norm.* and *Ops.* refer to normalisation operations, respectively.

linguistic patterns are consistent across different companies and if such uniformity could enhance the performance of a single, universally-trained model. A positive outcome could encourage industrial entities to collaboratively address this task, yielding mutual advantages.

4 Method

4.1 Task Formulation

In this work, we conceptualise the task of lexical normalisation and masking as an auto-regressive sequence-to-sequence learning task. Our approach involves training a Transformer-based encoder-decoder model to transform potentially noisy input sequences into their normalised counterparts. This methodology is an extension of the approach outlined by De Cao et al. (2020), which employs sentinel brackets for demarcating entity boundaries in auto-regressive entity linking.

We have adapted this approach to suit our specific requirements. Our model defines boundaries around both non-canonical words and phrases, as well as their canonical equivalents. For instance, an input sequence such as 'repl ace eng oil' is normalised to 'replace engine oil'. Using our encoding scheme, the sequence-to-sequence model represents this transformation in its output space as '{ repl ace } [replace] { eng } [engine] oil'. The model's output undergoes post-processing to yield the correctly formatted output, 'replace engine oil', by extracting canonical elements and unchanged tokens, as shown by '{ repl ace } [**replace**] { eng } [**engine**] **oil**'. This encoding technique and its application to various normalisation transformations is exemplified in Table 6.

Operation	1:1	`{ reply } [ replace ]`
	N:1	`{ repl ace } [ replace ]`
	1:M	`{ repleng } [ replace engine ]`
	N:0	`{ $$ } [ ]`
	N:M	`{ rep&re pl } [ repair and replace ]`

Table 6: Examples of the normalisation encoding scheme applied to different normalisation operations. Curly brackets (`{}`) denote a non-canonical span, whereas square brackets (`[]`) denote a canonical span.

While directly translating into normalised sequences (e.g., 'repl ace eng oil' → 'replace engine oil') may seem straightforward, it poses challenges for evaluation (see Appendix B). Ensuring alignment between input and output sequence translations is a complex task, as highlighted in the work of Sabet et al. (2020). Our encoding scheme directly addresses this challenge by explicitly capturing these transformations. Furthermore, our approach is particularly effective in token masking, as it naturally extends to an N:M operation (e.g., '{ UD01 } [<id>]', '{ blwnEN1 } [blown <id>]').

This methodology contrasts with the token-by-token normalisation strategy of Samuel and Straka (2021). Our approach requires only a single pass through the model, with the output sequence autoregressively generated via beam search decoding. Using this approach, each normalisation is conditioned on one another through the context provided by preceding tokens. This means that the model considers the entire input sequence and the part of the output sequence it has generated to predict each subsequent token. This contextual awareness allows for more cohesive and contextually appropriate normalisations, as the model can use the broader context to resolve ambiguities and infer the most probable normalisation for each token. In contrast, a token-by-token approach normalises each token in isolation, potentially missing the nuances of wider textual context.

4.2 Prefix Constrained Decoding

Building on the framework established by De Cao et al. (2020), our study also explores the use of prefix-constrained decoding to curtail the potential for model hallucination and ensure the alignment of input and output sequences. Prefix-constrained decoding is a technique where text generation is guided by constraints such as prefix tries or heuristics to ensure generated output adheres to specific conditions. This technique can be applied to maintain the alignment of input and output sequences during the decoding process for lexical normalisation. In contrast to entity linking, which relies on a closed set of semantic types to constrain generation, we experiment with this technique to limit the model to uncontrolled generation when generating a normalisation or masking pair; otherwise, it must copy the input sequence verbatim. The efficacy of prefix constraints in enhancing linguistic tasks, including entity recognition (Josifoski et al., 2022) and semantic parsing (Scholak et al., 2021), has been well-documented, supporting their application in our study.

4.3 Model Implementation and Parameters

We implement our sequence-to-sequence model as a Transformer encoder-decoder using the pretrained foundational model of ByT5 (Xue et al., 2022). ByT5, a token-free model, operates directly on byte sequences, enhancing its capacity to handle various languages and character sets without tokenization. All experiments and models are implemented using PyTorch and the Transformers library (Wolf et al., 2020) using PyTorch Lightning (Falcon, 2019) executed on a single Nvidia GeForce RTX 4080 graphics card. We use *google/byt5-small*, containing 299M parameters, fine-tuned in batches of 16 sequences.[5] Model optimisation uses AdamW with cross-entropy loss and a linear learning rate scheduler. Both source and target sequence lengths are set to 256 tokens, and the model runs for 20,000 steps with early stopping based on validation loss, employing a patience of 5 epochs. Our experiments with prefix constraints use logit renormalisation.

4.4 Evaluation

To measure the generalisation ability of a sequence-to-sequence model trained on our corpus, we evaluate them on the intrinsic word-level error reduction rate (E.R.R.), precision, and recall (van der Goot, 2019).[6] Here, E.R.R. is formulated as:

$$E.R.R. = \frac{TP - FP}{TP + FN} \tag{1}$$

E.R.R. values span from -1 to 1, with negative values indicating predominant incorrect normalisations by the model. A zero score signifies no alterations made by the model, and a score of 1 denotes perfect normalisation. In practice, we use the script provided as part of the Multilingual Shared Task (van der Goot et al., 2021), where we translate the encoded sequences into the traditional newline and tab-separated normalisation format for evaluation.

4.5 Baselines

To evaluate the performance of our sequence-to-sequence model on the MaintNorm corpus, we compare it against three normalisation methods:

Leave-As-Is (LAI): The LAI technique is characterised by its direct approach, retaining the original input without modification, resulting in a nominal E.R.R. of 0%.

Most Frequent Replacement (MFR): MFR employs a lexical database that associates each unigram (individual word) in the input with its most commonly observed replacement in the training

[5]HuggingFace google/byt5-small

[6]See Appendix A for evaluation details.

Company	Extra Data	MaintNorm (ours)			LAI			MFR			ÚFAL		
		P	*R*	*E.R.R.*	*P*	*R*	*E.R.R.*	*P*	*R*	*E.R.R.*	*P*	*R*	*E.R.R.*
A	N	**99.9**	95.8	95.2	0	0	0	**99.9**	91.7	90.9	99.8	92.0	91.0
	Y	**99.9**	**98.1**	**96.6**	0	0	0	**99.9**	91.7	90.9	99.9	92.1	91.3
B	N	98.9	94.6	90.0	0	0	0	**99.8**	93.9	90.2	99.6	91.0	85.5
	Y	99.7	**98.1**	**96.6**	0	0	0	**99.8**	93.9	90.2	99.6	91.7	86.5
C	N	99.4	95.2	89.1	0	0	0	**99.5**	89.9	78.6	99.4	86.6	71.9
	Y	**99.5**	**96.8**	**92.4**	0	0	0	**99.5**	89.9	78.6	99.1	86.6	71.5
A+B+C	-	99.7	97.5	95.8	0	0	0	99.8	93.0	89.4	99.5	90.2	85.0

Table 7: Summary of experiments evaluated on the respective hold-out test sets. *Extra data* refers to using the combined training data (A+B+C) but evaluated on the specific portions test-set. P, R, and E.R.R. refer to the precision, recall, and error reduction rate, respectively. **Bold** denotes the best-performing metric for each company.

corpus. During operation, the system substitutes each word with its prevalent counterpart. When an input word is novel and lacks a precedent in the database, it remains unaltered.

ÚFAL: The ÚFAL model (Samuel and Straka, 2021), based on the ByT5 pretrained language model (Xue et al., 2022), employs a token-by-token normalisation approach. It normalises each word separately, encapsulating it within specific tags for processing by ByT5, aligning with ByT5's pre-training objectives. Recognised as a leading method for multilingual lexical normalisation (van der Goot et al., 2021), ÚFAL was fine-tuned for our experiments using its default settings but without implementing its data augmentation strategies, which we reserve for future exploration.

5 Results

In this section, we examine the outcomes derived from developing the MaintNorm annotated corpus and our implementation of sequence-to-sequence modelling for lexical normalisation and masking within MSTs. The central objectives of this analysis are to address two key questions: Firstly, *what are the defining characteristics of lexical noise present in MSTs?* Secondly, *how effective is the application of sequence-to-sequence language modelling in executing lexical normalisation and masking as a combined task?*

5.1 MaintNorm Corpus Construction and Characterisation

In constructing the MaintNorm corpus, a significant observation across all three participating companies was their non-standard approach to casing. As highlighted in Table 5, the most prevalent normalisation operation involved the complete removal of casing, indicative of an excessive use of capital letters. It is noteworthy, however, that while fully capitalised tokens are rare within the corpus, they do occur and typically denote domain-specific acronyms such as 'TECO' (technically completed) and 'HAZ' (hazard), which are essential for domain experts.

Regarding the nature of normalisation transformations, MaintNorm primarily exhibits minimal N:M transformations, mirroring the tendencies observed in the WNUT corpus (Baldwin et al., 2015). This trend suggests a predominance of simpler, more direct normalisation methods within the corpus. Notably, a significant portion of the texts in MaintNorm, accounting for 94.8%, underwent at least one normalisation or masking operation. This rate was particularly high in two companies (A and B), where almost all texts in their respective portions of the corpus were subject to these operations. This extensive normalisation and masking process led to a substantial reduction (>50%) in vocabulary size across all three companies. This reduction underscores the impact of normalisation and masking on the diversity and complexity of the corpus vocabulary.

Table 5 further reveals that the characteristics of noise and masking in the maintenance communication language are consistent across companies despite their independent creation. The distributions of normalisation and masking operations highlight similar characteristics, such as the prevalence of normalisation through 1:1 transformations with high frequencies of character additions, whilst also having a high proportion of masks in the forms of `<id>`. Although `<sensitive>` and `<date>` masks appeared less frequently than `<id>` and `<num>`, their inclusion is crucial for maintaining privacy.

5.2 Sequence-to-Sequence Modelling

Here, we discuss the aspects of generalisation for a sequence-to-sequence model on the MaintNorm corpus. An overview of the experimental results is outlined in Table 7.

Comparative analysis with baseline methods. The sequence-to-sequence language model showcased notable efficiency in unified lexical normalisation and masking, achieving an E.R.R. above 90% across all experiments (refer to Table 7). Although the MFR baseline displayed unexpectedly robust performance, the difference between it and our model highlights the presence of non-mappable tokens. This suggests that the task of normalisation and masking may not be exceedingly challenging, which, albeit potentially less stimulating for researchers, is encouraging for practitioners aiming to implement these findings.

In contrast to our approach, MFR, akin to methods in prior studies (Hodkiewicz and Ho, 2016; Saetia et al., 2019; Akhbardeh et al., 2020), relies on dictionary replacement and cannot adapt to dynamic contexts with variable vocabularies. Using the same foundational model as the ÚFAL model allows for directly comparing encoding schemes. The results in Table 7 indicate superior performance of our encoding scheme across all dataset segments, likely due to its ability to contextually process the entire sequence during decoding, unlike ÚFAL's token-by-token method.

Although our model and encoding scheme are effective, we anticipate further enhancements by increasing the size of the pretrained language model and the number of beams in beam search decoding, which was limited to three due to resource constraints.

	A	B	C
Incorrect Predictions	56/2,059	48/2,202	70/2,050
Normalisation Errors	50	46	53
Masking Errors	6	2	7

Table 8: Error analysis of the best-performing models on their respective test sets from Table 7.

Comparative analysis: individual vs combined models. Evaluating model performance for individual companies against a unified model reveals distinct advantages in adopting a single, combined approach. This consolidated model notably enhances normalisation and masking capabilities, evidenced by a 1.4-6.6 E.R.R. improvement when leveraging additional training data. Although the single model approach appears superior, the performance of organisation-specific models, which closely rival the combined model using only a third of the data, is also noteworthy. Identifying the exact contributors to these performance disparities is challenging. However, qualitatively examining the corpora indicates common language use across the companies. This linguistic similarity suggests that merging the datasets creates a more substantial and varied corpus, enhancing the model's ability to generalise effectively.

Analysis of model errors. Despite achieving high precision and recall in normalisation and masking (see Table 7), our models are not entirely error-free, with error rates ranging from 2.2% to 3.4%. Table 8 outlines these errors. A closer qualitative analysis of incorrect predictions revealed that many errors originate from hapaxes and hapax legomena, causing inaccuracies or missed normalisation and masking opportunities. A common error pattern involves incorrectly handling concatenated corrections (e.g., '&8on' → 'and <num> on', '80A' → '<num> amperage'). Enhancing the MaintNorm corpus with a more diverse range of text samples will likely improve model performance by introducing a wider variety of linguistic scenarios, reducing the potential for such errors.

Effectiveness of encoding scheme and prefix-constrained decoding. Our model's high performance on the MaintNorm corpus, using a specific encoding scheme for lexical normalisation and masking, demonstrates its effectiveness in an autoregressive sequence-to-sequence framework. Although a notable challenge arises in data-scarce scenarios, the model struggles with encoding scheme assimilation, necessitating prefix-constrained decoding (see Table 9 in Appendix C). This issue could be mitigated through techniques such as pre-fine-tuning the models on synthetically generated corpora, following approaches similar to Dekker and van der Goot (2020) and Samuel and Straka (2021), and curriculum learning (Bengio et al., 2009). Our main experiments, as detailed in Table 7, achieve optimal results without constraints, benefiting from a robust training dataset.

While prefix-constrained decoding can effectively prevent hallucination and deviations from the encoding scheme, thereby avoiding misalignments between input and output sequences, its implementation is challenging. One notable issue is the degradation in error reduction efficiency, likely caused by logit renormalisation over constrained tokens. Our findings suggest that while the encoding scheme is effective for larger datasets of short texts, its application to smaller or complex corpora warrants further research. Although untested on other normalisation corpora like those in the multilingual shared task (van der Goot et al., 2021), we believe in the scheme's potential adaptability and plan to explore this in future work.

6 Conclusion and Future Work

In this paper, we have introduced the first corpus for normalising and masking maintenance short texts (MST), comprising 12,000 texts from the Australian mining and mineral processing sector. Our findings show that a unified approach to lexical normalisation and masking, using an encoder-decoder Transformer-based language model, delivers high performance on MSTs, surpassing existing state-of-the-art on our custom-constructed corpus. This methodology offers a viable pathway for industrial organisations to manage risk while releasing data, thereby facilitating research on technical language models in this vital commercial sector. We have made our code, corpus, and models publicly accessible under the MIT license. Looking ahead, we envisage expanding the scope of this dataset to encompass diverse maintenance contexts and enriching it with annotations from a broader range of annotators, which we believe will further augment its utility.

Acknowledgements

This research is supported by the Australian Research Council through the Centre for Transforming Maintenance through Data Science (grant number IC180100030). Additionally, Bikaun acknowledges funding from the Mineral Research Institute of Western Australia. Bikaun and Liu acknowledge the support from ARC Discovery Grant DP150102405.

References

Farhad Akhbardeh, Travis Desell, and Marcos Zampieri. 2020. MaintNet: A collaborative open-source library for predictive maintenance language resources. In *Proceedings of the 28th International Conference on Computational Linguistics: System Demonstrations*, pages 7–11, Barcelona, Spain (Online). International Committee on Computational Linguistics (ICCL).

Timothy Baldwin, Marie-Catherine de Marneffe, Bo Han, Young-Bum Kim, Alan Ritter, and Wei Xu. 2015. Shared tasks of the 2015 workshop on noisy user-generated text: Twitter lexical normalization and named entity recognition. In *Proceedings of the Workshop on Noisy User-generated Text*, pages 126–135.

Yoshua Bengio, Jérôme Louradour, Ronan Collobert, and Jason Weston. 2009. Curriculum learning. In *Proceedings of the 26th annual international conference on machine learning*, pages 41–48.

Tyler Bikaun, Tim French, Melinda Hodkiewicz, Michael Stewart, and Wei Liu. 2021. Lexiclean: An annotation tool for rapid multi-task lexical normalisation. In *Proceedings of the 2021 Conference on Empirical Methods in Natural Language Processing: System Demonstrations*, pages 212–219.

Tyler Bikaun and Melinda Hodkiewicz. 2021. Semi-automated estimation of reliability measures from maintenance work order records. In *PHM Society European Conference*, volume 6, pages 9–9.

Michael P Brundage, Thurston Sexton, Melinda Hodkiewicz, Alden Dima, and Sarah Lukens. 2021. Technical language processing: Unlocking maintenance knowledge. *Manufacturing Letters*, 27:42–46.

N De Cao, G Izacard, S Riedel, and F Petroni. 2020. Autoregressive entity retrieval. In *ICLR 2021-9th International Conference on Learning Representations*, volume 2021. ICLR.

Kelly Dekker and Rob van der Goot. 2020. Synthetic data for english lexical normalization: How close can we get to manually annotated data? In *Proceedings of the Twelfth Language Resources and Evaluation Conference*, pages 6300–6309.

William A Falcon. 2019. Pytorch lightning: The lightweight pytorch wrapper for high-performance ai research.

Yiyang Gao, Caitlin Woods, Wei Liu, Tim French, and Melinda Hodkiewicz. 2020. Pipeline for machine reading of unstructured maintenance work order records. In *Proceedings of the 30th. European Safety and Reliability Conference and 15th. Probabilistic Safety Assessment and Management Conference*. ESRA PSAM.

Bo Han and Timothy Baldwin. 2011. Lexical normalisation of short text messages: Makn sens a# twitter. In *Proceedings of the 49th Annual meeting of the Association for Computational Linguistics: Human language technologies*, pages 368–378.

Melinda Hodkiewicz and Mark Tien-Wei Ho. 2016. Cleaning historical maintenance work order data for reliability analysis. *Journal of Quality in Maintenance Engineering*, 22(2):146–163.

Martin Josifoski, Nicola De Cao, Maxime Peyrard, Fabio Petroni, and Robert West. 2022. Genie: Generative information extraction. In *Proceedings of the 2022 Conference of the North American Chapter of the Association for Computational Linguistics: Human Language Technologies*, pages 4626–4643.

Shenae Lee, Maria Vatshaug Ottermo, Stein Hauge, and Mary Ann Lundteigen. 2023. Towards standardized reporting and failure classification of safety equipment: Semi-automated classification of failure data for safety equipment in the operating phase. *Process Safety and Environmental Protection*, 177:1485–1493.

Vladimir I Levenshtein et al. 1966. Binary codes capable of correcting deletions, insertions, and reversals. In *Soviet physics doklady*, volume 10, pages 707–710. Soviet Union.

Ismini Lourentzou, Kabir Manghnani, and ChengXiang Zhai. 2019. Adapting sequence to sequence models for text normalization in social media. In *Proceedings of the International AAAI Conference on Web and Social Media*, volume 13, pages 335–345.

Sarah Lukens, Manjish Naik, Kittipong Saetia, and Xiaohui Hu. 2019. Best practices framework for improving maintenance data quality to enable asset performance analytics. In *Annual Conference of the PHM Society*, volume 11.

Benjamin Muller, Benoît Sagot, and Djamé Seddah. 2019. Enhancing bert for lexical normalization. In *Proceedings of the 5th Workshop on Noisy User-generated Text (W-NUT 2019)*, pages 297–306.

Hoang Nguyen and Sandro Cavallari. 2020. Neural multi-task text normalization and sanitization with pointer-generator. In *Proceedings of the First Workshop on Natural Language Interfaces*, pages 37–47.

Masoud Jalili Sabet, Philipp Dufter, François Yvon, and Hinrich Schütze. 2020. Simalign: High quality word alignments without parallel training data using static and contextualized embeddings. In *EMNLP 2020*, pages 1627–1643.

Kittipong Saetia, Sarah Lukens, Erik Pijcke, and Xiaohui Hu. 2019. Data-driven approach to equipment taxonomy classification. In *Proceedings of the PHM Society Conference*.

David Samuel and Milan Straka. 2021. Úfal at multilexnorm 2021: Improving multilingual lexical normalization by fine-tuning byt5. In *Proceedings of the Seventh Workshop on Noisy User-generated Text (W-NUT 2021)*, pages 483–492.

Torsten Scholak, Nathan Schucher, and Dzmitry Bahdanau. 2021. Picard: Parsing incrementally for constrained auto-regressive decoding from language models. In *Proceedings of the 2021 Conference on Empirical Methods in Natural Language Processing*, pages 9895–9901.

Joanna Sikorska, Sam Bradley, Melinda Hodkiewicz, and Ryan Fraser. 2020. Drat: Data risk assessment tool for university–industry collaborations. *Data-Centric Engineering*, 1:e17.

Dario Valcamonico, Piero Baraldi, Enrico Zio, Luca Decarli, Anna Crivellari, and Laura La Rosa. 2024. Combining natural language processing and bayesian networks for the probabilistic estimation of the severity of process safety events in hydrocarbon production assets. *Reliability Engineering & System Safety*, 241:109638.

Rob van der Goot. 2019. Monoise: A multi-lingual and easy-to-use lexical normalization tool. In *Proceedings of the 57th Annual Meeting of the Association for Computational Linguistics: System Demonstrations*, pages 201–206.

Rob van der Goot, Alan Ramponi, Arkaitz Zubiaga, Barbara Plank, Benjamin Muller, Iñaki San Vicente Roncal, Nikola Ljubešic, Özlem Çetinoğlu, Rahmad Mahendra, Talha Çolakoglu, et al. 2021. Multilexnorm: A shared task on multilingual lexical normalization. In *Seventh Workshop on Noisy User-generated Text (W-NUT 2021)*, pages 493–509. Association for Computational Linguistics.

Thomas Wolf, Lysandre Debut, Victor Sanh, Julien Chaumond, Clement Delangue, Anthony Moi, Pierric Cistac, Tim Rault, Rémi Louf, Morgan Funtowicz, et al. 2020. Transformers: State-of-the-art natural language processing. In *Proceedings of the 2020 conference on empirical methods in natural language processing: system demonstrations*, pages 38–45.

Linting Xue, Aditya Barua, Noah Constant, Rami Al-Rfou, Sharan Narang, Mihir Kale, Adam Roberts, and Colin Raffel. 2022. ByT5: Towards a token-free future with pre-trained byte-to-byte models. *Transactions of the Association for Computational Linguistics*, 10:291–306.

A Description of Evaluation Metrics

To assess the effectiveness of our models, we used precision (P), recall (R), and error reduction rate ($E.R.R.$), following the methodology outlined in (van der Goot, 2019). These metrics offer a comprehensive evaluation of test accuracy. Precision measures the accuracy of the normalisation model's replacements, while recall determines the model's ability to identify and correctly normalise anomalies. Together, these metrics complement the E.R.R., addressing its limitations in distinguishing between over-normalisation and under-normalisation. The definitions of precision, recall, and error reduction rate are as follows:

$$P = \frac{TP}{TP + FP} \tag{2}$$

$$R = \frac{TP}{TP + FN} \quad (3)$$

$$E.R.R. = \frac{TP - FP}{TP + FN} \quad (4)$$

Here, the TP (True Positive), FP (False Positive), and FN (False Negative) values are evaluated at the token level. They are conceptualised as follows:

- True Positive (TP): Words that required normalisation and were accurately normalised by the model.
- False Positive (FP): Words incorrectly normalised by the model despite not requiring normalisation.
- False Negative (FN): Words that required normalisation but were either inaccurately normalised or overlooked by the model.

B Description of Alignment Errors

Alignment errors arise when there's a mismatch between the input portion of the model's prediction and the ground truth, posing challenges to accurate evaluation. These errors can occur even when the model's normalisation predictions are technically correct, leading to complexities in the assessment process. The following examples demonstrate how alignment errors manifest within our encoding scheme:

1. Input: "`repl eng oil`"
2. Output (aligned, ground truth):
   "`{ repl } [ replace ] { eng } [ engine ] oil`"
3. Output (aligned, incorrect):
   "`{ repl } [ replacement ] eng oil`"
4. Output (misaligned, correct):
   "`replace { eng } [ engine ] oil`"
5. Output (misaligned, incorrect):
   "`rep { eng } [ engine ] oil`"

In these cases, converting the encoded outputs to the normalisation format of the shared task (van der Goot et al., 2021) results in alignment issues. For instance, example (4) shows a misalignment where the ground truth aligns "repl" to "replace", but the misaligned output aligns "replace" to "replace". As a result, such instances are incompatible with the evaluation script used in the shared task.

C Analysis of Alignment Errors

In Table 9, we analyse the correlation between the size of the corpus and alignment errors in our model. It's clear that a sufficiently large corpus enhances the model's comprehension of the encoding scheme, reducing alignment errors. This is primarily due to the model's improved ability to avert hallucination and the creation of incorrect structures in normalisation. On the other hand, with smaller corpora, the model is more prone to alignment errors. To counter this in smaller datasets, we implement prefix constraints in our encoding scheme. This method steers the model towards more precise alignment, thereby ensuring output accuracy even with limited data.

However, our analysis also reveals that while prefix-constrained decoding is beneficial for alignment, it may affect the model's overall error-reduction capabilities. This relationship between alignment accuracy and error reduction under prefix constraints poses an interesting area for future research.

Train Fraction	Train Size	Alignment Errors
0.1	960	179/1,200 (14.9%)
0.2	1,920	67/1,200 (5.6%)
0.3	2,880	56/1,200 (4.7%)
0.4	3,840	10/1,200 (0.8%)
0.5	4,800	7/1,200 (0.5%)
0.6	5,760	11/1,200 (0.9%)
0.7	6,720	4/1,200 (0.3%)
0.8	7,680	4/1,200 (0.3%)
0.9	8,640	0/1,200 (0.3%)
1.0	9,600	0/1,200 (0.0%)

Table 9: Overview of alignment errors in relation to corpus size, using a model trained on the combined corpus (A+B+C) and tested with a beam size of 3.

The Effects of Data Quality on Named Entity Recognition

Divya Bhadauria
University of Potsdam
Potsdam, Germany
divya.bhadauria@uni-potsdam.de

Alejandro Sierra-Múnera
Hasso Plattner Institute
Potsdam, Germany
alejandro.sierra@hpi.de

Ralf Krestel
ZBW - Leibniz Information Centre for Economics & Kiel University
Kiel, Germany
rkr@informatik.uni-kiel.de

Abstract

The extraction of valuable information from the vast amount of digital data available today has become increasingly important, making named entity recognition models an essential component of information extraction processes. This emphasizes the importance of understanding the factors that can compromise the performance of these models. Many studies have examined the impact of data annotation errors on NER models, leaving the broader implication of overall data quality on these models unexplored. In this work, we evaluate the robustness of three prominent NER models on datasets with varying amounts and types of noise. The results show that as the noise in the dataset increases, model performance declines, with a minor impact for some noise types and a significant drop in performance for others. The findings of this research can be used as a foundation for building more robust NER systems by enhancing dataset quality beforehand.

1 Introduction

Named entity recognition (NER) is an NLP task that identifies and categorizes mentions of named entities in texts into predefined categories within a given application context (Ehrmann et al., 2021). NER models are used in many downstream applications and are becoming an integral part of their implementation (Li et al., 2022). These models must be trained on task-specific data to work well with a specific application because an NER model learns the relationship between the data elements and applies this knowledge to find similar terms in the unseen data. If the model is trained on poor-quality data, it may not learn well and most likely fail to recognize or assign the wrong category to the named entities in new, unseen data.

The term "data quality" is used in information systems to measure the goodness of the data in fulfilling the requirements of a user (Wang and Strong, 1996). Data is considered high quality if it is suitable for the intended application and does not contain errors that can undermine its use (Hassenstein and Vanella, 2022).

With the advancement and easy access to digital technology, data in different domains is widely available and growing exponentially (Hassenstein and Vanella, 2022), thus creating the need to understand the fitness of the data for the desired application. This research aims to analyze the impact of various noise types to understand the effect of data quality on the performance of NER models.

The concept of data quality was discussed in detail by Wang and Strong (1996), and the idea was to look at the quality of data from the user's perspective and divide data quality into various categories to understand their origin and impact. This study analyzes the effect of four different types of noise: spelling errors, typo errors, optical character recognition (OCR) errors, and sentence shortening errors (SSE). These errors fall into the following data quality categories (Wang and Strong, 1996):

- The intrinsic quality dimension includes a subcategory called accuracy. It is concerned with the data's reliability and integrity. Spelling, typos, and OCR errors fall under this category, as the accuracy of any textual dataset is directly affected by characters, words, and even numeric values.
- Completeness is a quality dimension in the contextual category used to determine whether data is complete and appropriate for the chosen task. When sentence-shortening errors occur, context information is lost, affecting the data's completeness.

Many NER-specific ML models do not compare the performance based on the dataset quality. After a simple data cleaning step, the main focus is on finding suitable hyperparameters during training.

Proceedings of the Ninth Workshop on Noisy and User-generated Text (W-NUT 2024), pages 79–88
March 22, 2024 ©2024 Association for Computational Linguistics

There is no denying that hyperparameter tuning is an essential part of a well-trained model. However, all data-dependent models must be trained on high-quality data to make reliable future predictions on unseen data (Budach et al., 2022). The limited number of research (Hamdi et al., 2020; Bodapati et al., 2019) about the impact of data quality on NER systems creates a natural curiosity to question whether a model trained on good-quality data will make better predictions than a model trained on noisy data and if the NER-based NLP models should include data quality checks. This study observes the behavior of various models and tests their robustness with variable proportions of each error type and their combination on the CoNLL 2003 (Tjong Kim Sang and De Meulder, 2003), WNUT 16 (Strauss et al., 2016) and Ontonotes v5 (Pradhan et al., 2013) datasets. Specifically, the focus of this research is to answer the following questions:

- **RQ1:** What impact does data quality have on the performance of each NER model?
- **RQ2:** How do different types of individual noises affect NER model performance?
- **RQ3:** What effect does combining different types of noise have on the performance of an NER model?
- **RQ4:** What effect do different datasets with different noise types have on the performance of an NER model?

We published the code of our study in `https://github.com/HPI-Information-Systems/ner-text-quality-impact`

2 Background

The effect of OCR errors on the predictive capability of four NER models was investigated in a study by Hamdi et al. (2020). The results indicate a subsequent decline in the model's performance when trained on datasets containing OCR errors. The study also suggests that understanding the impact of the frequency of this error type before applying the models can enhance the performance of NER models. The study by Bodapati et al. (2019) investigates the robustness of NER models with capitalization errors. It demonstrates that the NER models trained with the customary training procedures do not perform well when tested against textual data with either capital or small-cased letters, and the model's predictive capability suffers greatly. Multiple studies have also been conducted to understand the impact of different types of noise on AI systems, and their results show that many state-of-the-art models are susceptible to even slight variations in data (Budach et al., 2022; Belinkov and Bisk, 2018; Náplava et al., 2021; Gudivada et al., 2017). When the performance of character level and word level processing models is compared, the former models are more resilient to changes in individual characters and can still understand the meaning and context of a word if there is a minor modification in the characters of the word, such as spelling or typo errors (Heigold et al., 2017).

Gudivada et al. (2017) also discusses some of the significant issues that machine learning (ML) models face as a result of poor data quality in the ML pipeline at two stages: training and testing. Even only a few outliers in the training dataset have been shown to cause instability in the learning process of the model and show how noisy data affects the prediction capabilities of the model. Al Sharou et al. (2021) discuss the intricate relationship between data quality and NLP systems, providing a distinction between different aspects of the noise types. It categorizes noise into two categories, good and bad, and explains how it can help NLP models make better predictions. It suggests that an error that seems detrimental to one kind of task can increase the accuracy of an NLP model curated for another domain. So, the data cleaning task should not be fixed for every NLP model, and without understanding the impact of various error types, it is a challenge to build reliable data validation systems.

With numerous studies demonstrating that data quality affects model performance, this study focuses primarily on analyzing the impact of various error types and their combination in the training and prediction phase of an NER model. The findings of this study can aid in the development of data cleaning or validation systems that are required before feeding any input data to an ML pipeline.

3 Noise Types in Text

In the real world, noise is present in all textual data. Different noise types have distinct origins, thus affecting the functioning of every model differently. The following noise types have been chosen to study their effect on NER model performance.

3.1 Spelling Errors

A correctly spelled word in any language is one whose spelling matches the dictionary spelling or, if not in the dictionary, is widely accepted by well-known writers and most speakers (Al Sharou et al., 2021). Any variation in these known spellings falls under the category of spelling errors.

3.2 Typographical Errors

Typo errors occur due to mistakes in typing and are also called typos or misprints (Shah and de Melo, 2020). As more people use the internet to connect and communicate, the emphasis is not on writing everything carefully, resulting in many typos in online texts. These errors may appear to be spelling mistakes, but they are distinct because typos occur due to fast typing or fingers slipping on the keyboard.

3.3 OCR Errors

Optical character resolution, or OCR, is a technological process of converting various digitized documents into a format that computers understand (Kissos and Dershowitz, 2016). The documents generated by the OCR process can be edited like any document typed on a computer. Two contributing factors to OCR errors are the poor image quality of the documents used and the use of different training instances for the OCR image classifier.

3.4 Sentence Shortening Errors

Sentence shortening errors or cut-off (Shen et al., 2020) is a prevalent noise in textual data where a certain amount of words are missing due to informal writing, very commonly seen on social media platforms or in automatic speech recognition systems (ASR) (Cunha Sergio and Lee, 2021). Such partial removal is used to check the robustness of context-based models, especially language models, such as BERT (Devlin et al., 2019), which infer the meaning of a word in the context of the entire sentence.

4 Models

This section briefly describes the three well-known NER models selected for this study. Each model uses a different architecture to identify and extract named entities. The first is a machine learning model, and the next two are deep learning models.

4.1 Condition Random Field

Conditional random fields (CRFs) is a discriminative machine learning model that predicts data points related to each other (Sutton and McCallum, 2010). A discriminative model uses the input data to predict the output class label by creating a direct mapping between the input data and the output label (Ng and Jordan, 2002). Patil et al. (2020) explains that the CRF model uses an undirected graphical model for the named entity identification. This graph connects each observation to other observations without any specific direction. Given the context of an observation, CRFs calculate the probability of it being a particular named entity. The CRF uses the concept of feature functions to know about the various features of each variable and thus understand the relationship between them. For the study of NER datasets (Sutton and McCallum, 2010), named-entity labels are dependent on their adjacent observation, so the simplest form of CRF, called the linear CRF, is used.

4.2 BERT

Bidirectional encoder representation from transformers (BERT), proposed by Devlin et al. (2019), is a powerful, well-known, and revolutionary model in the field of NLP. The first step of BERT is pre-training, where the model is trained on an unlabeled, unstructured large dataset to understand the bidirectional context, resulting in pre-trained language models. This pre-training step is self-supervised and can be completed without labeled data leveraging the masked language modeling and next sentence prediction training objectives. Our study uses 'bert-based-cased' pre-trained model for training the models on the selected datasets. The second step is fine-tuning, where the model is further trained using an additional output layer. This training uses labeled data of specific domains or genres to learn the parameters of the new layer and update the pre-trained parameters. For the specific case of NER, each token in a sentence has a classification head responsible for identifying the labels under the IOB scheme (Ehrmann et al., 2021).

4.3 BiLSTM + Flair Embeddings

Flair is an NLP library based on the PyTorch framework, which supports multiple tasks, such as named entity recognition, part-of-speech tagging, and text classification (Akbik et al., 2019). Flair introduces its own character-based embedding technique and provides support for various other embedding models. In this study, the Flair model uses the combination of Flair embeddings (Akbik et al., 2018) with classic word embeddings, e.g. GloVe (Pennington et al., 2014) for the CoNLL 2003 dataset, fastText (Bojanowski et al., 2017) for the OntoNotes v5 dataset, and GloVe(twitter) and fastText for the WNUT 16 dataset. Embeddings are created using the unified interface of the Flair library. This unified interface allows the implementation of various embeddings using the same code. The sequence labeling model of the Flair library is trained for NER using BiLSTMs to capture the information from both directions.

Each of the three models employs a different architecture to capture token and context meaning or any intricate information in the data. This diverse selection of models in this study is used to see which architecture is more resilient to the selected errors.

5 Datasets

Three well-known NER datasets are chosen for this experiment based on two criteria: the number of words with various class labels and the amount of noise in the dataset. The goal is to evaluate the models on small, moderate, and large datasets. All datasets contain information from different domains, and the noise level varies. Three text files containing the train, test, and validation sets are created for each dataset, following the IOB scheme. To have an idea of the amount of noise already present in the datasets, we measure existing misspellings using a spellchecker library.[1]

5.1 WNUT 16 Dataset

The first dataset selected for this research is the WNUT 16 dataset (Strauss et al., 2016). This dataset was created to analyze the challenges posed by the enormous amount of data generated on social media platforms, such as Twitter, which usually have user-generated noisy content. The WNUT 16[2] is a small-scale dataset as compared to the other two datasets considered for this study and consists of manually annotated tweets specially annotated to serve as a training ground for the NER systems. Out of the total words in the training and test set, $3,613$ (7.78%) and $7,274$ (11.75%) respectively are misspellings according to the spellchecker.

[1] https://pypi.org/project/pyspellchecker/

[2] https://github.com/jinpeng01/hgn

5.2 CoNLL 2003 Dataset

The second NER dataset selected for this study is the English CoNLL-2003 dataset (Tjong Kim Sang and De Meulder, 2003). The words in this dataset were annotated for four named entity types: person, location, organization, and miscellaneous. The English dataset was downloaded from the huggingface open source platform[3]. Out of the total words in the training and test set, $7,785$ (3.82%) and $2,584$ (5.56%) respectively are misspellings.

5.3 OntoNote v5 Dataset

The third dataset selected for this study is the OntoNotes v5 English dataset, the latest release in the OntoNotes (Pradhan et al., 2013) dataset series[4]. The dataset files were downloaded from the huggingface open source platform [5]. OntoNotes is a large-scale dataset, and along with classic NER entity types, it contains a large corpus of annotations. Out of the total words in the training and test set, $19,615$ (0.89%) and $2,822$ (0.12%) respectively are misspellings.

6 Experimental Setup

The most important task in this study is to create many different versions of train and test datasets with varying error types and rates. The subsections will briefly introduce the data augmentation steps, training process, and evaluation metrics selected for this study.

6.1 Dataset Modifications with Various Noise Types

The three datasets contain three files: train, validate, and test. The various noise types and their combinations are introduced in the train and test sets keeping the validation set untouched for all datasets in this study. For the WNUT 16 and CoNLL 2003 datasets, five datasets were generated from each train and test set for spelling, typos, OCR, and combination of all error types to conduct a thorough analysis. The error types are introduced using the NLPAug library.[6]

The number of word manipulations in a dataset varies for each error type. We decided, based on two separate studies, the minimum threshold for

[3] https://huggingface.co/datasets/conll2003

[4] https://doi.org/10.35111/xmhb-2b84

[5] https://huggingface.co/datasets/conll2012_ontonotesv5

[6] https://github.com/makcedward/nlpaug

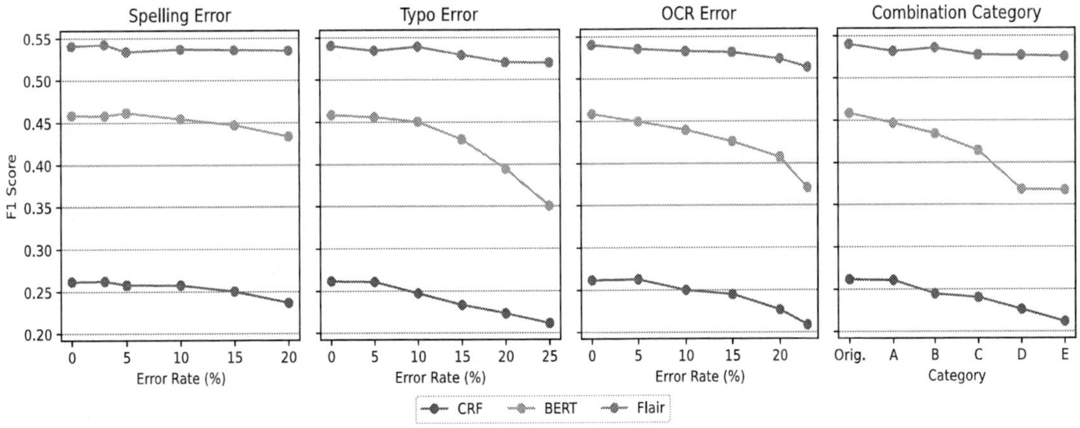

Figure 1: WNUT 16 dataset results with CRF, BERT, and Flair with various error rates for Spelling, Typo, OCR, and Combination of errors in train set

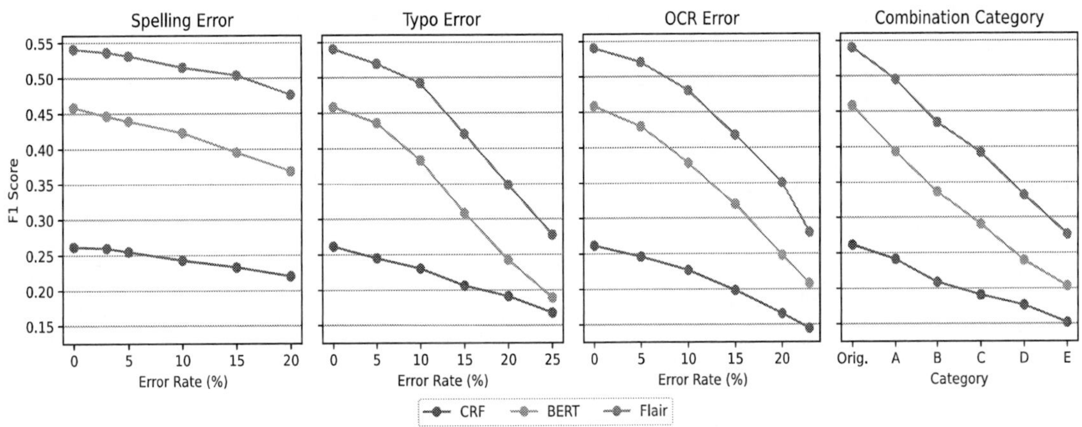

Figure 2: WNUT 16 dataset results with CRF, BERT, and Flair with various error rates for Spelling, Typo, OCR, and Combination of errors in test set

spelling (Flor et al., 2015) and typos (Rodríguez-Rubio and Fernández-Quesada, 2020) errors. The maximum threshold for OCR was taken from the study of Tong and Evans (2002), and errors are introduced in descending order from a higher to a lower number. The process of creating modified datasets with spelling, typo, and OCR errors is as follows:

- Five datasets are created for spelling errors with an increasing error rate of 3%, 5%, 10%, 15%, and 20%.
- Similar to spelling errors, five new datasets are generated for typos with the increasing error rate of 5%, 10%, 15%, 20%, and 25%.
- For OCR error, five datasets are created with an error rate of 5%, 10%, 15%, 20%, and 23%.

For the OntoNotes v5 dataset, we use only the lowest and highest error rates for each error type. As the model training using OntoNotes requires a much longer training time than the other two datasets, only two error rates are evaluated.

We follow a different process for SSE errors than the other error types. We divide the dataset into chunks of 450 words.[7] Then, we use a uniform distribution of 1 to 10 to remove words from the end of this chunk, thus creating a new dataset that simulates sentence shortening at the end of physical pages.

For the combination of errors, first, the SSE error

[7] On average, an A4 page contains 400 to 500 words, assuming it has a default margin, 12-point font size, and 1.5 line spacing. So, an average of 450 words per page is assumed for SSE errors.

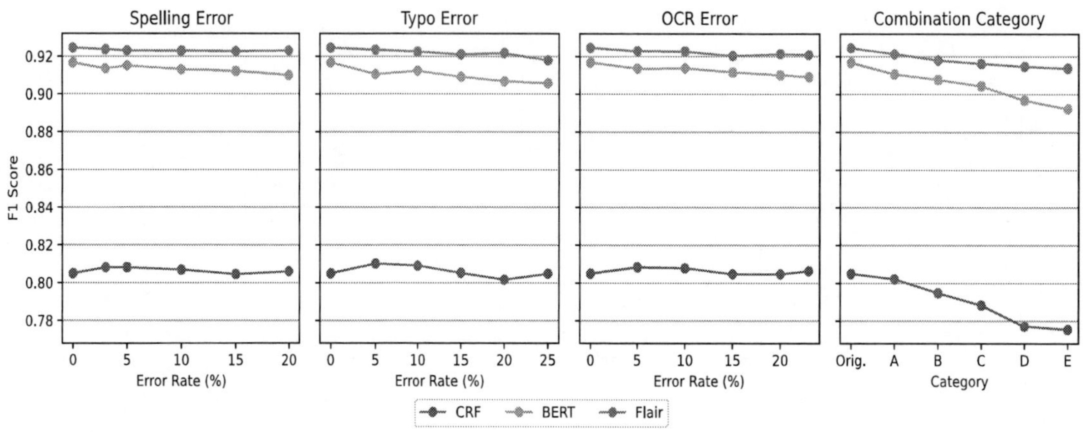

Figure 3: CoNLL 2003 dataset results with CRF, BERT, and Flair with various error rates for Spelling, Typo, OCR, and Combination of errors in train set

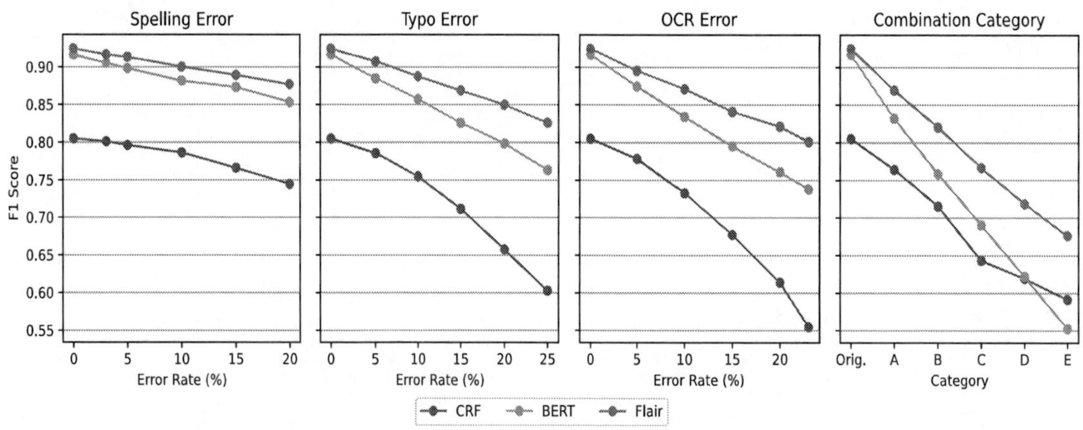

Figure 4: CoNLL 2003 dataset results with CRF, BERT, and Flair with various error rates for Spelling, Typo, OCR, and Combination of errors in test set

procedure is applied to the dataset, and then various combinations[8] of error rates are introduced to this dataset.

The process is repeated for two more seed values on the training set of each dataset, creating 15 modified training sets for each spelling, typo, OCR, and combination of errors and 3 datasets with SSE. Similarly, the test set of each dataset is infiltrated with various noise types but with only one seed value.

[8]Apply SSE then create five new datasets, A: 3% spelling error, 5% typos, and 5% OCR errors, B: 5% spelling error, 10% typos and 10% OCR errors, C: 10% spelling error, 15% typos and 15% OCR errors, D: 15% spelling error, 20% typos and 20% OCR errors, and E: 20% spelling error, 25% typos, and 23% OCR errors

6.2 Training Process

At first, each model is trained using the original train and validation sets. Then, for analyzing the impact of various noise types, the process is divided into two parts:

1. **Training the model with altered training datasets:** The model with the same configuration as the original dataset is trained with the modified train datasets. We make predictions on the unaltered test dataset to compare the model's performance with the original dataset.

2. **Testing the original model with noisy test datasets:** The model trained on the original dataset is used for predictions on noisy train datasets to analyze the effectiveness of models trained on less noisy data to predict noisy text.

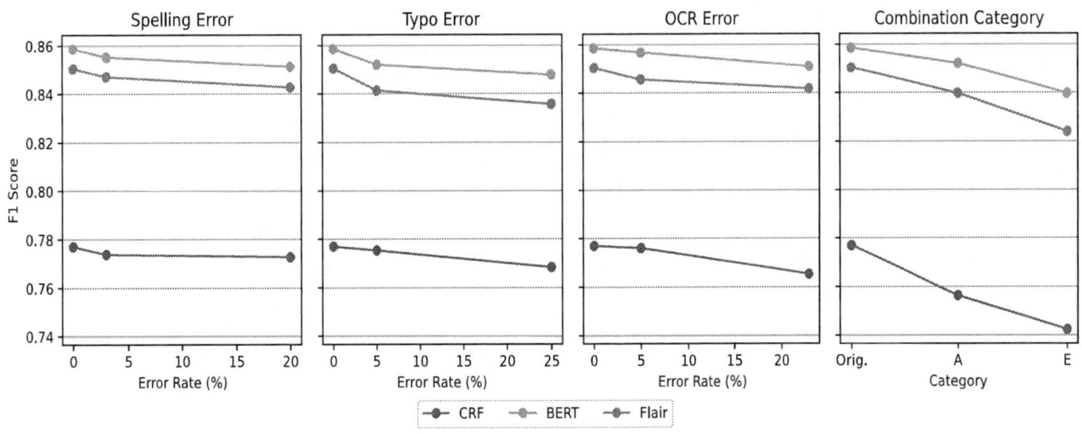

Figure 5: OntoNotes v5 dataset results with CRF, BERT, and Flair with various error rates for Spelling, Typo, OCR, and Combination of errors in train set

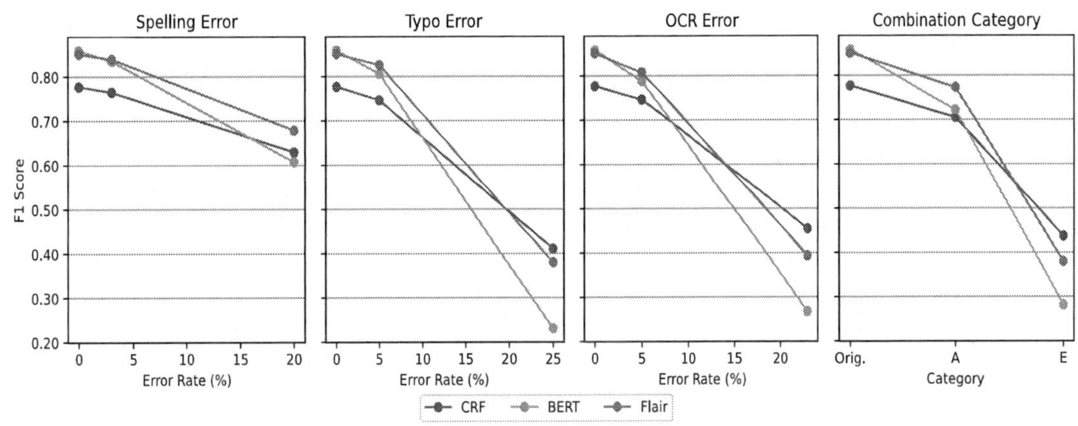

Figure 6: OntoNotes v5 dataset results with CRF, BERT, and Flair with various error rates for Spelling, Typo, OCR, and Combination of errors in test set

6.3 Evaluation Metrics

The results of all three models are presented using the micro-averaged F1 score, and for any further investigation, individual F1 scores with precision and recall for each class label are analyzed. We report the average over the different seeds.

7 Results

Two sets of experiments are performed for each model with a dataset, as mentioned in subsection 6.2. The results for each dataset are shown in two diagrams containing four subplots for spelling, typo, OCR, and combinations of all errors. The two figures for each dataset show the results with various error rates in the training and testing dataset. In plots, the numeric value 0 and the term "Orig." are used for a dataset without any added noise types. The term F1 score in all diagrams and table shows the micro F1 score obtained from all the experiments. The result of SSE for each dataset is shown in Table 1. The F1 score obtained after all experiments indicates that the SSE does not have any significant impact on the performance of the selected models.

7.1 WNUT 16 Dataset

Of all the models' performances on the WNUT 16 dataset, the BiLSTM combined with Flair embeddings has shown the best result on the original dataset, and models trained on a noisy training set. Figure 1 shows a constant decline in the performance of both the BERT and CRF models, and the most decline in performance is observed with the combinations of various error types (0.02 for Flair, 0.09 for BERT, and 0.05 for CRF).

Datasets	Model	Original	SSE	
			Train	Test
CoNLL 2003	CRF	0.8050	0.8041	0.8030
	BERT	0.9167	0.9146	0.9152
	Flair	0.9246	0.9252	0.9233
WNUT 16	CRF	0.2617	0.2626	0.2612
	BERT	0.4586	0.4534	0.4563
	Flair	0.5405	0.5384	0.5391
OntoNotes v5	CRF	0.7770	0.7630	0.7761
	BERT	0.8586	0.8578	0.8544
	Flair	0.8504	0.8450	0.8492

Table 1: The Table shows the F1 score obtained from all three models on each dataset for SSE. The train column contains the F1 score when SSE was introduced in the training set and the F1 score is obtained on the original test set. The test column contains the F1 score when the model trained on the original dataset is tested on a test set containing SSE errors.

Figure 2 shows that the model with the original WNUT dataset, when used on noisy test datasets with an increasing error rate, suffers a steep decline in prediction capability. For the combination of errors, BiLSTM combined with Flair embeddings F1 score decreased by 0.26, BERT by 0.26, and CRF by 0.09). The BiLSTM combined with Flair embeddings, which was very robust with errors in the training dataset, did not perform well on noisy test data.

7.2 CoNLL 2003 Dataset

Figure 3 shows the overall performance of each model on the CoNLL 2003 training datasets. The BiLSTM combined with Flair embeddings performed the best on the original dataset, but the CRF model is most robust towards individual errors. Its performance declines with a combination of errors. Out of all models, BERT's performance is affected by all error types, and the most decline in its performance is observed with the combination of errors where the F1 score has dropped from 0.9167 to 0.8924. Figure 4 shows the performance of the CoNLL 2003 model trained with the original dataset and tested on the noisy test dataset. The performance of CRF on noisy test datasets shows continuous declining performance.

7.3 OntoNotes v5 Dataset

Figure 5 shows the results of models trained on a noisy training set of the OntoNotes v5 dataset. The results of BiLSTM combined with Flair embeddings show robustness to individual errors, but performance suffers when multiple error types are combined. The performance of the BERT and CRF models does not degrade significantly.

The performance of models trained on the original OntoNotes v5 dataset declines continuously, similar to the results of the WNUT 16 and CoNLL 2003 on the test dataset. Figure 6 shows that the BiLSTMs with the Flair embeddings performance is the most affected by all individual and combination errors out of all models. The model's F1 score has come down from 0.8504 to 0.2302 with typo errors in the test dataset.

The observations with respect to the research questions stated in the introduction are as follows:

RQ1: What impact does data quality have on the performance of each NER model?
The quality of a dataset has a different impact on different architectures. The BiLSTM combined with Flair embeddings shows more resilience and the best F1 score on both the original and variations of the training dataset for the WNUT 16 and CoNLL 2003 datasets. With the variations of all noise types in the test set, all models show a steep decline in performance.

RQ2: How do different types of individual noises affect NER model performance?

Individual error analysis reveals that all models are more resistant to spelling errors than typos or OCR errors. Furthermore, for the NER task, removing a small percentage of data for SSE has little effect on model performance.

RQ3:What effect does combining different types of noise have on the performance of an

NER model?

A combination of all errors, even with a small percentage of each noise type, has always resulted in decreased performance for all models on all datasets.

RQ4: What effect do different datasets with different noise types have on the performance of an NER model?

On the high-quality CoNLL 2003 dataset, the performance of each model with increased noise is not affected as much as the addition of noise to the already noisy WNUT 16 datasets.

8 Conclusion

This paper investigated the effect of different types of textual noise on NER models by artificially adding noise to training and testing datasets at different rates. Our goal was to experiment with different levels of noise based on real-world, observed levels for each category. The results showed that each error has a different impact on the NER models, with the OCR and combination of all errors having the most significant impact. The influence of errors in the test dataset is severe compared to that in the training set, and in a few cases, the high error rate shows the models' inability to make useful predictions.

Acknowledgements

This research was partially funded by the HPI Research School on Data Science and Engineering.

References

Alan Akbik, Tanja Bergmann, Duncan Blythe, Kashif Rasul, Stefan Schweter, and Roland Vollgraf. 2019. FLAIR: An easy-to-use framework for state-of-the-art NLP. In *Proceedings of the 2019 Conference of the North American Chapter of the Association for Computational Linguistics (Demonstrations)*, pages 54–59, Minneapolis, Minnesota. Association for Computational Linguistics.

Alan Akbik, Duncan Blythe, and Roland Vollgraf. 2018. Contextual string embeddings for sequence labeling. In *COLING 2018, 27th International Conference on Computational Linguistics*, pages 1638–1649.

Khetam Al Sharou, Zhenhao Li, and Lucia Specia. 2021. Towards a better understanding of noise in natural language processing. In *Proceedings of the International Conference on Recent Advances in Natural Language Processing (RANLP 2021)*, pages 53–62, Held Online. INCOMA Ltd.

Yonatan Belinkov and Yonatan Bisk. 2018. Synthetic and natural noise both break neural machine translation.

Sravan Bodapati, Hyokun Yun, and Yaser Al-Onaizan. 2019. Robustness to capitalization errors in named entity recognition. In *Proceedings of the 5th Workshop on Noisy User-generated Text (W-NUT 2019)*, pages 237–242, Hong Kong, China. Association for Computational Linguistics.

Piotr Bojanowski, Edouard Grave, Armand Joulin, and Tomas Mikolov. 2017. Enriching word vectors with subword information. *Transactions of the Association for Computational Linguistics*, 5:135–146.

Lukas Budach, Moritz Feuerpfeil, Nina Ihde, Andrea Nathansen, Nele Noack, Hendrik Patzlaff, Felix Naumann, and Hazar Harmouch. 2022. The effects of data quality on machine learning performance.

Gwenaelle Cunha Sergio and Minho Lee. 2021. Stacked debert: All attention in incomplete data for text classification. *Neural Networks*, 136:87–96.

Jacob Devlin, Ming-Wei Chang, Kenton Lee, and Kristina Toutanova. 2019. Bert: Pre-training of deep bidirectional transformers for language understanding. In *North American Chapter of the Association for Computational Linguistics*.

Maud Ehrmann, Ahmed Hamdi, Elvys Linhares Pontes, Matteo Romanello, and Antoine Doucet. 2021. Named entity recognition and classification on historical documents: A survey.

Michael Flor, Yoko Futagi, Melissa Lopez, and Matthew Mulholland. 2015. Patterns of misspellings in 12 and 11 english: a view from the ets spelling corpus. volume 6.

Venkat N. Gudivada, Amy W. Apon, and Junhua Ding. 2017. Data quality considerations for big data and machine learning: Going beyond data cleaning and transformations.

Ahmed Hamdi, Axel Jean-Caurant, Nicolas Sidere, Mickaël Coustaty, and Antoine Doucet. 2020. Assessing and minimizing the impact of ocr quality on named entity recognition. Springer International Publishing.

Max J. Hassenstein and Patrizio Vanella. 2022. Data quality; concepts and problems. *Encyclopedia*, 2(1):498–510.

Georg Heigold, Günter Neumann, and Josef van Genabith. 2017. How robust are character-based word embeddings in tagging and mt against wrod scramlbing or randdm nouse?

Ido Kissos and Nachum Dershowitz. 2016. Ocr error correction using character correction and feature-based word classification. In *2016 12th IAPR Workshop on Document Analysis Systems (DAS)*, pages 198–203.

Jing Li, Aixin Sun, Jianglei Han, and Chenliang Li. 2022. A survey on deep learning for named entity recognition. *IEEE Transactions on Knowledge and Data Engineering*, 34(1):50–70.

Andrew Ng and Michael Jordan. 2002. On discriminative vs. generative classifiers: A comparison of logistic regression and naive bayes. *Adv. Neural Inf. Process. Sys*, 2.

Jakub Náplava, Martin Popel, Milan Straka, and Jana Straková. 2021. Understanding model robustness to user-generated noisy texts.

Nita Patil, Ajay Patil, and Bhausaheb Pawar. 2020. Named entity recognition using conditional random fields. *Procedia Computer Science*, 167:1181–1188.

Jeffrey Pennington, Richard Socher, and Christopher Manning. 2014. GloVe: Global vectors for word representation. In *Proceedings of the 2014 Conference on Empirical Methods in Natural Language Processing (EMNLP)*, pages 1532–1543, Doha, Qatar. Association for Computational Linguistics.

Sameer Pradhan, Alessandro Moschitti, Nianwen Xue, Hwee Tou Ng, Anders Björkelund, Olga Uryupina, Yuchen Zhang, and Zhi Zhong. 2013. Towards robust linguistic analysis using OntoNotes. In *Proceedings of the Seventeenth Conference on Computational Natural Language Learning*, pages 143–152, Sofia, Bulgaria. Association for Computational Linguistics.

Santiago Rodríguez-Rubio and Nuria Fernández-Quesada. 2020. Towards Accuracy: A Model for the Analysis of Typographical Errors in Specialised Bilingual Dictionaries. Two Case Studies. *Lexikos*, 30:386 – 415.

Kshitij Shah and Gerard de Melo. 2020. Correcting the autocorrect: Context-aware typographical error correction via training data augmentation. In *Proceedings of the Twelfth Language Resources and Evaluation Conference*, pages 6930–6936, Marseille, France. European Language Resources Association.

Dinghan Shen, Mingzhi Zheng, Yelong Shen, Yanru Qu, and Weizhu Chen. 2020. A simple but tough-to-beat data augmentation approach for natural language understanding and generation.

Benjamin Strauss, Bethany Toma, Alan Ritter, Marie-Catherine de Marneffe, and Wei Xu. 2016. Results of the WNUT16 named entity recognition shared task. In *Proceedings of the 2nd Workshop on Noisy User-generated Text (WNUT)*, pages 138–144, Osaka, Japan. The COLING 2016 Organizing Committee.

Charles Sutton and Andrew McCallum. 2010. An introduction to conditional random fields.

Erik F. Tjong Kim Sang and Fien De Meulder. 2003. Introduction to the CoNLL-2003 shared task: Language-independent named entity recognition. In *Proceedings of the Seventh Conference on Natural Language Learning at HLT-NAACL 2003*, pages 142–147.

Xiang Tong and David Evans. 2002. A statistical approach to automatic ocr error.

Richard Y. Wang and Diane M. Strong. 1996. Beyond accuracy: What data quality means to data consumers. 12(4):5–33.

Topic Bias in Emotion Classification

Maximilian Wegge[1] and **Roman Klinger**[1,2]
[1]Institut für Maschinelle Sprachverarbeitung, University of Stuttgart, Germany
[2]Fundamentals of Natural Language Processing, University of Bamberg, Germany
maximilian.wegge@ims.uni-stuttgart.de
roman.klinger@uni-bamberg.de

Abstract

Emotion corpora are typically sampled based on keyword/hashtag search or by asking study participants to generate textual instances. In any case, these corpora are not uniform samples representing the entirety of a domain. We hypothesize that this practice of data acquisition leads to unrealistic correlations between overrepresented topics in these corpora that harm the generalizability of models. Such topic bias could lead to wrong predictions for instances like "I organized the service for my aunt's funeral." when funeral events are overrepresented for instances labeled with sadness, despite the emotion of pride being more appropriate here. In this paper, we study this topic bias both from the data and the modeling perspective. We first label a set of emotion corpora automatically via topic modeling and show that emotions in fact correlate with specific topics. Further, we see that emotion classifiers are confounded by such topics. Finally, we show that the established debiasing method of adversarial correction via gradient reversal mitigates the issue. Our work points out issues with existing emotion corpora and that more representative resources are required for fair evaluation of models predicting affective concepts from text.

1 Introduction

Emotion analysis is typically formulated as the task of emotion classification, i.e., assigning emotions to textual units such as news headlines, social media or blog posts. Emotion classification is applied across various domains, ranging from political debates (Mohammad et al., 2014) to dialogs (Li et al., 2017) and literary texts (Mohammad, 2011), and enable further use cases such as analyzing emotions of social media users (e.g., in response to the COVID-19 pandemic, Zhan et al., 2022), identifying abusive language using emotional cues (Safi Samghabadi et al., 2020) or developing empathetic dialog agents, e.g., for emotional support (Liu et al., 2021).

Emotions are thereby modeled as either discrete classes of basic emotions (Ekman, 1992; Plutchik, 2001), within the vector space of valence and arousal (Russell, 1980), or as the result of the emoter's cognitive appraisal of the stimulus event (Scherer, 2005; Smith and Lazarus, 1990). Independent of which emotion theory is adopted, emotion data sets are commonly collected by searching for topics of interest, for instance with hashtags on social media (Schuff et al., 2017, i.a.) or by using specific subfora (Stranisci et al., 2022), in order to cover a variety of emotion labels instead of generally overrepresented ones. Another common approach is to ask study participants to report emotional episodes for a given emotion (Troiano et al., 2023, 2019; Scherer and Wallbott, 1994, i.a.). In that case, subjects are more likely to report important, long enduring, high-impact events than less relevant ones. Cases in which large corpora are uniformly sampled for annotation are comparably rare (Alm et al., 2005, i.a.).

We hypothesize that these established sampling procedures are harmful. They lead to topics overrepresented for specific emotions which allows the model to rely on spurious signals instead of actual emotion expressions. As an example, in *"I enjoyed my birthday party."* a model might learn to associate the topic of "party" with *joy*, instead of inferring the emotion from the text (here, the verb). That might then lead to wrong predictions for texts such as *"I did not like my party."*. We assume that this is also a reason for poor cross-corpus generalization of emotion classification (cf. Bostan and Klinger, 2018).

In this paper, we aim at understanding the prevalence and impact of this phenomenon in the context of emotion analysis. We answer the following research questions:

1. *Are emotion datasets biased towards topics?* We show that emotion datasets are biased towards topics, i.e., that there is a prototypical

Proceedings of the Ninth Workshop on Noisy and User-generated Text (W-NUT 2024), pages 89–103
March 22, 2024 ©2024 Association for Computational Linguistics

association of topics with emotion labels specific for each corpus.

2. *Is emotion classification influenced by topics?* Based on the observation of topic biases in datasets, we show that this bias also carries over to emotion prediction models.
3. *Can the influence of topics on emotion classification be mitigated?* We show that the robustness of emotion classifiers can be improved by using established debiasing methods which reduce the impact of the topic bias on the classifiers.

We perform the experiments on emotion self-report corpora (Scherer and Wallbott, 1994; Troiano et al., 2023; Hofmann et al., 2020), social media data from Twitter (Schuff et al., 2017) and Reddit (Stranisci et al., 2022), as well as on fictional stories (Alm et al., 2005). With these annotated corpora, we cover (i) a variety of domains and (ii) multiple emotion models.

2 Related Work

2.1 Emotion Classification

Computational approaches to emotion analysis often adopt categories inspired by theories of basic emotions (Ekman, 1999; Plutchik, 1982), by modeling emotions as six (*anger*, *fear*, *joy*, *sadness*, *disgust*, *surprise*) or eight (adding *anticipation*, *trust*) discrete classes. Alternatives include the use of the valence–arousal vector space to position emotion categories (Russell, 1980) or focus on the aspect that emotions are caused by events that undergo a cognitive evaluation (Scherer, 2005; Smith and Lazarus, 1990). In the latter case, emotions are represented by appraisal variables, including, for instance, if the event requires attention, if the person involved is certain about what is happening, if the outcome requires further effort, is pleasant, or if the person has been responsible or can control the situation.

The emotion model is sometimes, but not always, chosen based on the domain a corpus stems from. For instance, Schuff et al. (2017) reannotate a stance detection corpus with Plutchik's eight emotions due to their presumed universality. Alm et al. (2005) follow Ekman's model for a similar reason. Scherer and Wallbott (1994); Hofmann et al. (2020) choose a set of self-directed emotions because their data consists of self-reports. Troiano et al. (2023) use a larger set of emotions, and also annotate appraisal dimensions because of the prevalence of event descriptions in the texts they collected, similarly to Stranisci et al. (2022).

To develop automatic emotion classification methods, as in many areas of NLP, transformer-based pre-trained language models like BERT (Devlin et al., 2019) and RoBERTa (Liu et al., 2019) have been found to consistently outperform previous state-of-the-art approaches. These models are fine-tuned on domain-specific corpora. Bostan and Klinger (2018) show for 14 popular emotion datasets that a cross-corpus prediction performance is drastically lower than for in-corpus classification. We hypothesize that a major part of what makes a domain unique is the distribution of topics.

2.2 Bias

Bias has been found to affect various textual resources, including those to support hate-speech detection (Wich et al., 2020), sentiment analysis (Wang et al., 2021), machine translation (Stanovsky et al., 2019) or argument mining (Spliethöver and Wachsmuth, 2020). In general, the term bias refers to the phenomenon that machine learning models adopt latent, "non-generalizable features" (Shah et al., 2020) from the training data, such as domain-specific terms, contexts, or text styles. In consequence, the biased representation leads to erroneous results when applied to a domain where the alleged standard does not hold (cf. Hovy and Prabhumoye, 2021), which can lead to harmful impact on various groups in our society.

Topic bias originates in skewed topic representations. Wiegand et al. (2019), for instance, find the topic of *soccer* to be almost exclusively associated with abusive language, caused by the sampling procedure. In this paper, topic bias is understood to comprise two of these concepts: First, the association of certain emotion or appraisal labels with certain topics and second, the resulting bias in a classifier towards certain topics when predicting the emotion and appraisal labels.

Detection and Mitigation. For detecting bias contained within pre-trained models and word embeddings, Caliskan et al. (2017) introduce the Word Embedding Association Test (WEAT) and Kurita et al. (2019) investigate gender bias within BERT word embeddings. Wiegand et al. (2019) calculate the pointwise mutual information between words and abusive language annotations. Nejadgholi and Kiritchenko (2020) train a topic model on a dataset and perform a qualitative analysis of the result.

Bias mitigation is addressed at either the data or the modeling level. Wiegand et al. (2019) sample additional texts of the overrepresented class. Barikeri et al. (2021) augment training data by instance duplication, replacing the biased term with an inverse term. He et al. (2019) tackle the bias correction during training by developing an intentionally biased classifier in order to identify the features that exhibit bias. This information is then used to train a debiased classifier which compensates for the biased features. Qian et al. (2019) adapt the language model's loss function in order to mitigate gender bias, introducing a new term to the loss function that aims at equalizing the probability of male and female words. In the context of mitigating the influence of domains on classification, gradient reversal has proven effective (Ganin et al., 2015).

3 Methods & Experimental Setting

We will now explain our method for topic-bias detection in emotion corpora and then the experimental setting to evaluate established mitigation methods in this domain.[1]

Definitions. We consider six different corpora, where each corpus $c \in C$ is modeled as a tuple consisting of a set of topic labels T_c, a set of instances I_c and a set of annotation labels L_c, where L_c is either from the set of overall appraisals ($L_c \subseteq A_C$) or emotion labels ($L_c \subseteq E_C$), where $A_C \cap E_C = \varnothing$.

Further, each instance $i_c \in I_c$ consists of a text $s_{i,c} = (s_1, s_2, \ldots, s_n)$, a topic label $t_{i,c} \in T_c$ and a set of emotion or appraisal labels $L_{i,c} = \{a_j, \ldots, a_k\} \subseteq L_c$. Some of the corpora we consider are labeled with multiple, i.e., one or more emotions. Appraisals are always annotated in a multi-label setting.

3.1 Topic-based Bias Detection

Inspired by Wiegand et al. (2019); Nejadgholi and Kiritchenko (2020), we train separate emotion classifiers tasked with predicting either the emotion or appraisal label $a \in L_{i,c}$, for each topic $t_c^{\text{out}} \in T_c$ in a given corpus. In the subset of the corpus used for training the classifier (T^{train}), instances with the topic label t_c^{out} are excluded, i.e., $T_c^{\text{train}} = \{t_{i,c} | t_{i,c} \in T_c, t_{i,c} \neq t_c^{\text{out}}\}$. The number of classifiers trained for a given corpus c is thus equal to $|T_c|$.

[1]The repository to replicate our experiments will be made available via `https://www.bamnlp.de/resources/`.

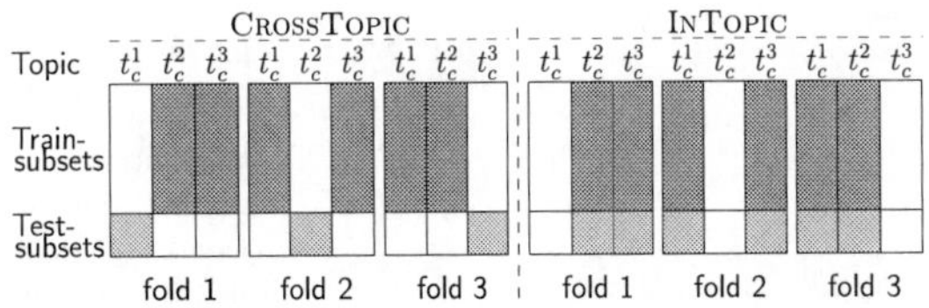

Figure 1: Visualization of the experimental setting for InTopic and CrossTopic predictions.

The classifiers are evaluated in two distinct settings: In the InTopic setting, multiple testsets are sampled from the corpus, one for each topic except t_c^{out}. Each testset is thus defined in relation to the respective held-out topic: $t_c^{\text{in}} = T_c \setminus \{t_c^{\text{out}}\}$. Thus, the union of all t_c^{in} per corpus reflects T_c^{train}. Therefore, a classifier trained on T_c^{train} is evaluated on all t_c^{in} of corpus c. For the CrossTopic setting, the classifier is evaluated on the held-out topic t_c^{out} which is not part of the training set T_c^{train}. In both settings, we calculate averages across folds which leads to a performance estimate whose comparisons are meaningful. Figure 1 visualizes this setup.

Topic Modeling. While emotion and appraisal annotations stem from the labels of the respective corpora, the topic labels need to be inferred from the data. We use BERTopic (Grootendorst, 2022), as it supports pre-trained transformer models to detect the semantic relations on sentence-level as well as HDBSCAN for clustering, averting the need of determining a fixed number of topics per dataset. This method has proven effective in previous research (Xu et al., 2022; Kellert and Mahmud Uz Zaman, 2022; Eklund and Forsman, 2022).

3.2 Bias Mitigation

We compare two established methods for debiasing the models with respect to topics.

Word Removal. As a straight-forward approach which still often shows a good performance (Dayanik and Padó, 2021, i.a.), the respective topic words are removed from the corpus. Specifically, we remove the most indicative words for each topic, according to the probabilities of the topic model.

Gradient Reversal. We compare this approach to the well-established method of adversarial learning through gradient reversal (Ganin et al., 2015). We extend the emotion/appraisal classifier by a topic predictor and gradient reversal layer, with the purpose of reversing the gradient (by multiplying it with $-\lambda$) of the following layer during backpropagation. Implementation details for all applied

	# Topics	∅ Topic	StD	Topic labels	# Instances	*Outlier*
ISEAR	10	525	290	love, exams, death, shame, school, animals, alcohol, accidents, fear, theft	7666	2412
SSEC	11	305	219	feminism, prayer, abortion, climate, clinton, twitter, trump, gay marriage, latino, swearing, patriotism	4870	1513
Tales	10	388	183	birds, flowers, tabitha twitchit, old english, piggies, royalty, dressmaking, hansel & gretel, boats, predators	10339	6457
enVENT	8	584	298	feelings, promotion, relationships, covid, dogs, graduation, pregnancy, driving	6600	1925
APPReddit	10	43	12	depression, everyday life, driving, love, romantic relationships, reddit, anger, death, platonic relationships, vaccination	780	352
enISEAR	13	58	25	death, dogs, accidents, theft, birth, food, affairs, UK politics, christmas, bullying, work, relationships, spooky	1001	245

Table 1: Number (#), average size (∅), standard deviation (StD), and manually assigned labels of the topics found by BERTopic for all corpora. All numbers exclude the outlier topic, whose number of instances is provided in the last column (*Outlier*). The topic labels are sorted by size, in decreasing order. The second to last column reports the number of all instances per corpus for reference. (We abbreviate the crowd-enVENT corpus in this paper as enVENT.)

methods are provided in Appendix A.

3.3 Data

We consider six corpora, each annotated for emotions or appraisal dimensions. We use the ISEAR (Scherer and Wallbott, 1994), SSEC (Stance Sentiment Emotion Corpus; Schuff et al., 2017) and Tales (Alm et al., 2005) corpora for emotion analysis and the APPReddit corpus (Stranisci et al., 2022) for appraisal analysis. From the enVENT (Troiano et al., 2023) and enISEAR (Troiano et al., 2019) corpora we use both annotation layers.

The corpora differ in size, annotation setup and – most relevant for us – in the way the instances are sampled and which topics are covered: ISEAR and enISEAR were created by asking study participants to report and describe events that caused a predefined emotion. ISEAR has been collected in an in-lab setup and enISEAR via crowdsourcing. Since participants were free to report any event that elicited one of the given emotions, they were also free in their choice of topic. This procedure is in fact expected to create a topic bias, because more important topics cause more intense emotions and are therefore more likely to be recalled. Therefore, Troiano et al. (2019) add diversification method to the otherwise similar setup. They mention topics that the study participants shall not report on.

In the SSEC corpus, Schuff et al. (2017) re-annotate Twitter posts originally collected by Mohammad et al. (2016). The original purpose of the text collection was to study sentiment and stance. Therefore, they have been collected with specific hashtags corresponding to topics "Atheism", "Climate Change is a Real Concern", "Feminist Movement", "Hillary Clinton", and "Legalization of Abortion". Arguably, we could have relied on these topics in the data, however for comparability in our experiments, we also use the topic modelling approach for this dataset.

The APPReddit corpus provides appraisal annotations of Reddit posts, sourced from subreddits mostly connotated with negative sentiment (Anger, offmychest, helpmecope anxiety, i.a.). The Tales corpus (Alm et al., 2005) features literary texts, specifically fairy tales by various authors. Here, sentences from uniformly sampled stories are the unit of annotation.

In order to enable inter-comparability, we map the varying annotation schemes onto a unified scheme. More information on the datasets is in Appendix B.

4 Results

We will now present the results to answer the research questions introduced in Section 1.

4.1 Are emotions biased towards topics?

Topic Modelling Results. Table 1 reports the results of the topic modeling at the overall corpus level, including the number of topics, the average size (number of instances) and the list of topic labels (L_c) for each corpus. The topic labels are defined manually, based on the ten most representative words for each topic.

The size of topics, i.e., the number of instances associated with it, varies across corpora (see ∅ and StD). The number of topics ranges from 8 (enVENT) to 13 (enISEAR), while ISEAR, Tales

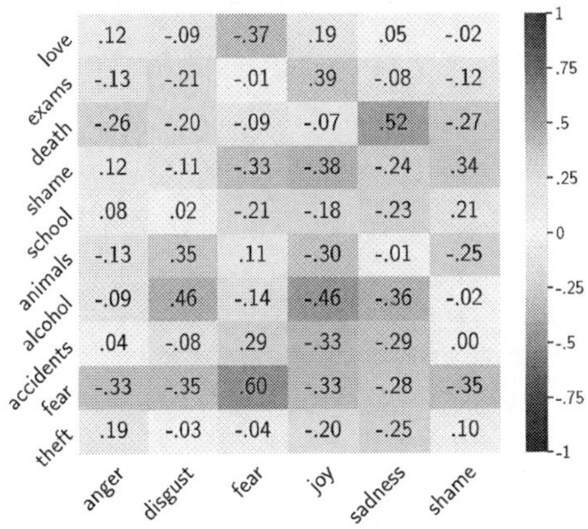

Figure 2: Normalized pointwise mutual information between topics and emotion annotations in ISEAR.

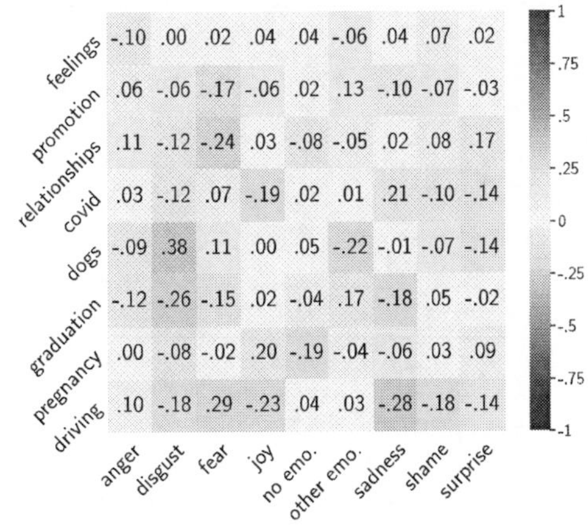

Figure 3: Normalized pointwise mutual information between topics and emotion annotations in ENVENT.

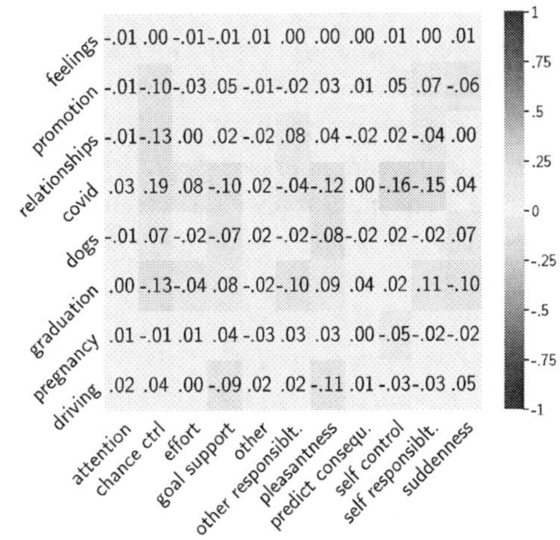

Figure 4: Normalized pointwise mutual information between topics and appraisal annotations in ENVENT.

and APPREDDIT comprise 10, ISEAR 11 topics.

An important finding is that, despite not being informed in a supervised manner regarding the emotion labels, the topics reflect the individual corpus' domain and sampling methods. ISEAR, ENISEAR and ENVENT, all of which are compiled by querying emotionally connotated event-descriptions, feature generic and everyday topics, e.g., *love*, *dogs* or *driving*. In SSEC the topic modeling corresponds to the keyword-based sampling based on the original intention to perform stance detection. In APPREDDIT, topics appear to be indicative of the subreddit they are sourced from. For instance, the topic of *depression* is related to the subreddit "mentalhealth". The variety of relationship-related topics (*romantic relationships*, *love*, *platonic relationships*) reflects the various subreddits revolving around these topics, e.g., "relationship advice" or "Dear Ex" (cf. Stranisci et al., 2022 for the exhaustive list of sampled subreddits). The topics in TALES appear most varied. Some topics correspond to generic concepts within fairytales (*birds*, *flowers*, *royalty*), while others are representative of specific fairy tales[2].

Emotion–Topic Relation. We will now look at the relation between emotions and topics from the dataset perspective. At first glance, such relations can already be observed in topics that revolve around specific emotions, such as *shame*, *fear* (both in ISEAR), *anger* (APPREDDIT) or, more general, *feelings* (ENVENT). In order to assess whether these equivalences on the lexical level are also present in the respective emotion annotations, we report the normalized pointwise mutual information between topics and their associated emotion annotations in Figures 2 and 3.[3] For ISEAR (Fig. 2), we observe that the topics of *shame* and *fear* are positively correlated with the emotion label of the same class. Further, emotionally correlated topics are *death* (with *sadness*), *alcohol* and *animals* (both *disgust*), *accidents* (*fear*) and *exams* with *joy* (all positive). Negative correlations can be observed for *alcohol* and *joy*, as well as for *love* and *fear*.

The observations for ENVENT are similar (Fig. 3), with positive correlations between *dogs* and *disgust* as well as *driving* and *fear*. Although these are consistent with correlations of similar topics in

[2]The most representative terms for the topic labeled as *Tabitha Twitchit* comprise the names of fictional characters from the kids stories by Beatrix Potter. Further, the topic *old english* appears to be based on lexical features alone (e.g., "thou", "thee", "thy").

[3]We focus our analysis on select datasets and report results for the remaining corpora in Appendix C.

		CROSSTOPIC					INTOPIC					$\Delta^{\text{INTOPIC}}_{\text{CROSSTOPIC}}$		
	Corpus	BL	WR	GR	$\Delta^{\text{BL}}_{\text{WR}}$	$\Delta^{\text{BL}}_{\text{GR}}$	BL	WR	GR	$\Delta^{\text{BL}}_{\text{WR}}$	$\Delta^{\text{BL}}_{\text{GR}}$	BL	WR	GR
Emotion	ISEAR	59	59	65	0	6	68	70	71	2	3	9	11	6
Emotion	ENISEAR	69	54	68	−15	−1	74	69	72	−5	−2	5	15	4
Emotion	SSEC	46	37	23	−12	−23	47	39	25	−8	−22	1	2	2
Emotion	TALES	84	84	82	0	−2	85	85	83	0	−2	1	1	1
Emotion	ENVENT	51	51	54	0	3	55	55	57	0	2	4	4	3
Emotion	Average	62	57	58	−5	−4	66	64	62	−2	−4	4	7	4
Appraisal	ENISEAR	70	56	54	−14	−16	75	57	56	−18	−19	5	1	2
Appraisal	ENVENT	63	61	44	−2	−19	64	61	45	−3	−19	1	0	1
Appraisal	APPREDDIT	66	56	56	−10	−10	68	55	56	−13	−12	2	−1	0
Appraisal	Average	66	57	51	−9	−15	69	57	52	−12	−17	3	0	1

Table 2: Results for CROSSTOPIC and INTOPIC experiments and differences between them for all experimental series. For each experimental setup, we show results for the baseline without debiasing (BL) and for the two debiasing methods of word removal (WR) and gradient reversal (GR).

ISEAR (*animals* and *disgust*, *accidents* and *fear*), the PMI values in ENVENT are consistently lower.

The ENVENT offers itself to compare the emotion–topic and appraisal–topic correlations (Figure 4). The highest positive correlation is between *covid* and *chance control*, i.e., *covid*-related events are appraised as out of control by the emoter. The topic of *covid* is further (slightly) negatively correlated with *self control* (thus, the complement to *chance control*) and *self responsibility*. This direct comparison on ENVENT shows that the correlations between topics and appraisals are less distinct than for emotions.

4.2 Is emotion classification influenced by topics?

What arises from the observation that topics and emotions (and topics and appraisals) are indeed correlated is the question whether this relation is reflected in classifiers. To this end, Table 2 shows results for CROSSTOPIC and INTOPIC experiments.

Following the assumption that emotion and appraisal classifiers are biased towards topics, the INTOPIC setting is hypothesized to score higher than the CROSSTOPIC setting. The difference between these two settings is shown in the $\Delta^{\text{INTOPIC}}_{\text{CROSSTOPIC}}$–BL column. Across all corpora, we see that all INTOPIC scores are higher than the CROSSTOPIC scores – the Δ is positive but varies: The highest discrepancy is observed for ISEAR (+9), while it is neglectable for SSEC, TALES and ENVENT (in the appraisal classification setting) and APPREDDIT (+2). In comparison, ENVENT (for emotion classification) as well as emotion and appraisal classification on ENISEAR show moderate improvement when evaluated INTOPIC (+4, +5, +5, respectively). Overall, the Δ values are similar (on average) between emotion and appraisal classification.

These results show that the topic influences the predictions negatively, but does not allow any insight if these results mostly stem from one emotion label or are the same across labels. To analyze this aspect, Figure 5 reports the F_1-scores obtained on each topic-specific subset for each held-out topic. The diagonal thus depicts the CROSSTOPIC setting. All other cells correspond to the INTOPIC setting.

The large Δ value reported for ISEAR in Table 2 leads to the diagonal values (CROSSTOPIC) in Figure 5 to be lower than the average of all other results of the same held-out topic (INTOPIC). However, the CROSSTOPIC scores are still comparably high. Particularly interesting is the topic of *death*. When this is absent from the training data, the classifier performs much worse on all testsets, both INTOPIC and CROSSTOPIC. Analogously, the topic *fear* appears to contain instances easier to classify, no matter which held-out topic is absent from the training data. The only exception is the mentioned topic *death*, and, although to a lesser extent, the CROSSTOPIC setting of the topic *fear*.

4.3 Can the influence of topics on emotion classification be mitigated?

To understand if the discrepancy between the CROSSTOPIC and INTOPIC results can be mitigated with debiasing methods, we show the results also in Table 2 (columns WR for word removal and GR for gradient reversal).

Do the mitigation methods lower the performance for each setting separately or do they im-

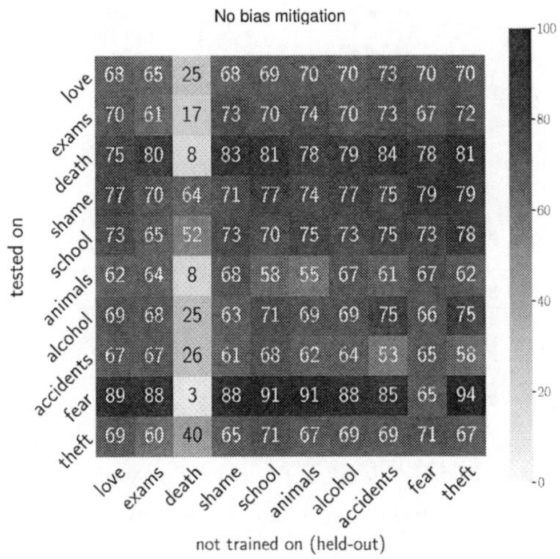

Figure 5: Micro-average F_1 for each topic-specific test set in ISEAR, for each held-out topic (CrossTopic/InTopic). No mitigation method is used (Bl setting).

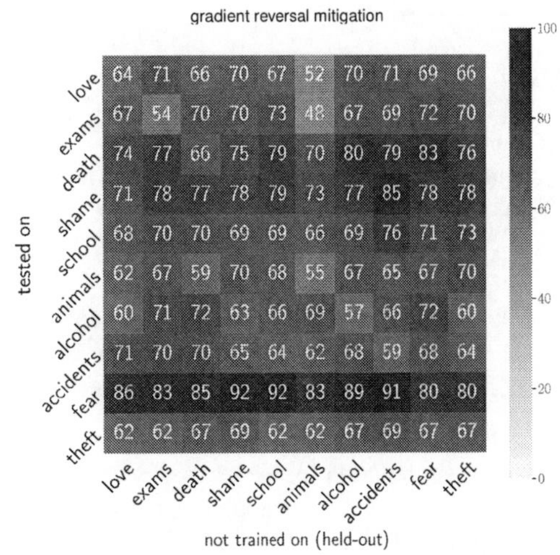

Figure 6: Micro-average F_1 for each topic-specific test set in ISEAR, for each held-out topic (CrossTopic/InTopic). Gradient reversal is used as a mitigation method (Gr setting).

prove it? The answer can be found in the $\Delta^{\text{BL}}_{\text{WR}}$ $\Delta^{\text{BL}}_{\text{GR}}$ columns. In the InTopic setting, most of these values are negative – the mitigation method removes information helpful for emotion classification. The only exception is the ISEAR corpus for emotion classification, where the method in fact improves the result. The negative difference is most pronounced for SSEC and nearly negligible for the other corpora for emotion classification. The results carry over to the CrossTopic setting: For SSEC, emotion classification performance is substantially lower, while the difference is neglectable for most other corpora. Only enISEAR (for emotion classification) shows a similarly significant drop in performance when Wr is applied. For ISEAR, however, the emotion classification is improved. To provide more detail on where this CrossTopic improvement takes place, we compare the detailed InTopic/CrossTopic results for the Bl- and Gr-settings in Figures 5 and 6, respectively. The direct comparison shows that the substantial impact of the topic *death* on CrossTopic emotion classification (Figure 5) is mitigated when applying the Gr-mitigation method (6).

Do the mitigation methods lower the performance discrepancy between the InTopic *and* CrossTopic *predictions?* To find the answer to this question, we compare the delta values Bl–Wr and Bl–Gr at the right of Table 2 ($\Delta^{\text{InTopic}}_{\text{CrossTopic}}$). A lower delta value for the mitigation method than for the Bl is an indicator that the method improves the classifier. In the emotion classification setup, this is the case for ISEAR and, to a lower extend, for enISEAR and enVENT. These are the corpora that are particularly designed to include event descriptions. However, there is a difference in performance between the mitigation methods. In the aforementioned corpora, an improvement can only be observed in the Gr-setting. When Wr is applied, ISEAR and enISEAR even show a decrease in performance.While the SSEC corpus would also have the potential to be improved with the method, the classifier relied too substantially on the topic information and cannot find enough signal for emotion classification such that the method may work.

For the appraisal prediction, we also observe an improvement for event-centered corpora enISEAR and APPReddit, but not for enVENT. Throughout all experiments, we observe that topic information removal is disadvantageous for appraisal prediction. We take this as an indicator that the classifiers indeed find information on the emotion expression outside of topic information. However, the appraisal information needs to be inferred from the topic of the text and cannot be found elsewhere.

5 Analysis

To provide an intuition how the predictions of the model changes with the topic mitigation, we show examples in Table 3. For each example sentence we see the corresponding topic label (according to the topic model), the gold emotion annotation and the CrossTopic-predictions with (Wr, Gr) or

ID	Text	Topic	Gold	CrossTopic BL	CrossTopic WR	CrossTopic GR
1	When one of my closest friends died unexpectantly	death	sadness	joy	disgust	**sadness**
2	When my uncle comes (3 times a year) for the traditional Christmas dinner with my grandparents and other relatives and is very drunk.	alcohol	disgust	anger	shame	**disgust**
3	When my fiancee travelled 2000 Km to visit me, and I hadn't seen her for 4 months.	love	joy	sadness	sadness	**joy**
4	Passing an exam I did not expect to pass.	exam	joy	fear	fear	fear
5	When I was admitted to a certain school as a student.	exam	joy	shame	shame	**joy**
6	Unexpected visit by a close friend, whom I hadn't seen for half a year.	love	sadness	sadness	fear	**sadness**

Table 3: Example predictions for instances from the ISEAR corpus, including assigned topic and gold emotion label. Predictions are reported for the CrossTopic-setting (trained on all instances except those labeled with respective topic in column *Topic*) when applying no mitigation method (BL), word removal (WR) and gradient reversal (GR). Predictions in **bold** represent correspondence with gold label.

without (BL) applying de-biasing methods.

Example 1 is assigned the topic *death* and is annotated with *sadness*. With no mitigation method applied, a CrossTopic-classifier (i.e., which has not seen any sentences belonging to the topic *death* during training) falsely predicts *joy* (BL). We hypothesize that the erroneous classification is due to a bias towards the topic of *love* (which is correlated with *joy*), represented by the term "friends". If word removal is applied, a different but equally incorrect label is predicted (*disgust*). Apparently, removing any words associated to topics from the input does mitigate the bias observed in the BL prediction, but removes too much information. However, when using gradient reversal, the bias is mitigated and the correct label *sadness* is predicted. Similar cases can be observed in Examples 2, 3, 5 and 6.

Example 4 shows a different pattern. Despite achieving de-biasing in the above cases, there are also examples where gradient reversal fails to mitigate the bias and predict the correct emotion label. None of the two mitigation methods leads to a correct prediction. Instead, all CrossTopic-classifiers assign *fear*. Presumably, this is because of the phrase "did not expect" which expresses a future-directed, misalignment with the predictability of events. This aspect might in itself be another possible form of appraisal bias.

6 Conclusion

We based our study on the observation that emotion analysis corpora are commonly sampled based on keywords or following other methods that are risky to lead to distributions that are not representative for the entirety of a domain. We contributed a better understanding how far this issue can be found in emotion corpora and if models fine-tuned on them rely on such spurious signals.

The analysis of topic distributions in emotion corpora yields that they are, indeed, biased towards topics. The degree of bias varies: Some corpora exhibit prototypical topics for certain emotions, while in others, only weak correlations between topic and emotion distribution can be observed. We hypothesize this is because of the respective sampling strategies: If the sampling method is biased, i.e., if certain topics are over-represented for a given emotion, topic bias emerges.

In the cases in which topic and emotion distributions are highly correlated, this topic bias is also found to be reflected in the resulting classifier. For mitigating this bias in emotion classifiers, gradient reversal proved to be useful. It allows the classifier to make use of available topic information without relying solely on it for making the classification decision.

Our results suggest that classifiers in which the topic bias is mitigated may have a higher performance across corpora, yet, this needs to be evaluated in future work. Further, we assume that prompt-learning or other few-shot modeling methods might suffer less from topic biases in corpora. If this is true, this opens a new research direction of selecting non-bias-inducing instances for emotion and appraisal classification.

Finally, the difference between topic–emotion and topic–appraisal correlations requires further analysis. We hypothesize that this is because appraisals are more closely related to events than general emotion labels.

Acknowledgements

This research has been conducted in the context of the CEAT project, KL 2869/1-2, funded by the German Research Foundation (DFG).

Limitations

We presented the first study on topics as unwanted confounders for emotion analysis. We focused on a set of popular corpora, but cannot make any judgements regarding corpora that we did not study. We are confident that similar effects can be found in other resources, but this still needs to be analyzed.

Another limitation is the pragmatic decision that the contextualized embeddings used by our emotion/appraisal predictors and the topic modeler are not the same. The representations used for topic clustering are provided by sentence-transformer models, while we leverage RoBERTa embeddings for emotion and appraisal classification. This potentially introduces an uncontrolled variance in our experiments. Using identical embedding models for both steps – or, alternatively, a joint embedding space – might reduce that variance and thus improve interpretability of the results.

Ethical Considerations

In our work, we do not develop or annotate corpora. We further do not collect data or propose new NLP tasks. Therefore, our work does not contribute potential biases originating from annotator or data selection. Instead, our goal is to understand biases better and contribute to a more fair emotion classification. We do not investigate how topic bias might cause harm in downstream applications.

Still, our topic analysis might be limited, for instance by the topic modeler chosen for the analysis and by the datasets that we studied. In real-world data applications, another topic modeling approach might be required. It is important to note that we do not make any statements which topics might have a negative impact on members of a society.

In general, emotion classifiers have a high potential to cause harm by making wrong predictions. Until the performance is on a higher, more reliable level and the effects of biases and other confounding variables are better understood, they should always be applied with caution. We propose that the analyses acquired with automatic emotion analysis methods should never be related to individuals. Instead, analysis should only be performed on an aggregated level.

References

Abien Fred Agarap. 2019. Deep learning using rectified linear units (relu).

Cecilia Ovesdotter Alm, Dan Roth, and Richard Sproat. 2005. Emotions from text: Machine learning for text-based emotion prediction. In *Proceedings of Human Language Technology Conference and Conference on Empirical Methods in Natural Language Processing*, pages 579–586, Vancouver, British Columbia, Canada. Association for Computational Linguistics.

Soumya Barikeri, Anne Lauscher, Ivan Vulić, and Goran Glavaš. 2021. RedditBias: A real-world resource for bias evaluation and debiasing of conversational language models. In *Proceedings of the 59th Annual Meeting of the Association for Computational Linguistics and the 11th International Joint Conference on Natural Language Processing (Volume 1: Long Papers)*, pages 1941–1955, Online. Association for Computational Linguistics.

Laura-Ana-Maria Bostan and Roman Klinger. 2018. An analysis of annotated corpora for emotion classification in text. In *Proceedings of the 27th International Conference on Computational Linguistics*, pages 2104–2119, Santa Fe, New Mexico, USA. Association for Computational Linguistics.

Aylin Caliskan, Joanna J. Bryson, and Arvind Narayanan. 2017. Semantics derived automatically from language corpora contain human-like biases. *Science*, 356(6334):183–186.

Erenay Dayanik and Sebastian Padó. 2021. Disentangling document topic and author gender in multiple languages: Lessons for adversarial debiasing. In *Proceedings of the Eleventh Workshop on Computational Approaches to Subjectivity, Sentiment and Social Media Analysis*, pages 50–61, Online. Association for Computational Linguistics.

Dorottya Demszky, Dana Movshovitz-Attias, Jeongwoo Ko, Alan Cowen, Gaurav Nemade, and Sujith Ravi. 2020. GoEmotions: A dataset of fine-grained emotions. In *Proceedings of the 58th Annual Meeting of the Association for Computational Linguistics*, pages 4040–4054, Online. Association for Computational Linguistics.

Jacob Devlin, Ming-Wei Chang, Kenton Lee, and Kristina Toutanova. 2019. BERT: Pre-training of deep bidirectional transformers for language understanding. In *Proceedings of the 2019 Conference of the North American Chapter of the Association for Computational Linguistics: Human Language Technologies, Volume 1 (Long and Short Papers)*, pages 4171–4186, Minneapolis, Minnesota. Association for Computational Linguistics.

Anton Eklund and Mona Forsman. 2022. Topic modeling by clustering language model embeddings: Human validation on an industry dataset. In *Proceedings of the 2022 Conference on Empirical Methods in Natural Language Processing: Industry Track*, pages

635–643, Abu Dhabi, UAE. Association for Computational Linguistics.

Paul Ekman. 1992. An argument for basic emotions. *Cognition & Emotion*, 6:169–200.

Paul Ekman. 1999. *Basic Emotions*, chapter 3. John Wiley & Sons, Ltd.

Yaroslav Ganin, Evgeniya Ustinova, Hana Ajakan, Pascal Germain, Hugo Larochelle, François Laviolette, Mario Marchand, and Victor Lempitsky. 2015. Domain-adversarial training of neural networks.

Maarten Grootendorst. 2022. Bertopic: Neural topic modeling with a class-based tf-idf procedure. *arXiv preprint arXiv:2203.05794*.

He He, Sheng Zha, and Haohan Wang. 2019. Unlearn dataset bias in natural language inference by fitting the residual. In *Proceedings of the 2nd Workshop on Deep Learning Approaches for Low-Resource NLP (DeepLo 2019)*, pages 132–142, Hong Kong, China. Association for Computational Linguistics.

Jan Hofmann, Enrica Troiano, Kai Sassenberg, and Roman Klinger. 2020. Appraisal theories for emotion classification in text. In *Proceedings of the 28th International Conference on Computational Linguistics*, pages 125–138, Barcelona, Spain (Online). International Committee on Computational Linguistics.

Dirk Hovy and Shrimai Prabhumoye. 2021. Five sources of bias in natural language processing. *Language and Linguistics Compass*, 15(8):e12432.

Olga Kellert and Md Mahmud Uz Zaman. 2022. Using neural topic models to track context shifts of words: a case study of COVID-related terms before and after the lockdown in April 2020. In *Proceedings of the 3rd Workshop on Computational Approaches to Historical Language Change*, pages 131–139, Dublin, Ireland. Association for Computational Linguistics.

Keita Kurita, Nidhi Vyas, Ayush Pareek, Alan W Black, and Yulia Tsvetkov. 2019. Measuring bias in contextualized word representations. In *Proceedings of the First Workshop on Gender Bias in Natural Language Processing*, pages 166–172, Florence, Italy. Association for Computational Linguistics.

Yanran Li, Hui Su, Xiaoyu Shen, Wenjie Li, Ziqiang Cao, and Shuzi Niu. 2017. DailyDialog: A manually labelled multi-turn dialogue dataset. In *Proceedings of the Eighth International Joint Conference on Natural Language Processing (Volume 1: Long Papers)*, pages 986–995, Taipei, Taiwan. Asian Federation of Natural Language Processing.

Siyang Liu, Chujie Zheng, Orianna Demasi, Sahand Sabour, Yu Li, Zhou Yu, Yong Jiang, and Minlie Huang. 2021. Towards emotional support dialog systems. In *Proceedings of the 59th Annual Meeting of the Association for Computational Linguistics and the 11th International Joint Conference on Natural Language Processing (Volume 1: Long Papers)*, pages 3469–3483, Online. Association for Computational Linguistics.

Yinhan Liu, Myle Ott, Naman Goyal, Jingfei Du, Mandar Joshi, Danqi Chen, Omer Levy, Mike Lewis, Luke Zettlemoyer, and Veselin Stoyanov. 2019. Roberta: A robustly optimized bert pretraining approach.

Ilya Loshchilov and Frank Hutter. 2019. Decoupled weight decay regularization.

Leland McInnes and John Healy. 2017. Accelerated hierarchical density based clustering. In *2017 IEEE International Conference on Data Mining Workshops (ICDMW)*, pages 33–42.

Leland McInnes, John Healy, and James Melville. 2020. Umap: Uniform manifold approximation and projection for dimension reduction.

Saif Mohammad. 2011. From once upon a time to happily ever after: Tracking emotions in novels and fairy tales. In *Proceedings of the 5th ACL-HLT Workshop on Language Technology for Cultural Heritage, Social Sciences, and Humanities*, pages 105–114, Portland, OR, USA. Association for Computational Linguistics.

Saif Mohammad, Svetlana Kiritchenko, Parinaz Sobhani, Xiaodan Zhu, and Colin Cherry. 2016. SemEval-2016 task 6: Detecting stance in tweets. In *Proceedings of the 10th International Workshop on Semantic Evaluation (SemEval-2016)*, pages 31–41, San Diego, California. Association for Computational Linguistics.

Saif Mohammad, Xiaodan Zhu, and Joel Martin. 2014. Semantic role labeling of emotions in tweets. In *Proceedings of the 5th Workshop on Computational Approaches to Subjectivity, Sentiment and Social Media Analysis*, pages 32–41, Baltimore, Maryland. Association for Computational Linguistics.

Isar Nejadgholi and Svetlana Kiritchenko. 2020. On cross-dataset generalization in automatic detection of online abuse. In *Proceedings of the Fourth Workshop on Online Abuse and Harms*, pages 173–183, Online. Association for Computational Linguistics.

Robert Plutchik. 1982. A psychoevolutionary theory of emotions. *Social Science Information*, 21(4-5):529–553.

Robert Plutchik. 2001. The Nature of Emotions. *American Scientist*, 89(4):344.

Yusu Qian, Urwa Muaz, Ben Zhang, and Jae Won Hyun. 2019. Reducing gender bias in word-level language models with a gender-equalizing loss function. In *Proceedings of the 57th Annual Meeting of the Association for Computational Linguistics: Student Research Workshop*, pages 223–228, Florence, Italy. Association for Computational Linguistics.

Ira J. Roseman. 1991. Appraisal determinants of discrete emotions. *Cognition & Emotion*, 5:161–200.

James Russell. 1980. A circumplex model of affect. *Journal of Personality and Social Psychology*, 39:1161–1178.

Niloofar Safi Samghabadi, Afsheen Hatami, Mahsa Shafaei, Sudipta Kar, and Thamar Solorio. 2020. Attending the emotions to detect online abusive language. In *Proceedings of the Fourth Workshop on Online Abuse and Harms*, pages 79–88, Online. Association for Computational Linguistics.

Klaus R. Scherer. 2005. What are emotions? and how can they be measured? *Social Science Information*, 44(4):695–729.

Klaus R Scherer and Harald G Wallbott. 1994. Evidence for universality and cultural variation of differential emotion response patterning. *Journal of personality and social psychology*, 66(2):310.

Hendrik Schuff, Jeremy Barnes, Julian Mohme, Sebastian Padó, and Roman Klinger. 2017. Annotation, modelling and analysis of fine-grained emotions on a stance and sentiment detection corpus. In *Proceedings of the 8th Workshop on Computational Approaches to Subjectivity, Sentiment and Social Media Analysis*, pages 13–23, Copenhagen, Denmark. Association for Computational Linguistics.

Deven Santosh Shah, H. Andrew Schwartz, and Dirk Hovy. 2020. Predictive biases in natural language processing models: A conceptual framework and overview. In *Proceedings of the 58th Annual Meeting of the Association for Computational Linguistics*, pages 5248–5264, Online. Association for Computational Linguistics.

Craig A. Smith and Richard S. Lazarus. 1990. Emotion and adaptation. *Handbook of Personality: Theory and Research*, pages 609–637.

Maximilian Spliethöver and Henning Wachsmuth. 2020. Argument from old man's view: Assessing social bias in argumentation. In *Proceedings of the 7th Workshop on Argument Mining*, pages 76–87, Online. Association for Computational Linguistics.

Gabriel Stanovsky, Noah A. Smith, and Luke Zettlemoyer. 2019. Evaluating gender bias in machine translation. In *Proceedings of the 57th Annual Meeting of the Association for Computational Linguistics*, pages 1679–1684, Florence, Italy. Association for Computational Linguistics.

Marco Antonio Stranisci, Simona Frenda, Eleonora Ceccaldi, Valerio Basile, Rossana Damiano, and Viviana Patti. 2022. APPReddit: a corpus of Reddit posts annotated for appraisal. In *Proceedings of the Thirteenth Language Resources and Evaluation Conference*, pages 3809–3818, Marseille, France. European Language Resources Association.

Enrica Troiano, Laura Oberländer, and Roman Klinger. 2023. Dimensional Modeling of Emotions in Text with Appraisal Theories: Corpus Creation, Annotation Reliability, and Prediction. *Computational Linguistics*, 49(1):1–72.

Enrica Troiano, Sebastian Padó, and Roman Klinger. 2019. Crowdsourcing and validating event-focused emotion corpora for German and English. In *Proceedings of the 57th Annual Meeting of the Association for Computational Linguistics*, pages 4005–4011, Florence, Italy. Association for Computational Linguistics.

Bo Wang, Tao Shen, Guodong Long, Tianyi Zhou, and Yi Chang. 2021. Eliminating sentiment bias for aspect-level sentiment classification with unsupervised opinion extraction. In *Findings of the Association for Computational Linguistics: EMNLP 2021*, pages 3002–3012, Punta Cana, Dominican Republic. Association for Computational Linguistics.

Maximilian Wich, Jan Bauer, and Georg Groh. 2020. Impact of politically biased data on hate speech classification. In *Proceedings of the Fourth Workshop on Online Abuse and Harms*, pages 54–64, Online. Association for Computational Linguistics.

Michael Wiegand, Josef Ruppenhofer, and Thomas Kleinbauer. 2019. Detection of Abusive Language: the Problem of Biased Datasets. In *Proceedings of the 2019 Conference of the North American Chapter of the Association for Computational Linguistics: Human Language Technologies, Volume 1 (Long and Short Papers)*, pages 602–608, Minneapolis, Minnesota. Association for Computational Linguistics.

Thomas Wolf, Lysandre Debut, Victor Sanh, Julien Chaumond, Clement Delangue, Anthony Moi, Pierric Cistac, Tim Rault, Remi Louf, Morgan Funtowicz, Joe Davison, Sam Shleifer, Patrick von Platen, Clara Ma, Yacine Jernite, Julien Plu, Canwen Xu, Teven Le Scao, Sylvain Gugger, Mariama Drame, Quentin Lhoest, and Alexander Rush. 2020. Transformers: State-of-the-art natural language processing. In *Proceedings of the 2020 Conference on Empirical Methods in Natural Language Processing: System Demonstrations*, pages 38–45, Online. Association for Computational Linguistics.

Xiao Xu, Gert Stulp, Antal Van Den Bosch, and Anne Gauthier. 2022. Understanding narratives from demographic survey data: a comparative study with multiple neural topic models. In *Proceedings of the Fifth Workshop on Natural Language Processing and Computational Social Science (NLP+CSS)*, pages 33–38, Abu Dhabi, UAE. Association for Computational Linguistics.

Hongli Zhan, Tiberiu Sosea, Cornelia Caragea, and Junyi Jessy Li. 2022. Why do you feel this way? summarizing triggers of emotions in social media posts. In *Proceedings of the 2022 Conference on Empirical Methods in Natural Language Processing*, pages 9436–9453, Abu Dhabi, United Arab Emirates. Association for Computational Linguistics.

A Implementation Details

Emotion/Appraisal Classifier. Following state-of-the-art approaches to emotion and appraisal classification (Demszky et al., 2020 Troiano et al., 2019), we fine-tune RoBERTa (Liu et al., 2019) as implemented in the Huggingface library (Wolf et al., 2020) on each corpus. For the classification, the output from the transformer layers is pooled and passed through a fully-connected dense layer (768 units). We apply ReLU activation (Agarap, 2019) and a dropout of 0.5 and a consecutive classification layer using softmax activation and binary cross-entropy loss for single-class classification (for ISEAR, Tales, and emotions in enVENT). For the multi-class classification task (SSEC, APPReddit, enISEAR and appraisals in enVENT), we apply a sigmoid activation and categorical cross-entropy loss instead. The learning rate is set to 5×10^{-5} across all experiments; the batch size is 16. We train each classifier for a maximum of 5 epochs and apply early stopping based on the validation accuracy (stops after two consecutive epochs without improvement). As optimizer, AdamW (Loshchilov and Hutter, 2019) is applied, weight decay is set to 10^{-5}. Results are averaged over three different runs for each classification task.

Topic Modeling. BERTopic consists of a pipeline of components for features representation, dimensionality reduction, clustering and topic. We use a pre-trained sentence embedding (all-MiniLM-L6-v2, as implemented in Huggingface) for feature extraction, Accelerated Hierarchical Density Clustering (HDBSCAN; McInnes and Healy, 2017) as a clustering method, Uniform Manifold Approximation (UMAP; (McInnes et al., 2020)) for dimensionality reduction and tf-idf for retrieving the topics within the clusters. Although HDBSCAN does not require a pre-determined number of topics, it can be tuned by setting hyperparameters for the minimum cluster size and controlling the amount of outliers allowed within a cluster. We adapt these hyperparameters to each corpus individually, depending on its size.

Word Removal. The list of topic words to be removed in each corpus consists of the ten most representative words of each topic within the dataset. The most representative words, i.e., the top k words per topic are determined by the probability that BERTopic assigns to each word, i.e., the word's probability to be assigned a certain topic label. Therefore, k is a hyperparameter determining the trade-off between general classification performance and topic-influence: Increasing k increases the potential impact of the de-biasing method (as less topic-specific features are available to the classifier), but, at the same time, decreases the general classification as less and less features are available overall. Further, by choosing a higher k, more words which are less representative for a given topic are removed as well, thus introducing noise to the experiment. Here, k is set to 10. Setting$k = 3$ or $k = 5$ were considered as well, but did not show a considerable change in performance compared to the non-mitigated baseline classifier (Bl). This hyperparameter choice is further supported by the observation that the top k representative words often comprise variations of the same word or concept. For example, in ISEAR, the ten most representative words for the topic *theft* consist of "theft", "stealing", "stole", "thief", "robbery", "thieves", "stolen", "borrowed", "robbers" and "cash". A higher k thus covers a broader range of morphological ("stealing", "stole", "stolen" and "thief", "thieves"), as well as semantic ("theft", "robbery") variation. The chosen topic words are not removed from the input, but substituted with "...". The number of masked topic words per corpus is summarized in Table 4.

	# topics	# masked topic words
ISEAR	10	100
SSEC	11	110
Tales	10	10
enVENT	8	80
APPReddit	10	100
enISEAR	13	130

Table 4: Number (#) of topics and the resulting number of removed (i.e., masked) topic words.

Gradient Reversal. The gradient reversal layer (GRL) is implemented as described by Ganin et al. (2015), with the purpose of reversing the gradient (by multiplying it with $-\lambda$) of the following layer during backpropagation. Since the layer has no trainable (nor non-trainable) weights associated with it, the GRL has no effect during a forward pass and acts as an identity transformation. For the InTopic-GR and CrossTopic-GR experiments conducted here, the GRL is added into the standard classifier architecture described above. The emotion classifier is coupled with an additional topic classification layer, equivalent to the single-class emotion classification layer, with the task of predicting the correct topic label $t_{i,c}$ for each instance. The topic classifier is connected via the GRL to the remaining layers of the network, i.e., the pre-trained RoBERTa model as well as the single dense layer. Since the gradient is reversed, all weights in the shared layer associated with the topic prediction task are decreased. A key factor in the implementation is the choice of λ as it regulates the impact of the GRL. Again, choosing λ is a trade-off between overall classification performance and de-biasing potency. To determine an optimal value for λ, standard emotion (or appraisal classifiers) are trained on each individual corpus for λ values of 0.1, 0.3, 0.5, 1 and 3. Across corpora, a significant decrease in performance can be observed for any $\lambda > 0.1$. Therefore, λ is set to 0.1 for all gradient reversal experiments.

B Data

Besides for their widespread use, the corpora are specifically selected for their variety in domain and text style. As bias in general and topic bias in particular is closely related to the respective dataset's domain, annotation and sampling methods of a dataset, the following overview puts emphasis on these aspects. We provide a detailed description of the datasets used in this investigation, emphasizing on each dataset's domain, annotation and sampling method. General corpus statistics are further provided in Table 6.

B.1 Corpora

ISEAR. The ISEAR corpus (Scherer and Wallbott, 1994) consists of 7,665 sentences which were sampled in an in-lab setting: Participants were presented with an emotion label and asked to report an event that elicited that particular emotion in them. Each event description is labeled with a single emotion from a set of eight (Ekman's basic emotions plus *shame* and *guilt*). Since participants were free to report any event that elicited one of the given emotions, they were also free in their choice of topic. However, since participants were asked to report events specific to certain emotions, sample bias could have been introduced to the corpus (under the assumption that there are prototypical events for certain emotions).

ENISEAR. The corpus consist of 1001 event descriptions that were originally compiled by (Troiano et al., 2019) as a complement to ISEAR. The event descriptions were sampled analogous to ISEAR, but in a crowd-sourcing setup (annotated for *joy*, *sadness*, *anger*, *fear*, *disgust*, *shame* and *guilt*). Here, ENISEAR also refers to the appraisal annotations which were added to the corpus by Hofmann et al. (2020): *Attention*, *certainty*, *effort*, *pleasantness*, *responsibility* and *control*. These additional annotations were provided by expert annotators.

SSEC. The Stance Sentiment Emotion Corpus (Schuff et al., 2017) consists of 4,868 Twitter posts. The original data stems from Mohammad et al. (2016) which Schuff et al. (2017) re-annotate for Plutchik's eight basic emotions. The annotations are conducted by trained expert annotators. Since the original dataset by Mohammad et al. (2016) was developed for stance detection, the instances were sampled using keywords (i.e., hashtags) that contain a particular stance in favor (e.g., "#Hillary4President") or against an entity ("#HillNo"). This type of keyword-based data sampling has been found to exhibit topic bias in related studies, e.g., on datasets of abusive language (Wiegand et al., 2019).

TALES. The TALES corpus (Alm et al., 2005) features 15,302 sentences from different fairytales. Sentences are labeled by experts with one of Ekman's basic emotions (*surprise* is split into *negative* and *positive surprise*). Emotions are annotated from the perspective of the respective character.

CROWD-ENVENT. Analogous to ENISEAR, the CROWD-ENVENT corpus (Troiano et al., 2023) consists of 6600 crowd-sourced, self-reported event descriptions. Each description is annotated for 21 appraisal dimensions[4], each rated on a scale between 1 and 5, as well as for emotions (Ekman's 6 basic emotions, plus *shame*, *pride*, *boredom*, *relief*, *trust*, *shame*, *guilt* and *no emotion*). Participants were free in their choice of topic, but the priming with an emotion label might influence the topic distribution (see ISEAR). In order to avoid oversampling descriptions of prototypical events, Troiano et al. apply a diversification method to foster more diverse event descriptions. The corpus additionally features crowd-sourced re-annotations of the event descriptions to investigate differences between the

[4]Suddenness, familiarity, event predictability, pleasantness, unpleasantness, goal relevance, own responsibility, others' responsibility, situational responsibility, anticipation of consequences, goal support, urgency, own control, others' control, situational control, acceptance of consequences, clash with internal standards and ideals, violation of (external) norms and laws, not consider, attention, effort.

Corpus	Size	Annotation	Domain	Class. Setting
ISEAR	7666	*joy, sadness, anger, fear, disgust, shame, guilt*	event descr.	single
SSEC	4870	Plutchik	tweets	multi
TALES	10339	Ekman + *no emotion*	fairy tales	single
CROWD-ENVENT	6600	Ekman + *shame, pride, bored., rel., trust, guilt, no*	event descr.	single
		21 appraisal dimensions		multi
APPREDDIT	780	*unexp., consist., cert., cntrl., resp.*	reddit posts	multi
ENISEAR	1001	*joy, sadness, anger, fear, disgust, shame, guilt*	event descr.	single
		attent., cntrl., circum., resp., pleasant., effrt., cert.		multi

Table 5: Corpus overview. Emotion/appraisal statistics for ENVENT/ENISEAR are reported separately.

reader's and writer's assessment of emotions and appraisals. However, these are not used here.

APPREDDIT. The APPREDDIT corpus (Stranisci et al., 2022) is annotated with appraisal dimensions. It comprises 780 reddit posts, where each posts contains at least one event description (1,091 events overall). The five appraisal labels (*certainty, consistency, control, unexpectedness, responsibility*) are based on (Roseman, 1991) and annotated by experts. The posts are sampled exclusively from a limited set of subreddits, mostly connotated with negative sentiment (Anger, offmychest, helpmecope anxiety, i.a.). This sampling procedure might introduce bias to the dataset.

B.2 Aggregated Annotation Scheme

As depicted above, the corpora differ in their annotation schemes. In order to provide a more comparable analysis, the individual annotations are mapped onto an inter-corpora annotation scheme. For emotions, *anger, disgust, fear, joy, sadness, shame, surprise, no emotion* and *other* are considered. This subset of emotion labels is based on basic emotions (Ekman, 1999). Beyond Ekman's six emotions, the list accounts for other labels that frequently occur (see Table 6 for an overview). The same procedure is applied to appraisal labels. However, approaches to appraisal classification are even more diverse in annotation than emotion datasets. To account for this variation, the inter-corpora labelset consists of 11 appraisal dimensions (suddenness, pleasantness, self control, chance control, self responsibility, other responsibility, goal support, predict consequences, attention, effort), however, only a subset of six labels is shared across two of the three corpora annotated with appraisals, while only two labels can be mapped to all three corpora (summarized in Table 7).

C Other Emotion–Topic Relations

Figures 7 and 8 show the results for topic–emotion associations for the TALES and the SSEC corpora, analogously to the other resources in Section 4.

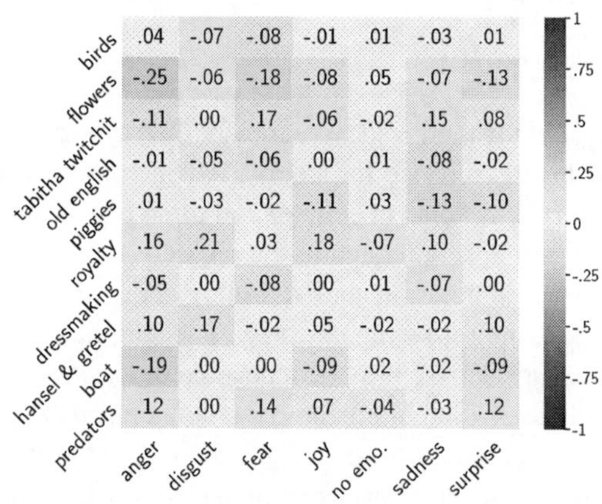

Figure 7: Normalized pointwise mutual information between topics and emotion annotations in TALES.

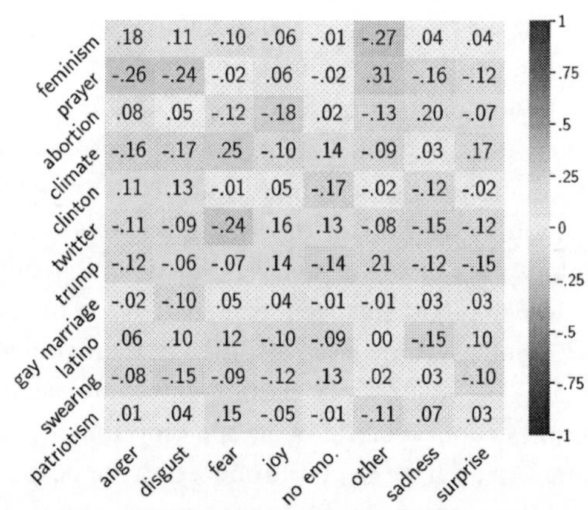

Figure 8: Normalized pointwise mutual information between topics and emotion annotations in SSEC.

Corpus	A	D	F	J	Sa	Sh	Su	No	O
ENVENT	550	550	550	550	550	550*	550	550	2,200*
ISEAR	1,096	1,096	1,095	1,094	1,096	2,189*	–	–	–
ENISEAR	143	143	143	143	143	286*	–	–	–
SSEC	1388	440	274	815	414	–	177	1552	1077*
TALES	302	40	251	579	340	–	144	8,683	–

Table 6: Number of instances of each emotion class (after mapping; the asterisk (*) indicates that this class includes mapped labels, i.e., combining multiple classes into one aggregated, but not simple one-to-one mapping of equivalent labels (happiness → joy).

Corpus	Attention	Pleasantness	Suddenness	Self Control	Chance Control	Self Responsibility	Other Responsibility	Predict Consequences	Goal Support	Effort	Other
APPREDDIT	–	–	307	307	–	400	457	748	312	–	–
ENVENT	4125	2261	3128	2142	1514	2597	3396	2841	2281	3210	6527*
ENISEAR	673	149	–	228	240	377	–	761	–	400	–

Table 7: Number of instances of each appraisal class (after mapping; the asterisk (*) indicates that this class includes mapped labels, either by simple one-to-one mapping (happiness → joy), or by combining multiple classes into one aggregated).

Stars Are All You Need: A Distantly Supervised Pyramid Network for Unified Sentiment Analysis

Wenchang Li
Sichuan University
liwenchang97@gmail.com

Yixing Chen
University Notre Dame
ychen43@nd.edu

Shuang Zheng
Dalian University of Technology
zhengshuang99@mail.dlut.edu.cn

Lei Wang
Meituan
wanglei46@meituan.com

John P. Lalor
University of Notre Dame
john.lalor@nd.edu

Abstract

Data for the Rating Prediction (RP) sentiment analysis task such as star reviews are readily available. However, data for aspect-category detection (ACD) and aspect-category sentiment analysis (ACSA) is often desired because of the fine-grained nature but are expensive to collect. In this work, we propose Unified Sentiment Analysis (Uni-SA) to understand aspect and review sentiment in a unified manner. Specifically, we propose a Distantly Supervised Pyramid Network (DSPN) to efficiently perform ACD, ACSA, and RP using only RP labels for training. We evaluate DSPN on multi-aspect review datasets in English and Chinese and find that in addition to the internal efficiency of sample size, DSPN also performs comparably well to a variety of benchmark models. We also demonstrate the interpretability of DSPN's outputs on reviews to show the pyramid structure inherent in unified sentiment analysis.

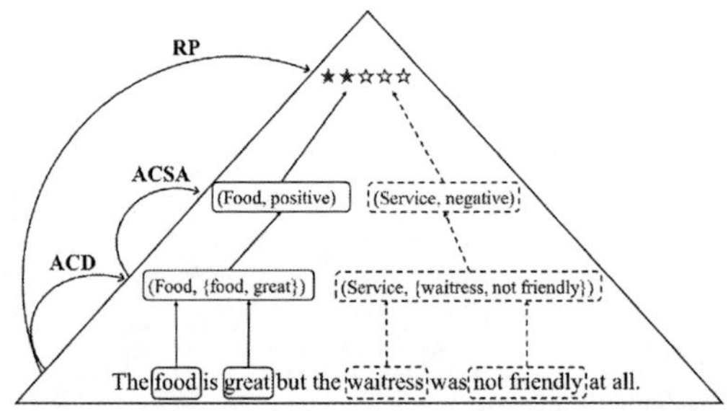

Figure 1: An overview of Unified Sentiment Analysis (Uni-SA). While ACD, ACSA, and RP can be performed individually, by leveraging the implicit pyramid structure of reviews, we can efficiently perform all three tasks with only RP labels.

1 Introduction

Consumers generate online reviews for millions of products and services in various contexts, including hotels, restaurants, products, and schools, on platforms such as Yelp, Amazon, and Tripadvisor. Firms can use online review data to better understand consumer behavior and build predictive models for their businesses (Zhang et al., 2023). Sentiment analysis of an entire document is a widely-used method for understanding unstructured consumer reviews at a high level (Liu and Zhang, 2012). In addition, fine-grained analysis of user generated content can detect aspects in documents (e.g., food quality and price in restaurant reviews). These aspects can be classified according to their sentiment (Schouten and Frasincar, 2015).

A holistic view of sentiment analysis includes three tasks: identifying aspects in the document (Aspect-Category Detection, ACD), classifying aspect sentiment (Aspect-Category Sentiment Analysis, ACSA), and classifying the overall sentiment of the document (Rating Prediction, RP).

For example, consider the review displayed in Figure 1: "*The food is great but the waitress was not friendly at all.*" Sentiment analysis models can first identify the aspects mentioned in this review via ACD (*Food*, *Service*), then predict their corresponding sentiment polarities with ACSA (*Food:Positive*, *Service:Negative*). Finally, an RP model will predict the star rating that a user would give for the review (two stars). With these methods, businesses can use both fine-grained and coarse-grained sentiment information to identify customer pain points and improve service quality.

Typically, NLP models consider ACD, ACSA, and RP independently. In some cases, ACD and ACSA are learned by a single model (e.g., Schmitt et al., 2018; Liu et al., 2021), but these two tasks are rarely connected to RP (Chebolu et al., 2023). However, star rating labels for RP are usually cheaper and easier to obtain than ACSA labels due to widespread availability of user-generated review text and stars online (Li et al., 2020a). More importantly, they can be considered a "coarse-grained synthesis" of ratings across aspects in the review (Bu et al., 2021). For example, if a user

Proceedings of the Ninth Workshop on Noisy and User-generated Text (W-NUT 2024), pages 104–118
March 22, 2024

states that the food is good, but the service quality is unacceptable, they will consider these two aspects together when giving an overall two-star rating (Figure 1), which implies that the aspect-level polarities inform the overall review of two stars (out of a possible five). This relationship provides an opportunity to unify the multiple tasks. Specifically in this work, we hypothesize that review-level star rating labels represent an aggregation of aspect-level sentiments, which themselves can be aggregated from word-level sentiments (Li et al., 2020c). To efficiently model this structure as a *pyramid structure*, we propose a Distantly Supervised Pyramid Network (DSPN) that requires *only RP labels* as signal to unify the three tasks of ACD, ACSA, and RP. We call this unified sentiment task Unified Sentiment Analysis (Uni-SA).

Contributions In this work, we make the following contributions:

- We introduce *Unified Sentiment Analysis* as a unified task of three key sentiment analysis tasks, specifically ACD, ACSA, and RP,
- We propose Distantly Supervised Pyramid Network (DSPN), a novel model for unified sentiment analysis. DSPN shows significant efficiency on training sample size with *only RP labels* as training input.
- We propose a novel aspect-attention mechanism for ACD to inform ACSA and capture the pyramid sentiment structure,
- We validate DSPN through experimental results on Chinese and English multi-aspect datasets and demonstrate the effectiveness and efficiency of DSPN.[1]

2 Unified Sentiment Analysis

Before describing our model, we first define our notation and present the unifying framework of Uni-SA. We borrow notation from the prior work where possible and introduce new notation as needed for consistency across tasks (Pontiki et al., 2016). For reference, we have included a comprehensive notation table in the appendices (Appendix A). Our corpus is a collection of *reviews* $\mathbf{R} = \{R_1, R_2, \ldots, R_{|\mathbf{R}|}\}$. Each review R_i consists of a sequence of word tokens (hereafter "words"): $R_i = \{t_i^{(1)}, t_i^{(2)}, \ldots, t_i^{(n)}\}$.

[1]Code available at https://github.com/nd-ball/DSPN

2.1 Aspect-Category Detection

In the ACD task, there are N predefined aspect categories (hereafter "aspects"): $A = \{A_1, A_2, \ldots, A_N\}$. The set of aspects present in R_i is defined as: $A_{R_i} = \{A_{R_i}^{(1)}, A_{R_i}^{(2)}, \ldots, A_{R_i}^{(K)}\}$, where $K \leq N$. To train unsupervised ACD models, the required training data is simply $\mathbf{R}$.

2.2 Aspect-Category Sentiment Analysis

For a given review R_i and one of its aspects $A_{R_i}^{(j)}$, the goal of ACSA is to predict the polarity of the aspect: $\hat{y}_{A_{R_i}^{(j)}}$. Aspect polarity is typically binary (*positive* or *negative*) or categorical (with a third option of *neutral*). Supervised ACSA models require review-aspect-polarity triples: $\{R_i, (A_{R_i}^{(j)}, y_{A_{R_i}^{(j)}})_{j=1}^{K}\}_{i=1}^{|\mathbf{R}|}$. In the case of multi-aspect ACSA, there are multiple aspects present in each review, and therefore ACSA requires $K \times |\mathbf{R}|$ labels, a factor of K larger than in RP.

2.3 Rating Prediction

Given a review R_i, RP aims to predict the star rating $\hat{y}_{R_i}$. Supervised RP models requires review-sentiment tuples: $\{(R_i, y_{R_i})\}_{i=1}^{|\mathbf{R}|}$

2.4 Model Running

Typically ACD, ACSA, and RP are considered standalone tasks. Here we propose a unified approach, where with training data of *only* RP labels, a model can output present aspects (ACD), the sentiment of those aspects (ACSA), and an overall document-level sentiment score (RP). This approach uses training labels from a single task to efficiently learn multiple distinct sentiment analysis tasks.

More specifically, for a model M, the training data required is the same as the RP task: $\{(R_i, y_{R_i})\}_{i=1}^{|\mathbf{R}|}$. At run-time, the model provides three outputs for a new review R_i: (1) The predicted aspects present in the review ($\hat{A}_{R_i}$), (2) the sentiment polarity of each identified aspect ($\hat{y}_{A_{R_i^{(j)}}} \forall A_{R_i^{(j)}} \in \hat{A}_{R_i}$), and (3) the overall sentiment prediction for the review ($\hat{y}_{R_i}$).

3 Distantly Supervised Pyramid Network

In this section, we describe DSPN for Uni-SA. The overall model architecture is illustrated in Figure 2.

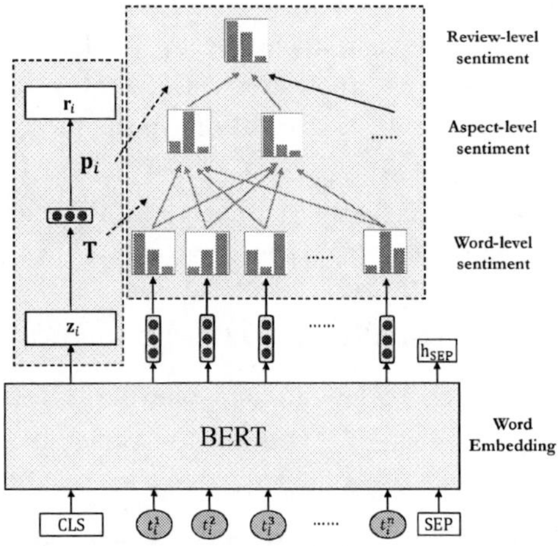

Figure 2: Overall architecture of DSPN. Aspect embedding matrix $\mathbf{T}$ is used to calculate the distance between words and aspects, which is regarded as the word-level attention weights for each aspect. Aspect importance $\mathbf{p}_i$ is learned by Module 1 and is used as the attention weights of aspects.

3.1 Module 1: Aspect-Category Detection

For the ACD task, we utilize an autoencoder-style network (He et al., 2017). For a review R_i, the input sequence X_i is constructed as $\{[CLS], t_i^{(1)}, t_i^{(2)}, \ldots, t_i^{(n)}, [SEP]\}$. We use BERT (Devlin et al., 2019) to generate embeddings for each example, $\mathbf{z}_i$.

To generate aspect embeddings, we first set the aspect and keyword map dictionary for each aspect. Then for each aspect, we use BERT to encode the sentence composed of key words related to the aspect and obtain its output as the initial embedding of the aspect. In this way, we initialize the aspect embedding matrix $\mathbf{T}$. [2] Lastly, Module 1 performs sentence reconstruction at the aspect-level through a linear layer:

$$\mathbf{z}_i = \text{BERT}(X_i) \tag{1}$$

$$\mathbf{p}_i = \text{softmax}(\mathbf{W_1} \cdot \mathbf{z}_i + \mathbf{b_1}) \tag{2}$$

$$\mathbf{r}_i = \mathbf{T}^\top \cdot \mathbf{p}_i \tag{3}$$

where $\mathbf{r}_i$ is the reconstructed sentence embedding and $\mathbf{p}_i$ is the aspect importance vector.

The loss function for Module 1 is defined as a hinge loss to maximize the inner product between the input sentence embedding and its reconstruction while minimizing the inner product between the input sentence embedding and randomly sampled negative examples:

$$L(\theta_{\text{ACD}}) = \sum_{R_i \in \mathbf{R}} \sum_{j=1}^{m} \phi_{R_i,j} + \lambda_{\text{ACD}} U(\theta) \tag{4}$$

$$\phi_{R_i,j} = max(0, 1 - \mathbf{r}_i \mathbf{z}_i + \mathbf{r}_i \mathbf{n}_j) \tag{5}$$

where $\mathbf{n}_i$ represents each negative sample, and $U(\theta)$ represents the regularization term to encourage unique aspect embeddings (He et al., 2017).

The aspect embedding matrix $\mathbf{T}$ and aspect importance vector $\mathbf{p}_i$ are inputs for attention calculation in DSPN's pyramid network (Module 2).

3.2 Module 2: Pyramid Sentiment Analysis

Module 2 is based on the intuition that the sentiment of a review is an aggregation of the sentiments of the aspects contained in the review (Bu et al., 2021). In addition, the sentiment of an aspect is an aggregation of the sentiments of the words indicating that aspect, forming a three-layer structure. We propose using a pyramid network to capture this structure, and we can use easy-to-obtain RP ratings as training labels.

3.2.1 Word Sentiment Prediction Layer

We use the hidden vector of each word output by BERT to obtain word representations, where $\mathbf{h}_i^{(j)}$ is the representation of the j-th word. We use two fully connected layers to produce a word-level sentiment prediction vector:

$$\mathbf{w}_i^{(j)} = \mathbf{W_3} \cdot ReLU(\mathbf{W_2} \cdot \mathbf{h}_i^{(j)} + \mathbf{b_2}) + \mathbf{b_3} \tag{6}$$

3.2.2 ACSA with Aspect Attention

We can calculate the similarity of words and aspects using the word representations and the aspect embedding matrix $\mathbf{T}$ output by Module 1. This similarity will be treated as the attention weights of words for the aspect. When predicting aspect-level sentiment, for the k-th aspect, the sentiment S_a^k is computed as:

[2] There are N predefined aspects in ACD task, and many prior works have identified the representative words for each one of them (Bu et al., 2021; Wang et al., 2010). For example, "staff", "customer", and "friendly" can be the representative words for "Service" aspect. Based on this, we proposed to firstly construct a sentence that contains top representative words, then use the embedding of this sentence as the initial embedding for the aspect.

Dataset	Language	MA	MAS	Split	Reviews	Overall Sentiment			Aspect Sentiments		
						Pos.	Neu.	Neg.	Pos.	Neu.	Neg.
TripDMS	English	100%	100%	Train	23,515	8,998	5,055	9,462	64,984	34,200	43,391
				Val	2,939	1,161	613	1,165	8,174	4,245	5,349
				Test	2,939	1,079	647	1,213	8,002	4,355	5,437
ASAP	Chinese	95.97%	63.85%	Train	36,850	29,132	5,241	2,477	77,507	27,329	17,299
				Val	4,940	3,839	784	317	10,367	3,772	2,373
				Test	4,940	3,885	717	338	10,144	3,729	2,403

Table 1: Statistics of the datasets. **MA** is the percentage of multi-aspect instances in the dataset and **MAS** is the percentage of multi-aspect multi-sentiment instances.

$$d_k^{(j)} = \mathbf{T}_k^\top \cdot \mathbf{h}_i^{(j)} \tag{7}$$

$$a_k^{(j)} = \frac{\exp(d_k^{(j)})}{\sum_{m=1}^{n} \exp(d_k^{(m)})} \tag{8}$$

$$S_a^k = softmax(\sum_{j=1}^{n} \mathbf{w}_i^{(j)} a_k^{(j)}) \tag{9}$$

3.2.3 Review Prediction

Review-level sentiment S_r is computed by:

$$S_r = softmax(S_a \cdot \mathbf{p}_i) \tag{10}$$

Here $\mathbf{p}_i$ is the aspect importance vector output by Module 1 (§3.1), which is regarded as the attention weights of aspects in a review. S_a is the matrix concatenation of aspect-level sentiments across the K aspects in the review.

3.3 Loss

For the RP task, as each prediction is a 3-class classification problem, the loss function is defined by the categorical cross-entropy between the true label and the model output:

$$L(\theta_{\text{RP}}) = -\sum_i S_{gold} \cdot log(S_r) \tag{11}$$

We jointly train DSPN for RP and ACD by minimizing the combined loss function:

$$L(\theta) = \lambda L(\theta_{\text{ACD}}) + L(\theta_{\text{RP}}) \tag{12}$$

where λ is the weight of ACD loss. Although no direct supervision is required for ACSA, due to the construction of DSPN, the model inherently learns aspect sentiment predictions.

4 Experiments

4.1 Datasets

To validate DSPN's contribution as an efficient and effective model for unified sentiment analysis, we experiment with two datasets. Statistics of the two datasets are given in Table 1. While DSPN can learn ACD, ACSA, and RP with only RP labels, we require datasets for our benchmarking that have ACD, ACSA, and RP labels.[3]

ASAP ASAP is a Chinese-language restaurant review dataset from a leading e-commerce platform in China (Bu et al., 2021). ASAP includes RP labels and ACSA labels. RP labels are categorical on a 5-star scale. ACSA labels are categorical (*positive, negative, neutral*) for each aspect#attribute [4] identified in the review text (Pontiki et al., 2016). For ACSA we aggregate sentiment at the entity level for a total of five aspects: {Food, Price, Location, Service, Ambience} by majority vote.

TripDMS TripDMS is an English-language hotel review dataset from Tripadvisor.com (Wang et al., 2010; Yin et al., 2017). TripDMS RP labels are categorical on a 5-star scale. ACSA labels are categorical (*positive*, *negative*, *neutral*) for seven aspects: {Value, Room, Location, Cleanliness, Check-in, Service, Business}.

4.2 Evaluation

DSPN's main contribution is accurate and efficient unified sentiment analysis via distant supervision. We therefore compare DSPN to existing ACD, ACSA, and RP models.

4.2.1 Aspect-Category Detection

In the ACD task, we compare DSPN with fully unsupervised ABAE (He et al., 2017). To more fairly compare with the prior work, we replace the underlying encoder of ABAE with a BERT encoder and update the aspect embedding matrix $\mathbf{T}$ initialization accordingly. We call this ABAE-BERT and

[3] To the best of our knowledge, these datasets are the only ones with RP and ACSA labels for us to evaluate performance.

[4] ASAP defines 5 aspects and 18 attributes.

		Efficiency			Performance		
		Parameters (MM)	Labels (thousands)	Training Time (minutes)	ACD (F1)	ACSA (Acc)	RP (Acc)
TripDMS	ABAE-BERT (ACD)	91.2	0	40	92.3		
	AC-MIMML-BERT (ACSA)	105	164.6	55		64.3	
	BERT-ITPT-FiT (RP)	82.7	23.5	102			72.4
	Pipeline	278.9	188.1	197	92.3	**64.3**	72.4
	DSPN	**102.9**	**23.5**	**95**	**92.7**	53.2	**72.5**
	Delta	-63.1	-87.5	-51.8	0.43	-17.3	0.14
ASAP	ABAE-BERT (ACD)	97.5	0	42	80.1		
	AC-MIMML-BERT (ACSA)	107.2	184.3	55		77.2	
	BERT-ITPT-FiT (RP)	91	36.9	110			80.3
	Pipeline	295.7	221.1	207	**80.1**	**77.2**	80.3
	DSPN	**111**	**36.9**	**88**	79.4	65.4	**81.3**
	Delta	-62.5	-83.3	-57.5	-0.87	-15.3	1.3

Table 2: Comparison between DSPN and a high-performance pipeline approach to unified sentiment analysis.

		Efficiency			Performance		
		Parameters (MM)	Labels (thousands)	Training Time (minutes)	ACD (F1)	ACSA (Acc)	RP (Acc)
TripDMS	ABAE	3.1	0	15	91.2		
	GCAE	4.2	164.6	5		55.1	
	BERT-Feat	80.2	23.5	35			71.4
	Pipeline	**87.5**	188.1	**55**	91.2	**55.1**	71.4
	DSPN	102.9	**23.5**	95	**92.7**	53.2	**72.5**
	Delta	17.60	-87.50	72.73	1.64	-3.45	1.54
ASAP	ABAE	3.1	0	15	79.4		
	GCAE	4.4	184.3	6		70.3	
	BERT-Feat	80.8	36.9	42			79.2
	Pipeline	**88.3**	221.1	**63**	**79.4**	**70.3**	79.2
	DSPN	111	**36.9**	88	**79.4**	65.4	**81.3**
	Delta	25.71	-83.33	39.68	0.00	-6.97	2.65

Table 3: Comparison between DSPN and a high-efficiency pipeline approach to unified sentiment analysis.

report its performance.[5] In the experiment, we follow previous work (Ruder et al., 2016; Ghadery et al., 2019) and use thresholding to assign aspects whose probability exceeds a given threshold to the corresponding review. We choose the threshold that produces the best performance ($1e^{-4}$) in our experiment. We evaluate ACD using F1 score to determine the quality of the identified aspects (He et al., 2017).

4.2.2 Aspect-Category Sentiment Analysis

For ACSA, we use several strong supervised ACSA models. Our benchmark models include non-BERT models: GCAE (Xue and Li, 2018), End2end-LSTM/CNN (Schmitt et al., 2018), and AC-MIMLLN (Li et al., 2020c) as well as BERT-based models: AC-MIMLLN-BERT (Li et al., 2020c) and ACSA-Generation (Liu et al., 2021). We use accuracy to evaluate ACSA (Li et al., 2020b).

4.2.3 Rating Prediction

The RP task a text classification task. Therefore, we compare DSPN with several BERT fine tuning strategies (Sun et al., 2019): BERT-Feat, BERT-FiT, and BERT-ITPT-FiT. Consistent with prior work (e.g., Aly and Atiya, 2013; Mudinas et al., 2012), we convert the 5-star RP rating into three classes (Negative, Neural, and Positive). To evaluate RP models, we use accuracy.

4.2.4 Implementation details

We implement models in PyTorch. The batch sizes are set to 32 for all models. Non-BERT models are optimized by the Adam optimizer, while BERT models use BERTAdam optimizer. We set the learning rate as 5e-5, and use early stopping with a pa-

[5] In ABAE-BERT, we don't need to manually define the meaning of aspect by looking at the nearest K words in the embedding space.

tience of 3 during training. We set the negative samples as 5 due to GPU constraints. We report results averaged over five runs.

5 Results

5.1 Overall Performance

To compare DSPN to the existing models, we compare DSPN with a pipeline approach. We create two pipelines: a *high performance* pipeline where we use the best performing model for each task in the pipeline, and a *high efficiency* model, where we use the most efficient benchmark model in terms of parameters in our pipeline.

Tables 2 and 3 presents the results of our comprehensive benchmarking. We first note that DSPN is the *only model capable of performing all three tasks*. What's more, DSPN is able to perform all three tasks with only supervision for the RP task. For RP, DSPN outperforms all of our benchmark models. On TripDMS, DSPN demonstrates stronger F1 score in ACD task than ABAE. On both datasets, our proposed ABAE-BERT outperforms original ABAE, demonstrating that incorporating large language models leads to higher quality aspects.

DSPN's performance on ACSA is lower than the supervised benchmarks. This is to be expected as DSPN's only supervision is RP labels. From an efficiency point of view, ACSA models require 164,605 labels on TripDMS to learn one task (ACSA), while DSPN only requires 23,515 labels (86% fewer) to learn three tasks. Based on an 86% size gap, DSPN performance is 17% lower than the best-performing supervised model for ACSA. Similarly for ASAP, based on an 80% size gap, DSPN performance is 15% lower than the best-performing supervised model for ACSA. In fact, DSPN outperforms the fully-supervised End2end-CNN baseline model.

Our single-task benchmarks serve to set the "upper-bound" of performance for the task when given a fully labeled dataset. However, if for a given dataset, only RP labels exist, then DSPN is the only method for learning all three tasks.

Considering that DSPN does not use any aspect-level labels, that the effectiveness of DSPN is comparable to supervised models on the ACSA task is a strong empirical validation of the unified sentiment analysis framework in general and the DSPN architecture in particular. [6]

[6]Results for all benchmarking models are presented in the Appendix for completeness.

Model	Rest-14	Rest-15	Rest-16	MAMS
ACSA-G	78.43	71.91	73.76	70.30
JASen	26.62	19.44	23.23	14.74
AX-MABSA	49.68	42.74	36.47	29.74
DSPN	30.01	18.23	24.01	12.79

Table 4: ACSA results on datasets with no RP labels. Benchmark results are from (Kamila et al., 2022). ACSA-G is supervised, JASen and AX-MABSA are weakly supervised, and DSPN is distantly supervised.

5.2 DSPN on No-rating Datasets

We have shown DSPN's effectiveness using two datasets that include both review-level star rating labels (for RP) and aspect-level sentiment annotations (for ACSA). However, a large number of current ACSA datasets do not contain rating data (RP), such as Rest-14 (Pontiki et al., 2014), Rest-15 (Pontiki et al., 2015), Rest-16 (Pontiki et al., 2016) and MAMS (Jiang et al., 2019). In order to enable DSPN to run on such datasets, we use the *aggregate value* of aspect ratings as the training labels instead of the star rating labels given by users. What's more, we can also evaluate our distant supervision model against existing weakly supervised ACSA models.

Table 4 shows that DSPN performs comparably to the JASen (Huang et al., 2020) model, which uses a small number of keywords for each aspect-polarity pair as supervision. *This result indicates that RP is not simply an average over ACSA labels, and that the RP labels used by DSPN provide a strong signal.*

Moreover, we conduct a simple additional experiment. In the experiment, we utilize several unsupervised sentiment analysis tools (VADER (Hutto and Gilbert, 2014), TextBlob (Loria, 2018), and Zero-shot text classification (Yin et al., 2019)) to directly generate sentiment labels, which will replace the star rating labels given by users for training. We name the version of DSPN as UPN (U for unsupervised), and here we report the ACSA results of DSPN and UPN on TripDMS (Table 5).

5.3 Quality Analysis

5.3.1 Case Study

In order to visualize and analyze DSPN's performance, we first take two reviews from TripDMS as examples (Figure 3a). For each example, the trained DSPN model takes the review text as in-

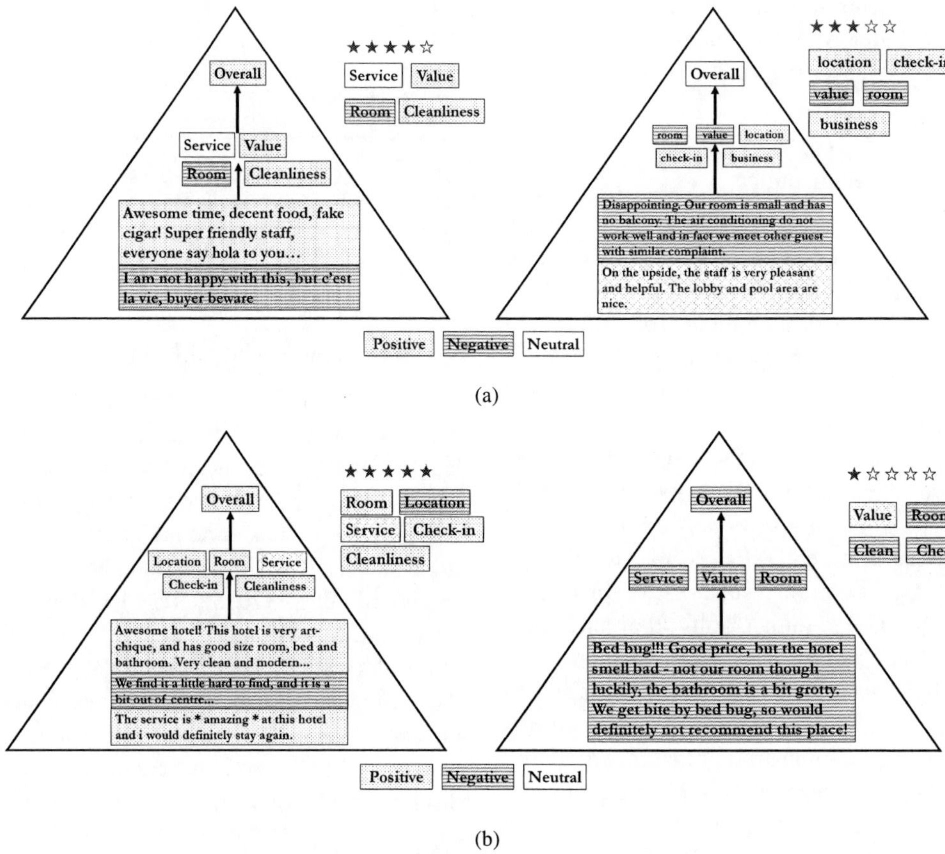

Figure 3: Case studies of correct predictions (3a) and incorrect predictions (3b). True RP and ACSA labels are outside of the pyramid, DSPN's predictions are within the pyramid. For space, we show a portion of the review.

Model	Label Source	Performance
DSPN	Star ratings	0.532
UPN	TextBlob	0.502
UPN	VADER	0.511
UPN	Zero-shot	0.533

Table 5: DSPN results compared to a fully unsupervised pyramid network (UPN).

put, and first outputs word-level sentiment predictions. Then, DSPN (i) identifies aspect keywords via word attention calculation; (ii) obtains the aspect importance; (iii) calculates aspect-level sentiment through the sentiments of their key words, and lastly (iv) combines aspect sentiment with aspect importance to predict the final review-level sentiment ("Overall" in Figure 3).

For case 1 in Figure 3a, DSPN correctly labels the review as positive, and also correctly identifies and labels the *Service*, *Value*, *Room*, and *Cleanliness* aspects with no aspect-level annotations. For case 2, DSPN gives correct predictions on word-, aspect-, and review-level sentiments.

5.3.2 Error Analysis

To exemplify errors in DSPN, we examine two examples of error cases from TripDMS in Figure 3b. We find that DSPN is sometimes influenced by extreme star rating labels. For example, for case 1 in Figure 3b, DSPN gives correct word-level sentiments, but tends to give positive prediction at aspect level due to the overall 5-star rating. Similarly for case 2, DSPN gives negative predictions on all three levels due to 1-star rating. This is to be expected as DSPN's only supervision is star rating labels.

6 Related Work

Sentiment analysis is a widely-studied area of NLP across ACD, ACSA, and RP. Several recent reviews provide comprehensive overviews of the state of the field (Liu and Zhang, 2012; Schouten and Frasincar, 2015). Below we describe the most relevant work.

6.1 Aspect-Category Detection

Extant ACD methods are either rule-based, supervised, or unsupervised. Rule-based methods (e.g., Hai et al., 2011; Schouten et al., 2014) heavily depend on manually defined rules and domain knowledge. Supervised methods (e.g., Toh and Su, 2016; Xue et al., 2017) require that each review is labeled with a subset of the predefined aspect categories. Unsupervised models (e.g., Titov and McDonald, 2008; Brody and Elhadad, 2010; Zhao et al., 2010) typically extract aspects by implicitly finding word co-occurrence patterns in the corpus. The ABAE model (He et al., 2017) uses an autoencoder-style network to extract aspects in a fully unsupervised manner, and is the foundation of our Module 1. Recently, Tulkens and van Cranenburgh (2020) proposed a simple aspect detection model that utilize a POS tagger and word embeddings, with a contrastive attention mechanism that outperforms more complex models. In our work, we utilize a novel aspect-attention mechanism to use ACD model outputs as part of the ACSA task.

6.2 Aspect-Category Sentiment Analysis

Most ACSA methods in the literature are supervised (Schouten and Frasincar, 2015; Li et al., 2020c; Liu et al., 2021) and require costly and time-consuming data annotation at the aspect level. Unsupervised LDA-based ACSA models (e.g., Zhao et al., 2010; Xu et al., 2012; García-Pablos et al., 2018) often rely on external resources such as part-of-speech tagging and sentiment word lexicons. These LDA-based models can suffer from a topic resembling problem (Huang et al., 2020). To address this, Huang et al. (2020) proposed a weakly-supervised approach that can learn a joint aspect-sentiment topic embedding. However, this method can only be applied to documents with a single annotated aspect, which degenerates the task to RP. Recently, Kamila et al. (2022) proposed an exteremely weakly supervised ACSA model, AX-MABSA, which gives a strong performance on ACSA without using any labelled data. However, the model relies on a single word for each class, making it difficult to select a representative word for the "neutral" class. In this work, we propose a distantly supervised pyramid network to efficiently perform ACSA task with only star rating labels.

6.3 Rating Prediction

RP is modeled as a multi-class classification task, and is well-studied (e.g., Ganu et al., 2009; Li et al., 2011; Liu and Zhang, 2012; Chen et al., 2018). There is also a significant body of literature on semi-supervised and unsupervised approaches to RP (Pugoy and Kao, 2021; Yao et al., 2017; Boteanu and Chernova, 2013).

6.4 Multi-Task Sentiment Analysis

There has been work in jointly learning ACSA and RP (Bu et al., 2021), leveraging RP information for ACSA (Yin et al., 2017; Li et al., 2018; He et al., 2018), and leveraging ACSA information for RP (Cheng et al., 2018; Wu et al., 2019). Prior work on document-level multi-aspect sentiment classification predicted user's ratings on different aspects of products or services (Yin et al., 2017; Li et al., 2018). By adding user information and star rating labels, the methods give strong performances. In each of these cases, the extra information augments the task labels, improving performance at the cost of efficiency. Other works (Bu et al., 2021; Fei et al., 2022) have done ACD and ACSA via joint learning; these methods require costly and time-consuming aspect-level data annotation, hindering efficiency. Schmitt et al. (2018) proposed joint learning models to simultaneously perform ACD and ACSA in an end-to-end manner. To the best of our knowledge, this is the first work to learn all three tasks simultaneously using a single task source for supervision.

7 Conclusion

In this paper, we introduce *unified sentiment analysis* to connect three important sentiment analysis tasks. To perform the task, we propose a Distantly Supervised Pyramid Network (DSPN) that shows significant efficiency advantage by only using star rating labels for training. Experiments conducted on two multi-aspect datasets demonstrate the good performance of DSPN on RP and ACD as well as the effectiveness with only RP labels as supervision.

DSPN's performance demonstrates the validity of considering sentiment analysis holistically and this empirical evidence shows that it is possible to use signal from a single task (RP) to efficiently and effectively learn three tasks. We hope this work spurs research on leveraging one label source for efficient learning for multiple tasks.

8 Limitations

There are several limitations to this work that shed light on promising avenues for future research.

Aspect and Review Sentiment Mismatch DSPN uses star rating labels for training. However, the user rating may not be consistent with the overall sentiment of the review text, thus generating the noise of distant labels. This is because the user may not have written all the aspects in the review, or the user's sentiment is heavily dominated by a certain aspect. It is not obvious how to model this within DSPN. While attention should address this to an extent, future work could consider methods from label noise research.

Evaluation Data Availability Another limitation has to do with data availability. There are a number of ACSA and RP datasets separately in the literature. However, it is very rare that datasets support unified sentiment analysis, i.e. they include both aspect-level sentiments and review-level star rating labels. Therefore, we were restricted to TripDMS and ASAP as the only two datasets available for our main evaluation. However, we feel that by demonstrating the capability of DSPN on one English dataset and one Chinese dataset helps demonstrate the generalization capability of the model. We encourage future work on the creation of more datasets with both ACSA and RP labels to drive further research in unified sentiment analysis.

Unsupervised ACD A final limitation concerns ACD. We compare to ABAE as our ACD module is unsupervised. However, there are supervised ACD methods in the literature, including some that do ACD and ACSA jointly. Future work can investigate injecting further supervision into the unified sentiment analysis task for ACD and/or ACSA.

9 Ethics Statement

The authors state that this research was conducted in accordance with the ACL Code of Ethics. We note that our experiments are on two controlled datasets and do not provide any guarantees of effectiveness or performance on out-of-domain data. In addition, although we experiment with English and Chineses languages, we cannot make claims as to how our research performs on other languages, including low-resource languages.

References

Mohamed Aly and Amir Atiya. 2013. Labr: A large scale arabic book reviews dataset. In *Proceedings of the 51st Annual Meeting of the Association for Computational Linguistics (Volume 2: Short Papers)*, pages 494–498.

Adrian Boteanu and Sonia Chernova. 2013. Unsupervised rating prediction based on local and global semantic models. In *2013 AAAI Fall Symposium Series*.

Samuel Brody and Noemie Elhadad. 2010. An unsupervised aspect-sentiment model for online reviews. In *Human language technologies: The 2010 annual conference of the North American chapter of the association for computational linguistics*, pages 804–812.

Jiahao Bu, Lei Ren, Shuang Zheng, Yang Yang, Jingang Wang, Fuzheng Zhang, and Wei Wu. 2021. Asap: A chinese review dataset towards aspect category sentiment analysis and rating prediction. In *Proceedings of the 2021 Conference of the North American Chapter of the Association for Computational Linguistics: Human Language Technologies*, pages 2069–2079.

Siva Uday Sampreeth Chebolu, Franck Dernoncourt, Nedim Lipka, and Thamar Solorio. 2023. Survey of aspect-based sentiment analysis datasets. In *IJCNLP-AACL 2023*.

Chong Chen, Min Zhang, Yiqun Liu, and Shaoping Ma. 2018. Neural attentional rating regression with review-level explanations. In *Proceedings of the 2018 World Wide Web Conference*, pages 1583–1592.

Zhiyong Cheng, Ying Ding, Lei Zhu, and Mohan Kankanhalli. 2018. Aspect-aware latent factor model: Rating prediction with ratings and reviews. In *Proceedings of the 2018 world wide web conference*, pages 639–648.

Jacob Devlin, Ming-Wei Chang, Kenton Lee, and Kristina Toutanova. 2019. Bert: Pre-training of deep bidirectional transformers for language understanding. In *Proceedings of the 2019 Conference of the North American Chapter of the Association for Computational Linguistics: Human Language Technologies, Volume 1 (Long and Short Papers)*, pages 4171–4186.

Hao Fei, Jingye Li, Yafeng Ren, Meishan Zhang, and Donghong Ji. 2022. Making decision like human: Joint aspect category sentiment analysis and rating prediction with fine-to-coarse reasoning. In *Proceedings of the ACM Web Conference 2022*, pages 3042–3051.

Gayatree Ganu, Noémie Elhadad, and Amélie Marian. 2009. Beyond the stars: Improving rating predictions using review text content. In *International Workshop on the Web and Databases*.

Aitor García-Pablos, Montse Cuadros, and German Rigau. 2018. W2vlda: almost unsupervised system for aspect based sentiment analysis. *Expert Systems with Applications*, 91:127–137.

Erfan Ghadery, Sajad Movahedi, Masoud Jalili Sabet, Heshaam Faili, and Azadeh Shakery. 2019. Licd: A language-independent approach for aspect category detection. In *European Conference on Information Retrieval*, pages 575–589.

Zhen Hai, Kuiyu Chang, and Jung-jae Kim. 2011. Implicit feature identification via co-occurrence association rule mining. In *International Conference on Intelligent Text Processing and Computational Linguistics*, pages 393–404.

Ruidan He, Wee Sun Lee, Hwee Tou Ng, and Daniel Dahlmeier. 2017. An unsupervised neural attention model for aspect extraction. In *Proceedings of the 55th Annual Meeting of the Association for Computational Linguistics (Volume 1: Long Papers)*, pages 388–397.

Ruidan He, Wee Sun Lee, Hwee Tou Ng, and Daniel Dahlmeier. 2018. Exploiting document knowledge for aspect-level sentiment classification. In *Proceedings of the 56th Annual Meeting of the Association for Computational Linguistics (Volume 2: Short Papers)*, pages 579–585.

Jiaxin Huang, Yu Meng, Fang Guo, Heng Ji, and Jiawei Han. 2020. Weakly-supervised aspect-based sentiment analysis via joint aspect-sentiment topic embedding. In *Proceedings of the 2020 Conference on Empirical Methods in Natural Language Processing (EMNLP)*, pages 6989–6999.

Clayton Hutto and Eric Gilbert. 2014. Vader: A parsimonious rule-based model for sentiment analysis of social media text. In *Proceedings of the international AAAI conference on web and social media*, volume 8, pages 216–225.

Qingnan Jiang, Lei Chen, Ruifeng Xu, Xiang Ao, and Min Yang. 2019. A challenge dataset and effective models for aspect-based sentiment analysis. In *Proceedings of the 2019 Conference on Empirical Methods in Natural Language Processing and the 9th International Joint Conference on Natural Language Processing (EMNLP-IJCNLP)*, pages 6280–6285.

Sabyasachi Kamila, Walid Magdy, Sourav Dutta, and MingXue Wang. 2022. Ax-mabsa: A framework for extremely weakly supervised multi-label aspect based sentiment analysis. In *Proceedings of the 2022 Conference on Empirical Methods in Natural Language Processing*, pages 6136–6147.

Avinash Kumar, Pranjal Gupta, Nisarg Kotak, Raghunathan Balan, Lalita Bhanu Murthy Neti, and Aruna Malapati. 2022. Barlat: A nearly unsupervised approach for aspect category detection. *Neural Processing Letters*, 54(5):4495–4519.

Fangtao Li, Nathan Nan Liu, Hongwei Jin, Kai Zhao, Qiang Yang, and Xiaoyan Zhu. 2011. Incorporating reviewer and product information for review rating prediction. In *Twenty-second international joint conference on artificial intelligence*.

Junjie Li, Haitong Yang, and Chengqing Zong. 2018. Document-level multi-aspect sentiment classification by jointly modeling users, aspects, and overall ratings. In *Proceedings of the 27th International Conference on Computational Linguistics*, pages 925–936.

Qiudan Li, Daniel Dajun Zeng, David Jingjun Xu, Ruoran Liu, and Riheng Yao. 2020a. Understanding and predicting users' rating behavior: A cognitive perspective. *INFORMS Journal on Computing*, 32(4):996–1011.

Yuncong Li, Zhe Yang, Cunxiang Yin, Xu Pan, Lunan Cui, Qiang Huang, and Ting Wei. 2020b. A joint model for aspect-category sentiment analysis with shared sentiment prediction layer. In *China National Conference on Chinese Computational Linguistics*, pages 388–400.

Yuncong Li, Cunxiang Yin, Sheng-hua Zhong, and Xu Pan. 2020c. Multi-instance multi-label learning networks for aspect-category sentiment analysis. In *Proceedings of the 2020 Conference on Empirical Methods in Natural Language Processing (EMNLP)*, pages 3550–3560.

Ming Liao, Jing Li, Haisong Zhang, Lingzhi Wang, Xixin Wu, and Kam-Fai Wong. 2019. Coupling global and local context for unsupervised aspect extraction. In *Proceedings of the 2019 conference on empirical methods in natural language processing and the 9th international joint conference on natural language processing (EMNLP-IJCNLP)*, pages 4579–4589.

Bing Liu and Lei Zhang. 2012. A survey of opinion mining and sentiment analysis. In *Mining text data*, pages 415–463. Springer.

Jian Liu, Zhiyang Teng, Leyang Cui, Hanmeng Liu, and Yue Zhang. 2021. Solving aspect category sentiment analysis as a text generation task. In *Proceedings of the 2021 Conference on Empirical Methods in Natural Language Processing*, pages 4406–4416.

Steven Loria. 2018. textblob documentation. *Release 0.15*, 2.

Ling Luo, Xiang Ao, Yan Song, Jinyao Li, Xiaopeng Yang, Qing He, and Dong Yu. 2019. Unsupervised neural aspect extraction with sememes. In *IJCAI*, pages 5123–5129.

Andrius Mudinas, Dell Zhang, and Mark Levene. 2012. Combining lexicon and learning based approaches for concept-level sentiment analysis. In *Proceedings of the first international workshop on issues of sentiment discovery and opinion mining*, pages 1–8.

Maria Pontiki, Dimitrios Galanis, Haris Papageorgiou, Ion Androutsopoulos, Suresh Manandhar, Mohammad Al-Smadi, Mahmoud Al-Ayyoub, Yanyan Zhao,

Bing Qin, Orphée De Clercq, et al. 2016. Semeval-2016 task 5: Aspect based sentiment analysis. In *International workshop on semantic evaluation*, pages 19–30.

Maria Pontiki, Dimitrios Galanis, Harris Papageorgiou, Suresh Manandhar, and Ion Androutsopoulos. 2015. Semeval-2015 task 12: Aspect based sentiment analysis. In *Proceedings of the 9th international workshop on semantic evaluation (SemEval 2015)*, pages 486–495.

Maria Pontiki, Dimitris Galanis, John Pavlopoulos, Harris Papageorgiou, Ion Androutsopoulos, and Suresh Manandhar. 2014. SemEval-2014 task 4: Aspect based sentiment analysis. In *Proceedings of the 8th International Workshop on Semantic Evaluation (SemEval 2014)*, pages 27–35.

Reinald Adrian Pugoy and Hung-Yu Kao. 2021. Unsupervised extractive summarization-based representations for accurate and explainable collaborative filtering. In *Proceedings of the 59th Annual Meeting of the Association for Computational Linguistics and the 11th International Joint Conference on Natural Language Processing (Volume 1: Long Papers)*, pages 2981–2990.

Sebastian Ruder, Parsa Ghaffari, and John G Breslin. 2016. Insight-1 at semeval-2016 task 5: Deep learning for multilingual aspect-based sentiment analysis. In *Proceedings of the 10th International Workshop on Semantic Evaluation (SemEval-2016)*, pages 330–336.

Martin Schmitt, Simon Steinheber, Konrad Schreiber, and Benjamin Roth. 2018. Joint aspect and polarity classification for aspect-based sentiment analysis with end-to-end neural networks. In *Proceedings of the 2018 Conference on Empirical Methods in Natural Language Processing*, pages 1109–1114.

Kim Schouten and Flavius Frasincar. 2015. Survey on aspect-level sentiment analysis. *IEEE Transactions on Knowledge and Data Engineering*, 28(3):813–830.

Kim Schouten, Flavius Frasincar, and Franciska De Jong. 2014. Commit-p1wp3: A co-occurrence based approach to aspect-level sentiment analysis. In *Proceedings of the 8th International Workshop on Semantic Evaluation (SemEval 2014)*, pages 203–207.

Chi Sun, Xipeng Qiu, Yige Xu, and Xuanjing Huang. 2019. How to fine-tune bert for text classification? In *Chinese Computational Linguistics: 18th China National Conference, CCL 2019, Kunming, China, October 18–20, 2019, Proceedings 18*, pages 194–206. Springer.

Ivan Titov and Ryan McDonald. 2008. Modeling online reviews with multi-grain topic models. In *Proceedings of the 17th international conference on World Wide Web*, pages 111–120.

Zhiqiang Toh and Jian Su. 2016. Nlangp at semeval-2016 task 5: Improving aspect based sentiment analysis using neural network features. In *Proceedings of the 10th international workshop on semantic evaluation (SemEval-2016)*, pages 282–288.

Stéphan Tulkens and Andreas van Cranenburgh. 2020. Embarrassingly simple unsupervised aspect extraction. In *Proceedings of the 58th Annual Meeting of the Association for Computational Linguistics*, pages 3182–3187.

Cong Wan, Shan Jiang, Cong Wang, Ying Yuan, and Cuirong Wang. 2020. A novel sentence embedding based topic detection method for microblogs. *IEEE Access*, 8:202980–202992.

Hongning Wang, Yue Lu, and Chengxiang Zhai. 2010. Latent aspect rating analysis on review text data: a rating regression approach. In *Proceedings of the 16th ACM SIGKDD international conference on Knowledge discovery and data mining*, pages 783–792.

Chuhan Wu, Fangzhao Wu, Junxin Liu, Yongfeng Huang, and Xing Xie. 2019. Arp: Aspect-aware neural review rating prediction. In *Proceedings of the 28th ACM International Conference on Information and Knowledge Management*, pages 2169–2172.

Xueke Xu, Songbo Tan, Yue Liu, Xueqi Cheng, and Zheng Lin. 2012. Towards jointly extracting aspects and aspect-specific sentiment knowledge. In *Proceedings of the 21st ACM international conference on Information and knowledge management*, pages 1895–1899.

Wei Xue and Tao Li. 2018. Aspect based sentiment analysis with gated convolutional networks. In *Proceedings of the 56th Annual Meeting of the Association for Computational Linguistics (Volume 1: Long Papers)*, pages 2514–2523.

Wei Xue, Wubai Zhou, Tao Li, and Qing Wang. 2017. Mtna: a neural multi-task model for aspect category classification and aspect term extraction on restaurant reviews. In *Proceedings of the Eighth International Joint Conference on Natural Language Processing (Volume 2: Short Papers)*, pages 151–156.

Huaxiu Yao, Min Nie, Han Su, Hu Xia, and Defu Lian. 2017. Predicting academic performance via semi-supervised learning with constructed campus social network. In *International Conference on Database Systems for Advanced Applications*, pages 597–609.

Wenpeng Yin, Jamaal Hay, and Dan Roth. 2019. Benchmarking zero-shot text classification: Datasets, evaluation and entailment approach. In *2019 Conference on Empirical Methods in Natural Language Processing and 9th International Joint Conference on Natural Language Processing, EMNLP-IJCNLP 2019*, pages 3914–3923. Association for Computational Linguistics.

Yichun Yin, Yangqiu Song, and Ming Zhang. 2017. Document-level multi-aspect sentiment classification as machine comprehension. In *Proceedings of the 2017 conference on empirical methods in natural language processing*, pages 2044–2054.

Zelin Zhang, Kejia Yang, Jonathan Z Zhang, and Robert W Palmatier. 2023. Uncovering synergy and dysergy in consumer reviews: A machine learning approach. *Management Science*, 69(4):2339–2360.

Wayne Xin Zhao, Jing Jiang, Hongfei Yan, and Xiaoming Li. 2010. Jointly modeling aspects and opinions with a maxent-lda hybrid. In *Proceedings of the 2010 Conference on Empirical Methods in Natural Language Processing*, page 56–65.

A Notation

For clarity and consistency, we provide a comprehensive description of the notation we use in this article (Table 6).

Variable	Description	Dimension
d_w	Embedding dimension	$\mathbb{R}^{768}$
$\mathbf{R}$	Reviews in our dataset	-
R_i	i-th review consisted of a sequence of word tokens	$\mathbb{R}^{n \times d_w}$
n	Number of word tokens in R_i	$\mathbb{R}^{100}$
$t_i^{(j)}$	j-th word in R_i	$\mathbb{R}^{1 \times d_w}$
A	Predefined aspect categories	$\mathbb{R}^{N}$
A_{R_i}	The set of aspects present in R_i	$\mathbb{R}^{K}(K \leq N)$
$A_{R_i}^{(j)}$	j-th aspect in A_{R_i}	$\mathbb{R}^{1 \times d_w}$
$y_{A_{R_i}^{(j)}}$	Sentiment polarity of $A_{R_i}^{(j)}$	$\mathbb{R}^{3}$
y_{R_i}	Star rating of R_i	$\mathbb{R}^{3}$
M	Model	-
$\hat{A}_{R_i}$	Prediction of A_{R_i}	-
$\hat{y}_{A_{R_i}^{(j)}}$	Prediction of $y_{A_{R_i}^{(j)}}$	$\mathbb{R}^{3}$
$\hat{y}_{R_i}$	Prediction of y_{R_i}	$\mathbb{R}^{3}$
$\mathbf{X}_i$	Input sequence	$\mathbb{R}^{n \times d_w}$
$\mathbf{z}_i$	Sentence embedding of $\mathbf{X}_i$ (pooler_output of BERT)	$\mathbb{R}^{n \times d_w}$
$\mathbf{T}$	Aspect embedding matrix	$\mathbb{R}^{N \times d_w}$
$\mathbf{T}_k$	Embedding of k-th aspect	$\mathbb{R}^{1 \times d_w}$
$\mathbf{r}_i$	Reconstructed sentence embedding	$\mathbb{R}^{1 \times d_w}$
$\mathbf{p}_i$	Weight vectors of K aspect embeddings (aspect importance)	$\mathbb{R}^{N \times d_w}$
$L(\theta_{ACD})$	Loss function of ACD task (Module 1)	-
λ_{ACD}	Weight of regularization term	-
$U(\theta)$	Regularization term	-
n_j	Each negative sample	$\mathbb{R}^{1 \times d_w}$
$\mathbf{h}_i^{(j)}$	hidden state of j-th word (last_hidden_state of BERT)	$\mathbb{R}^{1 \times d_w}$
$\mathbf{w}_i^{(j)}$	Sentiment prediction vector of j-th word	$\mathbb{R}^{1 \times d_w \times 3}$
$d_k^{(j)}$	Distance between j-th word and k-th aspect	-
$a_k^{(j)}$	Attention weight of j-th word towards k-th aspect	-
S_a^k	Prediction of aspect-level sentiment	$\mathbb{R}^{N \times 3}$
S_r	Prediction of review-level sentiment	$\mathbb{R}^{3}$
S_a	Matrix concatenation of S_a^k	$\mathbb{R}^{K \times 3}$
S_{gold}	True review-level sentiment (star rating labels)	$\mathbb{R}^{3}$
$L(\theta_{RP})$	Loss function of RP task (Module 2)	-
λ	Weight of $L(\theta_{ACD})$	-
$L(\theta)$	Overall loss function	-

Table 6: Description of variables in our formulation.

B Additional Error Analyses

For a more comprehensive analysis, we look into the DSPN errors in more detail. Due to the imbalanced label distribution in the original data (Table 1), DSPN tends to predict more extreme sentiment polarities (positive or negative) on TripDMS, and tends to predict positive sentiments on ASAP. The confusion matrices for aspect-level sentiments predicted by DSPN are consistent with the distribution of the original data (Tables 7a and 7b).

True \ Pred	Neg	Neu	Pos	Total
Neg	3,511	982	944	5,437
Neu	1,672	884	1,799	4,355
Pos	1,962	1,560	4,480	8,002
Total	7,145	3,426	7,223	17,794

(a) Confusion Matrix of DSPN on TripDMS

True \ Pred	Neg	Neu	Pos	Total
Neg	589	521	1,293	2,403
Neu	260	712	2,757	3,729
Pos	127	760	9,257	10,144
Total	976	1,993	13,307	16,276

(b) Confusion Matrix of DSPN on ASAP

Table 7: DSPN confusion matrices.

C Budget Constraint Experiment

For a more direct comparison between DSPN and the supervised ACSA models, we designed a budget-constraining experiment. Specifically, we randomly selected ACSA labels for TripDMS and ASAP so that the supervised models have the same training set size as DSPN.

In this setting, DSPN's performance is closer to the supervised models' performance (Table 8). In particular, DSPN outperforms both End2end-LTSM and End2end-CNN on ASAP. Overall, the supervised models still outperform DSPN, but this is to be expected given that the labels used for training are ACSA labels. DSPN is trained to perform RP, but is also able to perform ACSA in a way that is comparable to these supervised models under the same budget constraint.

D Benchmarking Details

- End2end-LSTM/CNN: The method uses an end-to-end network for ACSA. It can simultaneously perform aspect category detection and aspect-level sentiment analysis.

Model	TripDMS	ASAP
End2end-LSTM	0.542	0.651
End2end-CNN	0.536	0.649
GCAE	0.540	0.701
AC-MIMLLN	0.614	0.758
AC-MIMLLN-BERT	0.639	0.766
ACSA-Generation	0.602	0.758
DSPN (Ours)	0.532	0.654

Table 8: ACSA results when all models are trained with the same amount of data.

- GCAE: This method is a simple and effective supervised model based on convolutional neural networks and gating mechanisms.
- AC-MIMLLN: It utilized multi-instance multi-label learning for ACSA and found that the aspect-level sentiment can be regarded as an aggregation of the word-level sentiments indicating the aspect.
- AC-MIMLLN-BERT: It replaces the embedding layer for ACSA and the multi-layer Bi-LSTM in AC-MIMLLN with the BERT.
- ACSA-generation: This is the first method that solve ACSA task with natural language generation paradigm, and achieved good results.
- BERT-Feat: BERT as features.
- BERT-FiT: BERT + Fine-Tuning as features.
- BERT-ITPT-FiT: BERT + withIn-Task Pre-Training + Fine-Tuning as features.

E On Sentence Reconstruction for ACD

Sentence reconstruction is standard for unsupervised ACD task. Table 9 shows that sentence reconstruction is widely used and effective for this task.

F Additional Benchmarking

Tables 10, 11, and 12 present the comprehensive results of our benchmarking. We selected our pipeline models from these benchmarks based on predictive performance and efficiency.

Reference	Mechanism	Datasets	Performance
(He et al., 2017)	sentence reconstruction	CitySearch, BeerAdvocate	SOTA
(Kumar et al., 2022)	seed words + sentence reconstruction + adversarial training	CitySearch, Laptop	SOTA
(García-Pablos et al., 2018)	topic model	CitySearch	Competitive results
(Liao et al., 2019)	multiple context modeling + representation reconstruction	SemEval 14, 15, 16	SOTA
(Luo et al., 2019)	lexical semantic enhancing + sentence reconstruction	CitySearch, BeerAdvocate	SOTA
(Wan et al., 2020)	sentence embedding + sentence reconstruction	Sina microblog	Effective results
This paper	sentence reconstruction + multi-task learning + distant supervision	ASAP, TripDMS	Comparable results

Table 9: Mechanisms Used in Unsupervised ACD Task

	TripDMS			ASAP		
Model	**Accuracy**	**Params**	**Train Time**	**Accuracy**	**Params**	**Train Time**
DSPN	70.5	5.28M	12min	78.5	6.1M	13min
DSPN-BERT	72.5	102.92M	95min	81.3	111M	88min
BERT-Feat	71.4	80.15M	35min	79.2	80.8M	42min
BERT-FiT	72.2	81M	37min	81	81.25M	30min
BERT-ITPT-FiT	72.4	82.7M	102min	80.3	91M	110min

Table 10: Comprehensive RP Results

	TripDMS			ASAP		
Model	**F1**	**Params**	**Train Time**	**F1**	**Params**	**Train Time**
DSPN	92.7	5.28M	12min	78.6	6.1M	13min
DSPN-BERT	92.7	102.92M	95min	79.4	111M	88min
ABAE	91.2	3.1M	15min	79.4	3.1M	15min
ABAE-BERT	92.3	91.2M	40min	80.1	97.5M	42min

Table 11: Comprehensive ACD Results

	TripDMS			ASAP		
Model	**Accuracy**	**Params**	**Train Time**	**Accuracy**	**Params**	**Train Time**
DSPN	51.4	5.28M	12min	64.4	6.1M	13min
DSPN-BERT	53.2	102.92M	95min	65.4	111M	88min
End2end-LSTM	57.4	5.3M	8min	66.1	6.22M	8min
End2end-CNN	57.9	5.12M	7min	65.2	5.32M	7min
GCAE	55.1	4.23M	5min	70.3	4.4M	6min
AC-MIMLLN	62.1	31M	50min	76	31.2M	50min
AC-MIMLLN-BERT	64.3	105M	55min	77.2	107,2M	55min
ACSA-generation	64.1	142M	208min	76.1	145.18M	210min

Table 12: Comprehensive ACSA Results

Author Index

Association for Computational Linguistics
209 N. Eighth Street
Stroudsburg, Pennsylvania 18360

ISBN 978-1-7138-9465-0

9 781713 894650

CURRAN ASSOCIATES INC.
proceedings.com